EVALUATIONS OF US POETRY SINCE 1950, VOLUME 1

RECENCIES SERIES: RESEARCH AND RECOVERY IN TWENTIETH-CENTURY AMERICAN POETICS

MATTHEW HOFER, SERIES EDITOR

RECENCIES

This series stands at the intersection of critical investigation, historical documentation, and the preservation of cultural heritage. The series exists to illuminate the innovative poetics achievements of the recent past that remain relevant to the present. In addition to publishing monographs and edited volumes, it is also a venue for previously unpublished manuscripts, expanded reprints, and collections of major essays, letters, and interviews.

Also available in the Recencies Series:

For additional titles in the Recencies Series, please visit unmpress.com.

EVALUATIONS OF US POETRY SINCE 1950

Volume 1

Language, Form, and Music

Edited by Robert von Hallberg and Robert Faggen

University of New Mexico Press | Albuquerque

ISBN 978-0-8263-6313-8 (paper)
ISBN 978-0-8263-6314-5 (electronic)

Library of Congess Control Number: 2021944761

Founded in 1889, the University of New Mexico sits on the traditional homelands of the Pueblo of Sandia. The original peoples of New Mexico—Pueblo, Navajo, and Apache—since time immemorial have deep connections to the land and have made significant contributions to the broader community statewide. We honor the land itself and those who remain stewards of this land throughout the generations and also acknowledge our committed relationship to Indigenous peoples. We gratefully recognize our history.

Cover illustration: courtesy of DesignCuts.com
Designed by Felicia Cedillos
Composed in Minion Pro 10.25/14.25

CONTENTS

FORM

MUSICALITY

Introduction

ROBERT FAGGEN AND ROBERT VON HALLBERG

Academia

Imagine two college students in a classroom waiting for their literature instructor to arrive. They have prepared for the day's class, but one says to the other: "I don't know why we had to read X. It's dull—and difficult, too." Not an altogether implausible scenario, even in a contemporary poetry course. A comment like that about a Romantic poetry course is less plausible, only because that course is more settled into required readings. The case for a modern poetry course is only a little less settled: Pound, Eliot, Frost, Stevens, Williams, H. D., Moore, and Hart Crane, say; then possibly Zukofsky and Stein. Eight major poets and a couple of others formerly known as minor writers—that is a curricular form one recognizes. A strenuous selection has been made for most periods of poetry; the years after World War II are an exception. Selection is what critics do, even if only indirectly. Their interpretive and historical essays advocate implicitly the merits of particular poets. Compilers of anthologies and textbooks make available to general readers and students the poems that critics seem to esteem, even if the ground of that esteem is not well marked. Poets neglected by critics may yet survive in anthologies, provided that their work draws the attention of younger poets. In fact, the efforts of critics alone may not be enough to canonize particular poets. Hugh Kenner's advocacy failed in the case of Louis Zukofsky; that of Richard Bridgman and Donald Sutherland, in that of Gertrude Stein. Both writers are now in anthologies, though, thanks to younger poets.

Back to those students, and their instructor. Fifty-five minutes of class discussion ensue, most of it thematic interpretation. Then for ten minutes the instructor speaks of the historical situation of X's writing, the evolution of a genre and a style, say, which leads to ten more minutes on connections between the poems and the social and economic history of the period. Class ends, and the students chat some more. The first one says she now realizes that they studied X in order to understand better the historical context of poetry in this period. The second one isn't sure that that is what he wanted from the course. He's been taking courses in the History Department and is accustomed to a broader range of evidence for general claims and more rivalry among the claims presented. He took the poetry course, he says, because he loves poetry. He writes poems, and may take creative writing rather than another literature course next semester. She admits to some love of poetry and has taken a number of literature courses, but class discussion in those courses seldom went in that direction.

Do historical explanations of literature adequately meet the interests of students? Few students come to literature courses out of historical curiosity, though many develop that interest. More come rather to understand why poems capture their affection. Teachers face the challenge less of creating interest in poetry than of amplifying an existent interest.

In what form is critical judgment best expressed? We favor the explicit one of Johnson, Pound, Winters, and Bloom. In putting together these volumes, we asked contributors to identify their criteria, even though evaluation is not entirely a measurement of conformity to criteria. Michael W. Clune argues persuasively that "[j]udgment is a process of disclosing particular features and qualities"—largely through interpretation. This process begins with curiosity and uncertainty, not with an agenda. "We [critics] are often speaking of show-ing [people] new criteria," he writes. "The [literary] work satisfies a desire we didn't know we could have; it exemplifies a principle we didn't know existed; it manifests a new quality . . . a quality we don't yet have a name for."[1] He speaks for the indefiniteness and implicitness of the critical process, and his words accurately render the feel of a literary education. Nonetheless, these two volumes record an effort to do the other thing: to formulate judgments plainly, as if in response to a student's question about the worth of a poem, when everyone wants to speak definitely. Are the chapters below as direct as Johnson, Pound, Winters, and Bloom? Certainly not, but our authors have responded to that charge. And Clune explains well why that effort is con-straining. We wanted explicitness not to settle standards of literary apprecia-tion but to facilitate discussion of the value of particular poems. A great deal is known about how to interpret poetry, but not about how to assess it. F. R. Leavis's account of the objective of evaluation is pertinent:

Essentially, a critical judgment has the form, "This is so, isn't it?" . . .
What, of its nature, the critical activity aims at, in fact, is an exchange, a
collaborative exchange, a corrective and creative interplay of judgments.
For though my judgment asks to be confirmed and appeals for
concurrence in a recognition that the thing is *so*, the response I expect at
best will be of the form, "Yes, but—," the "but" standing for qualifications,
corrections, shifts of emphasis, refinements, additions.[2]

When we began to plan this collection, we quickly made an impossibly long
list of poets whose work might, in the eyes of our various colleagues, be the
subject of an essay. Forty names: many of them not mentioned in these pages.
We truly regret some omissions and do not intend the list of those included
as an adequate selection of the best poets of our period. For some poets
whose work we wanted to represent here, we were unable to find a ready
critic. We worked finally from our critics' enthusiasms. We could not pay for
essays, nor effectively insist on particular poets. No canon is offered here. Yet
selections will soon be made, if not by critics, then by editors alone; literary
curricula favor a half-dozen poets to a half century. While waiting for the
anthologies, we might tell students and one another more about why one
poem rather than another warrants continued attention.

Suspicion of evaluation in literary criticism, while not new, has been consequential in the past half-century.[3] In 1957 Northrop Frye wrote derisively of
evaluation: "The demonstrable value-judgment is the donkey's carrot of literary criticism."[4] "Every increase of appreciation," he claimed, "has been right
and every decrease wrong: . . . criticism has no business to react against things,
but should show a steady advance toward undiscriminating catholicity."[5]
Anthologies thicken without critical debate. New poets are added to subsequent editions. In a democratic literary culture, readers push back against
tastemakers. Even T. S. Eliot felt that urge in 1920, before he had himself
become a tastemaker: "The critic must not coerce, and he must not make
judgments of worse and better. He must simply elucidate: the reader will form
the correct judgment for himself."[6] A critic need not even name a relevant
value. Judgment takes care of itself. Within a year he was of a different mind:
"[O]ur standards vary with every poet whom we consider. All we can hope to
do, in the attempt to introduce some order into our preferences, is to clarify
our reasons for finding pleasure in the poetry we like."[7] He did see the point

of stating reasons for approving of particular poems. Harold Bloom made this point more recently: "Judgments of literary value have no significance if not rendered explicit." But he added: "Any literary academic who issues a judgment of aesthetic value—better, worse than, equal to—risks being summarily dismissed as a rank amateur."[8] Evaluation is rarely even discussed in academic settings. Frye objected that evaluative arguments do not illuminate a text: "Every deliberately constructed hierarchy of values in literature known to me is based on a concealed social, moral, or intellectual analogy."[9] Resentment of impure judgment has pushed evaluation off the table entirely—and not for Frye alone. He sought to establish literary study on an intellectual basis resembling that of biology, chemistry, or philology. And that dream is not entirely dead.

Evaluation takes a distinctive form in contemporary letters. Scholars of Romantic or Renaissance poetry may defer to established canons when making up syllabi for courses. Although the earlier historical periods are now and then unsettled by evaluative challenges, their established canons are supported by critical commentary. Concerning poetry since 1950, there are instead taste-encampments. What distinguishes their judgments from those of communities of earlier literary interest—scholars of Renaissance and Romantic poetry—is that taste-camps present no sustained critical examination of their rivals' judgments. James Merrill's readers, for instance, are rarely Adrienne Rich's or Charles Bernstein's. Yet judgments of one camp by another are systematically enforced. This has been true for decades. Rival camps preserve their coherence with taciturnity and disdain rather than debate. The outcome is that students and general readers can draw on only thin accounts of the merits and limits of writers within all camps. All camps appear to be held together more by sensibility than by literary ideas. Close, sustained comparison of writers from separate areas of the contemporary scene could change this.

Both scholars and critics write for students of literature. In contemporary poetry courses, students make their way through improvised reading lists. They contribute to the formation of a curriculum by testing the poets on offer. Those who leave them cold are unlikely to be included when the course is next offered. Readers of contemporary poetry—not only in academic settings—constantly ask whether a particular text has a claim to repeated attention. Literary critics more than scholars write for just such an audience.

Critics of contemporary writing face a constantly expanding number of texts; the work of selection is nearly unavoidable. Leavis observed: "You can't, as some scholars seem to suppose you can, have the poem in a kind of neutral possession, and then proceed to value it or not as you choose—or leave the critic to do the valuing. Any reading of a poem that takes it as a poem involves an element of implicit valuation."[10] To accept a poem is to preserve it for rereading. This curatorial activity is familiar even to general readers. They speak easily of poems recalled, exactly because the mass of contemporary writing is unmanageably large and destined to be lost. Readers build community by naming those texts that have become poems for them. Critics do the same, only they are better equipped to justify their selections than are students or general readers. Literary critics can explain how the literary values known to readers of earlier eras affect the open set of ongoing writing. The challenge to academic readers is to attain sufficient abstraction in one's taste to allow one to recognize the longevity and mobility of literary values. "The real concern of the evaluating critic," Frye said, "is with positive value, with the goodness, or perhaps the genuineness, of the poem, rather than with the greatness of its author."[11] The chapters that follow express positive value judgments to encourage memory of particular poems and poets.

Form

Eliot prizes poems whose parts come together remarkably: "It is not the 'greatness,' the intensity, of the emotions, the components, but the intensity of the artistic process, the pressure, so to speak, under which the fusion takes place, that counts."[12] Esteem for formal coherence dominated poetic theory from the late 1920s until 1960—and motivated great works of criticism. In essays but also college textbooks, the New Critics pressed the proposition that the essence of poetry is form. Its truth is obvious in great stanzaic verse, especially the English sonnet with its closing couplet. Shakespeare's ability to fuse three quatrains and a couplet is sometimes wondrous; the whole self-evidently exceeds the sum of its parts. Eliot wanted to reduce the prominence of subject matter and emotion in literary criticism. The pressure, he stresses, is that of craft, or the strength of a poet's engagement with language, for that is a poet's "artistic process." What the philosopher Christine Korsgaard says of the general phenomenon is true: "There is a terrible self-sufficiency about the most beautiful things, as if all they need is to be what they individually are."[13] Even in the 1960s, after *Howl* (1956) and *Life Studies* (1959), poets and critics continued to speak of poetic form as "organic." What they meant was specifically compatible with Eliot's view. They referred to something transcendent that occurs in the assembling of words and lines.

In the mid-1960s the notion of form inherited from the New Critics was rendered metaphysical by poets who nonetheless considered themselves at odds with New Critical doctrine. Here is Denise Levertov in 1965:

> A partial definition . . . of organic poetry might be that it is a method of apperception, i.e., of recognizing what we perceive, and is based on an intuition of an order, a form beyond forms, in which forms partake, and of which man's creative works are analogies, resemblances, natural allegories.[14]

Not diction, syntax, or rhythm but something other than these knowable elements of a poem are her concern. She draws on a familiar literary version of Platonism, as does Cal Bedient when he speaks of the poem's relation to a source beyond the poet. The critics assembled here do not speak of inspiration, but the formalism of the past century retains vestiges of this ancient notion that are still consequential. One sees here how radical the poetics of Language writers means to be, for Charles Bernstein and Marjorie Perloff would have none of transcendent form. For them, poems are constructed by plan, as buildings are. When the plans are followed, the building is complete; nothing extra should be added to the plans of the architect and engineer. It makes sense that Perloff finds precedent for Bernstein's poetry in Pope.

Charles Olson famously quoted Robert Creeley in 1950: "FORM IS NEVER MORE THAN AN EXTENSION OF CONTENT."[15] Together they meant to undermine the regnant concept of poetic form as a counterforce to statement. Jonathan F. S. Post appreciates Anthony Hecht's poems as outcomes of a dialectic between brutal subject matter and elaborate, refined syntax and prosody. The New Critical sense of form as oppositional was perfect for Hecht's project: he could hear the collision of violence and craft—content and form—and imagine a severe art appropriate to the atrocities and abuses of the mid-twentieth century. Post credits Hecht with engaging the Holocaust in 1960, before other English-language poets had turned to topical subjects. Post repeatedly refers to the strength and power, and emotional impact, of Hecht's poems. Their ground note is suffering. Post quotes Seamus Heaney on form as resistance to necessity—genocide, bombardment, massacre, riot, chaos. Poets known as formalists ought to be not merely those who write in meter and stanzas, but those like Hecht and J. V. Cunningham, who demonstrate the significant functions of conventional forms.

A realized form has its parts where they are meant to stay. Some poems, however, dramatize the arrival of form, or a struggle between statement and silence. Nigel Smith shows that the setting of words to music entails tension between tempo and utterance, a tension audible in song but pertinent to lyric poetry generally. When a text is full, the music must make space or meet a tempo that accommodates the words; Joni Mitchell's "Raised on Robbery" is an instance. Smith especially appreciates songwriters like Bob Dylan and Mitchell who push against an audience's sense of a "proper distribution of syllables . . . into the available musical space." Fluency, "verbal exuberance," challenges musical forms and produces a sense of excess, excitement. Songwriters move words around within the form of a melody, and one hears that negotiation as a drama. Smith is particularly drawn to songs that speed up articulation in order to fit a musical measure. The dominant voice of lyric poetry is reflective, contemplative, that of someone figuring something out, often slowly. However, one recalls Tom Raworth's unusual delivery of some of his poems at a rapid pace, the line breaks mostly inaudible. These performances were disorienting because one rarely hears verse proceed so rapidly, although some stage productions of Elizabethan verse sound too quick to modern audiences. Raworth seemed to wish to get the poem on an unfamiliar frequency, one so high that semantics were subordinated to sounds—a reversal of the usual ratio.[16] The pleasure is not in rendering a sonic profile primary and a semantic chain secondary, but in the revelation of forms one had not previously heard so directly. Think of the great vocalist Jon Hendricks, and his collaboration with Dave Lambert and Annie Ross on "Cloudburst." Nigel Smith's claim is that analysis of the popular song should help one hear more of the play of forms in lyric poems. Raworth would have understood.

Recognizable forms are a hard sell: achieved, we say, meaning settled; enduring, meaning marmoreal, we say too, overbearing or funereal, not charming. The sense of something true said memorably is a very old appeal of poetry. Is it now anachronistic? Does literary history admit of anachronism? For some of the best critics, it may. Consider Charles Bernstein, who likes the roughness of fresh efforts, the awkwardness of something differently conceived, and imperfectly executed. The most valuable poem, in his view, is imperfect. "I prefer art that opens up possibilities rather than art that perfects a possibility. That may mean liking 'lesser' poems to 'greater' ones." A lesser poem may have something hopeful about it, indicating a future, an evolution in view. Marjorie Perloff defends Bernstein's poetry against the charge of formlessness. She makes the argument, derived in part from Roman Jakobson, that formal structures are functional, valid, whether they connect semantic, phonic, or even orthographical elements of a text. This matters because one knows these kinds of elements very differently. One understands semantic resemblances, hears phonic ones, and sees orthographic ones. She shows that these elements all operate in Bernstein's "The Lives of the Toll Takers." That is, if one is accustomed to thinking of form in connection with prosody or genre or figure alone, one may not recognize the variousness of form in Bernstein, or Ezra Pound, or Shakespeare's sonnets, for that matter, or one may see it but not feel it, and therefore not appreciate these poets adequately. She advocates an especially wide range of feeling in the reading of experimental poems. Hear this, see that, and understand this other thing: altogether, that is poetic form, and ready to be felt.

After 1960 many poets expressed reservations about rhetorical as much as prosodic form. Linda Gregerson imagines a poet with rhetorical designs on readers but a medium that constantly surprises. In her chapter in this volume, she states that poetry is "a collaborative medium," and certainly poets know that their intentions are only part of an equation. Histories of usage, syntactic structures, prosodic patterns, and vowel echoes also determine what poems say, not just how they say it; and then eventually readers construct their own interpretations. Like many readers, Gregerson is attracted by a mobile voice: changeability is her value, nothing final. Stephen Yenser similarly praises Elizabeth Bishop's "errancy," "wandering," and "deviation." It's the strangeness of her voice that intrigues him, as it did Merrill. Yenser characterizes her "signature tone" as "sweetbitter"; he is not concerned, as Gregerson is, with the civic or political sense of mixed feelings, but at the level of style he is on her wavelength. Langdon Hammer affirms at the end of his chapter herein the justness of Merrill's "dualistic sensibility"— the notion that there is a plus and minus to everything. Our collective peace, Gregerson suggests (and we concur), might be enhanced by more provisionality in our intellectual discourse. Politicians now show little interest in collaboration, which one reasonably thinks would be the payoff for resurrection of the subjunctive in public policy discussions. While this stiffness is a recent phenomenon in Washington, it has characterized literary culture since the appearance of Olson's "Projective Verse" (1950).

One distinguishes poetic from ordinary language by means of some notion of the aesthetic, although that category has lost much legitimacy in literary interpretation. One wants poems to be consequential, maybe even poets to address the controversies of their time—as Milton, Marvell, Dryden, Blake, Wordsworth, Yeats, Eliot, and Pound all did. The status of poetic statement is directly at issue in the chapters (in volume 2) by John Shoptaw on ecopoetry, Charles Altieri on Rich's political advocacy, and Sarah Nooter on Sharon Olds's explicitness. Traditionally, poetic language is memorable, ready for recitation and the stonecutters. Stephen Yenser and John Farrell (in this volume), and Richard Strier and Patrick Morrissey (in volume 2), do speak for artful phrasing by Elizabeth Bishop, Charles Wright, Robert Hass, and August Kleinzahler, respectively, and for good reason. Exactness of expression is difficult. Gregerson, however, speaks cogently for provisional expression. Critics who esteem memorable formulations also want change and variety within careers and even individual poems. "Fugitive," "erratic," "deliberately discontinuous," "fallibility"—these qualities, Gregerson argues, are valuable in poems. In social and political policy, in regulations and laws, one rightly wants utterances open to revision, reinterpretation, repeal. This is no more than democratic political deliberation. Why should poetry be different? Without a sense of the aesthetic (or of decorum), the question is unanswerable.

Magnitude

Why is the unity of some works of art thought "terrible," as Korsgaard says? How might coherence elicit fright? A beauty that does not serve ends other than itself is a cause for fear, she says, presumably because it violates the ordinary sense of things as valuable for some purpose. To be made to recognize the existence of a value that needs no external justification arouses fear, because it suggests that one has misunderstood the order of things. Instrumental reasoning may be subordinate to something else. However hard it is to argue that the value of poetry lies in truth-telling, or in beauty, that is what is asked of high art. Eliot claimed that the "peculiarity of all great poetry . . . is merely a peculiar honesty."[17] He did not refer to the circulation of commonplaces; the repeated term indicates the opposite of generality. He referred in particular to Blake's eccentricity, which he called "peculiarly terrifying." He may well have had in mind the adagia of *The Marriage of Heaven and Hell*. Louise Glück said that the "true, in poetry, is felt as insight. It is very rare, but beside it other poems seem merely intelligent comment."[18] This Germanic term, insight, refers to unusually penetrating, intermittent vision. A philosophical argument is sustained; an insight is not. Insight appears independent of reasoning, or of context. How it is arrived at is beside the point. Literary criticism has a term for the power of strange, unsustainable truth: the sublime.

Angus Fletcher said that "the value of the most eccentric works falls on another scale [from that of Shakespeare's sonnets], yet it is not easy to say exactly what that scale measures. It seems to measure a literary activity akin to the production of the sublime."[19] One does not dispute the truth of a lightning bolt; one acknowledges it, and hopes to move on. The poets of our period who tried to write something akin to the sublime? They are few: Robert Lowell, at the start of his career; Frank Bidart, more persistently; Ronald Johnson and Robert Duncan, too. A lonely band, after the modernists. This may be the one just sense in which one speaks of a falling off after *Four Quartets* and *The Pisan Cantos*.[20] "Strangeness for me is *the* canonical quality," Harold Bloom says, "the mark of sublime literature."[21] The poetry of the past half century has rarely been sublime; it has been more civic in its attention, agreeable in its idioms. For decades, this grand measure has been admired from afar, but suspiciously.

Cal Bedient begins his chapter on poetic ambition, in volume 2, with three criteria concerning magnitude: the first is that poetry "speak[s] a language that comes from behind the work, not from within it"; the second, that it express a vision of the largeness of life itself; the third, "that the work be in the final form of the full promise of its assumptions, a fresh demonstration of possibilities." His second criterion gets at the discontinuity between the generation born in the 1880s and those born in the 1920s and 1930s. The United States has seen extraordinary expansion since 1945: of the economy and state apparatus; of its extraterritorial involvement; of research universities and colleges; and of technology. But poetry has seemed stubbornly secondary to its immediate past.[22] Bedient credits Jorie Graham for answering to aspirations of the modernists, when some of her contemporaries regarded modernism as a wrong turn. Merrill's *The Changing Light at Sandover* "countered the seriousness and monumentality of modernism as embodied by Eliot and the Eliot-influenced New Criticism," Langdon Hammer writes, "at the same time that it rejected the professionalism of the creative writing programs." John Wilkinson praises Charles Olson's explicit engagement of his predecessors. When we speak of Whitman as the father of American poetry, we take for granted the magnitude of the art that had come to seem dubious after 1945. Large spirits, seeing others grandly, are rightly called magnanimous; maybe too-this or too-that for companionship, but candidates for greatness. No one wanted an abject poetry, but some important poets did want to turn down the volume after Pound's arrest.

Poetry is a conservative art insofar as its traditions are constantly renewed by living poets. The term "sublime" is infrequently invoked by recent critics; most (aside from Bloom) are shy of its grandeur. But it remains a measure. Something similar may be said of "unity." Critics recognize a need to explain alternatives to this concept of poetic success. No one speaks of Arnold's "high seriousness," but the concept bears on Post's analysis of Anthony Hecht. Sianne Ngai has recently argued that our live aesthetic categories are deliberately diminutive: "zany," "cute," and "interesting" have currency in discussions of the visual arts.[23] There is less reason in the criticism of poetry to generate new rubrics for advocacy. Poets are not constrained to styles by market forces. A poet may revive a diction or prosodic or rhetorical form by force of will and skill, as J. V. Cunningham has demonstrated. Thanks to paper and pencil, we can have the poetry we want, regardless of immediate precedent, as Pound and Eliot demonstrated.

Academia, Again

Back again to the classroom. We have seen a reduction of judgment not simply to feelings or to the irrational but to one's personal background as determined by categories of race, class, and gender. An evaluation of a work answers no doubt to particular interests, but should they be so limited? This problem was made pointedly clear to one of us while serving on a doctoral oral examination. The student's main field was Renaissance drama; her secondary field was American poetry. She had taken written examinations, and the committee of three professors—two in Renaissance literature and one in American poetry—would then question her further. Most of the examination was taken up with questions about the Renaissance. I had only ten minutes left to ask questions about American poetry. On the written exam, the student discussed two poems, Williams's "Portrait of a Lady" and Plath's "Daddy." So, I asked two questions. The first was: "What contemporaries of Williams wrote poems with the same or similar title?" She knew of Pound's but not of Eliot's. I then moved on to "Daddy" and asked, "Is this a good poem?" Her answer was simple and startling: "You're Jewish, aren't you?" I probably looked puzzled enough for her to respond, "No, it's a good thing." I ignored that and stated that I just wanted her to tell me about her evaluative criteria. The dissertation director abruptly ended the examination, and the student left the room fairly distressed. She passed the exam, but I'm not sure that I did. And her dissertation adviser scolded me for asking the question about "Daddy." "You sounded like Jesse Helms," she said.

I might have framed the question in a more specific way—"Does Plath successfully construct a voice in the poem?" or "Is her transformation of the personal to the mythic effective?" Of course, the latter version could readily lead one to ask whether it is extravagant to use the Holocaust as a metaphor for one's personal rage against a parent. Extravagant? OK, unethical? The student assumed that my own critical concerns came purely from my personal background. One would hope that an evaluation is not so rigidly predictable. That said, is it wrong to be concerned about ethical and moral concerns in relation to aesthetics? Are those complex categories strictly separable? Almost anyone who evaluates a work of art is concerned with how an artist engages an audience, with the means used to persuade and move us.

Critics assess the success or failure of those strategies with a wide range of criteria, many of which cannot be determined by the critic's origin.

We hope to have made clear—by our citations—that the efforts of literary critics going back to Plato remain indispensable. When Bloom says that strangeness is the essential canonical value, he is near Socrates on the madness of poets, and that is something to ponder. The suspicion of evaluation that began in the mid-1950s intensified in the early 1980s for a decade of debate about canon formation. John Guillory effectively ended that debate in 1993 with a study, as acute now as then, of institutional settings of evaluation.[24] Recent books by Sianne Ngai, Rita Felski, Andrew H. Miller, and Michael Clune indicate that a return to evaluation is now underway, although selection has been a constant issue with regard to contemporary writing.[25] We join these recent critics in reminding our discipline of the need for evaluation. They ask what immediately pleases students. Felski's overarching term is "hooked." Miller examines the allure of vicarious being, "other lives." These terms seek the intelligent sense of first readings of texts— mostly narratives. The criticism of poetry is rich with terms of esteem that are differently oriented. What does one think after multiple readings, after discussion with others, after considering counterintuitive critical responses? Critics often summon attention to a poem read without feeling. They pull one back, a little shamefaced, to poems one might have better noticed. Not: What does it feel like to read this poem? But: And now what do you think? Ngai, Felski, and Miller, too, want to urge considered readings on students, but these critics begin with less skepticism toward first reading than has been the custom. The chapters that follow concern what most deserves considered admiration.

R. F.

R. v. H.

Notes

1. Michael W. Clune, *A Defense of Judgment* (Chicago: University of Chicago Press, 2021), 85, 96.
2. F. R. Leavis, *Valuation in Criticism and Other Essays*, ed. G. Singh (Cambridge: Cambridge University Press, 1986), 277–78. Eva Schaper discusses this

Enlightenment idea in John Gilbert Cooper and Voltaire in her essay "The Pleasures of Taste" (in *Pleasure, Preference and Value: Studies in Philosophical Aesthetics*, ed. Eva Schaper [Cambridge: Cambridge University Press, 1983], 40–42).

3. See Barbara Herrnstein Smith, "Contingencies of Value," in *Canons*, ed. Robert von Hallberg (Chicago: University of Chicago Press, 1984), 5–40.

4. Northrop Frye, *Anatomy of Criticism* (Princeton, NJ: Princeton University Press, 1957), 20.

5. Ibid., 25.

6. T. S. Eliot, *The Sacred Wood* (1920; London: Methuen, 1960), 11.

7. T. S. Eliot, *Selected Essays* (New York: Harcourt, Brace and World, 1960), 267–68.

8. Harold Bloom, *Anatomy of Influence* (New Haven, CT: Yale University Press, 2011), 17.

9. Frye, *Anatomy of Criticism*, 23

10. Leavis, *Valuation*, 279.

11. Frye, *Anatomy of Criticism*, 27.

12. Eliot, *The Sacred Wood*, 55.

13. Christine M. Korsgaard, "The Dependence of Value on Humanity," in *The Practice of Value*, by Joseph Raz, Christine M. Korsgaard, Robert Pippin, and Bernard Williams (Oxford: Clarendon Press, 2003), 78.

14. Denise Levertov, "Some Notes on Organic Form," in *The Poet in the World* (New York: New Directions, 1973), 7.

15. Robert Creeley, quoted in Charles Olson, "Projective Verse" (1950), in Charles Olson, *Human Universe and Other Essays*, ed. Donald Allen (New York: Grove Press, 1967), 51–52.

16. See PennSound for a recording of Raworth's "Errory," a poem published in 1996 and discussed interestingly by Charles Bernstein, Al Filreis, Michael Hennessey, and Marjorie Perloff; PoemTalk, podcast no. 50, http://jacket2.org/podcasts/state-error-poemtalk-50.

17. Eliot, *The Sacred Wood*, 151.

18. Louise Glück, *Proofs and Theories: Essays on Poetry* (Hopewell, NJ: Ecco Press, 1994), 45.

19. Angus Fletcher, *Colors of the Mind: Conjectures on Thinking in Literature* (Cambridge, MA: Harvard University Press, 1991), 260.

20. Allen Grossman commented on this notion in conversation with Mark Halliday: "I think one of the reasons for the absence of a sentiment of vital contemporaneity among persons of your generation [born just after World War II] lies in the willed disavowal of majority by the productive poets who were dominant during the time when you were educated. It seems as if Yeats and Eliot, Pound and Stevens used up the idea of greatness or implicated that idea in complex ways with aspects of the civilization . . . that produced the Second World War." Allen

Grossman, *Against Our Vanishing*, ed. Mark Halliday (Boston: Rowan Tree, 1981), 34–35.

21. Bloom, *Anatomy of Influence*, 19.

22. Critics of postwar poetry have complained of modest advocacy. John Guillory has written well of Eliot's strategic pursuit of a minor voice in "The Ideology of Canon-Formation: T. S. Eliot and Cleanth Brooks," in *Canons*, ed. Robert von Hallberg (Chicago: University of Chicago Press, 1984), 337–62; but generally the modernists were not exemplars of diminution in their poems.

23. Ngai does not argue that these concepts have purchase on recent discussion of poetry, though she does sense a connection between cuteness and the brevity of Williams and O'Hara. "Interesting" is used in conversation to recommend poems, and just about anything else, but in public criticism of poetry the term has no authority. "Cute" has no currency in conversation or print concerning poetry. "Zany" could be used to describe some poems, Ed Dorn's *Gunslinger* and some of Charles Bernstein's work, or Frank O'Hara's, but poetry critics have not put the term into play. Sianne Ngai, *Our Aesthetic Categories: Zany, Cute, Interesting* (Cambridge, MA: Harvard University Press, 2012), 3, 18–19.

24. John Guillory, *Cultural Capital: The Problem of Literary Canon Formation* (Chicago: University of Chicago Press, 1993), esp. 269–340. See, too, Barbara Herrnstein Smith, *Contingencies of Value: Alternative Perspectives for Critical Theory* (Cambridge, MA: Harvard University Press, 1991). For fuller references to the debate on canon formation, see Guillory, *Cultural Capital*, 343n5.

25. Ngai, *Our Aesthetic Categories*; Rita Felski, *Hooked: Art and Attachment* (Chicago: University of Chicago Press, 2020); Andrew H. Miller, *On Not Being Someone Else: Tales of Our Unled Lives* (Cambridge, MA: Harvard University Press, 2020); and Clune, *A Defense of Judgment*.

VOICE

CHAPTER 1

On Voice as a Category of Analysis; or, Lyric Address

LINDA GREGERSON

I'D LIKE TO suggest that we revive the category of voice as an object of analysis, retrieving it from the discredited realm of mystification ("I haven't found my voice yet") and from denigration as a naïve delusion about the a priori status of the self. Voice—and I refer to the specifically rhetorical construction of voice, the who's-speaking-to-whom part—has gone largely missing from recent discussions of the lyric poem, sidelined by attention to thematics or to formal lenses that fail to capture both the rigor and the subtlety of vocal navigation. For this purpose it helps, I think, to look at early English-language experiments with the construction of "voice" in all its provisionality and rhetorical complexity.

What are the evaluative underpinnings of this examination? I am interested in flexibility and range, a mobile alliance between the semantic and the symptomatic modes of meaning making; I hope to see our conversations about form acknowledge the turns of rhetoric to be as crucial as the turns of syntax, the deployments of meter and line break, and the construction of verbal figure. I would also hope that a more explicit attention to rhetorical voice might give us more flexible ways of contemplating—and inhabiting—the present "identitarian" moment, in which the crucial issues of racial, sexual, ethnocultural, regional, and dis/ability status are too often treated as exclusively thematic issues, divorced from all but the most obvious considerations of poetic method. Rhetorical voicing: old-fashioned name for an ever-immediate and foundational property of language. A genealogy of lyric voice might help us to identify unexpected affinities and distinctions; might even, in an ideal world, enable us to read more generously across the spectrum of as-yet-uncanonized work. Not least, it might provide an analytical framework and a descriptive vocabulary that move us decisively beyond outdated oppositional thinking. "Authorial intent" vs. "language writes us": powerful (and useful) propositions that too easily harden into mantras. The lyric poem has always been a collaborative construct, one part poet, one part reader or auditor, one part the complex network of purpose and momentums and materialities that constitute its medium.

1. Thomas Wyatt

To suggest the range of vocal construction I have in mind, a range that comprehends the work of T. S. Eliot as well as William Shakespeare, Anne Carson as well as John Ashbery, I'd like to adduce just four examples, one of which, for brevity's sake, I trust to be virtually self-explanatory. The first of these is a poem from the sixteenth century, by Sir Thomas Wyatt. I have written about Wyatt at greater length elsewhere,[1] but his work is so foundational for rhetorical voicing in the English-language lyric that I have to adduce his example once again. I refer to his extraordinarily limber play with lyric address, the built-in-front-of-our-very-eyes impression of speaker and occasion. Wyatt cultivates a kind of vocal gesture—fugitive, erratic, deliberately discontinuous—we have since come to regard as the hallmark of personality. Experimenting with voice-as-characterological-symptom, he conjures the figment of an individuated speaking persona, one who is biased, irritable, and rhetorically unstable. The innovation lies not in the quality of strong feeling—to speak of and with strong feeling is as old as poetry itself— nor in the reference to biographical and social circumstance: this too is old. The innovation lies in method, the symptom-effect or vocal signature that suggests, by way of back formation, a socially embedded, distinctive personality. Wyatt's contribution is consequential precisely because his method is at odds with the fully contextualized monologue that will reach its apotheosis in the work of Robert Browning.

Classical guides to rhetoric, assiduously studied by English schoolboys and incorporated into sixteenth-century English handbooks, offer counsel on what the rhetor must be, or seem to be; how the speaker must construct a self of words in order to suggest a presence behind the words, a presence that secures the efficacy of words. From the perspective of rhetoric, meaning is not the semantic premise but the measurable consequence of eloquence, an effect or manipulable impression, as when one spirit contrives to subdue another, as in, I *mean* to make you mine. Rhetoric emphasizes the transitive aspects of linguistic production, the conspiracy of words with power. The power to mold opinion is an emanation of the speaker's person, or so the classical rhetoricians frankly posit: a thing is so because I who say it is so am a reliable person. And you are willing to believe what I say, or to behave as if you do, because the self you see in the mirror of my words, the space I invite you to inhabit as interlocutor, is a self, or a space, you like. Rhetoric invents its audience, too. There was a time when this model of concentrated will-to-produce-a-world sounded not only naïve from a theoretical standpoint but hopelessly out of touch. No longer. If the instruments of rhetorical efficacy have been altered almost beyond recognition, if inarticulateness itself has been formidably "weaponized" in the public sphere, the mechanics of who-recruits-whom to the collaborative production of meaning look uncannily like those described in the ancient rhetorics. Augustine called his professorship in rhetoric the "chair of lies," and he believed that conscience required him to abandon it.

What is the role of lyric in a culture all too prone to manipulation? An urgent question, and one to which I'll return. But first, some background on technique. The special innovation of lyricists in sixteenth-century England was to combine the flamboyant manipulations of rhetorical persuasion with the quasi-dramatic enactment of Petrarchan love-longing. In Wyatt, as in Sidney, Shakespeare, and a host of subsequent writers, the speaker implicit behind the lyric is at once a technical virtuoso and a creature capable of linguistic self-betrayal. Idiosyncrasies of phrasing, gaps in logic, ostensibly inadvertent lapses of proportion begin to be cultivated as symptoms of personality or clues to dissonant subtext. This turns the handbook premise against itself: rhetorical power is found to inhere not only in demonstrated mastery but also, paradoxically, in mastery's breakdown. The most compelling word is found to be the word that makes its own fallibility, and that of its speaker, most palpably felt.

Wyatt's most famous adaptation of Petrarch is deliberately pitched at the opposite end of the rhetorical spectrum from its original, which reports a transcendent vision of the beloved.[2]

> Whoso list to hunt, I know where is an hind,
> But as for me, helas, I may no more.
> The vain travail hath wearied me so sore,
> I am of them that farthest cometh behind.
> Yet may I by no means my wearied mind
> Draw from the deer, but as she fleeth afore
> Fainting I follow. I leave off therefore
> Sithens in a net I seek to hold the wind.
> Who list her hunt, I put him out of doubt,
> As well as I may spend his time in vain.
> And graven with diamonds in letters plain
> There is written her fair neck round about:
> "*Noli me tangere* for Caesar's I am,
> And wild for to hold though I seem tame."[3]

"Whoso list to hunt, I know where is an hind." Grounded, demotic, shot through with aggrievement and insinuation, the poem begins by conjuring not only a speaker with an ax to grind but also an implied inner audience. And this audience, like the speaker, has attributes. It is gendered; it is "interested." Wyatt's poem begins in a kind of locker room vernacular, male. You want to try your luck? he says; I can point you in the right direction. "Whoso list to hunt, I know where is an hind." And almost immediately, the first of several turnings: "But as for me, helas, I may no more." This modulates, almost, to the more orthodox Petrarchan lover's complaint. Almost, but not quite. For the speaker is pointedly not alone with his suffering, not even in the special sense of lyric complaint, which always inhabits the paradoxical public/private domain of that-which-is-written-to-be-read. This speaker has hunted with others who are *in the game*: "The vain travail hath wearied me so sore, / I am of them that farthest cometh behind." The deprivation of which he complains, in other words, is relative as well as absolute; the problem is not merely the beloved's coldness or inaccessibility but the social insult of a poor competitive showing.

The instabilities of renunciation and continued entanglement have been amply noted in this sonnet before, but for my purposes, the key point is that they *both solicit and evade* a psychological reading. On one level, the inconsistent push-and-pull ("I may no more," "I follow," "I leave off") suggests the turmoil of captive desire and thus the symptoms of a psyche under pressure. The symptom-effect again. But this is one level only: we do not find ourselves inside a single, coherent subjectivity in "Whoso List to Hunt." Producing the effects of psychological instability, and exceeding them as well, is something else: an instability of rhetorical proposition. From the knowing pseudo-confidentiality of line 1, which conjures an inner audience of fellow cynics, the speaker segues to a complaint mode in which that audience is vaporized. The second quatrain inhabits a different speaking-and-listening cosmos altogether; we have moved from quasi-dramatic to lyric mode. Even within that lyric mode, the speaking persona seems to waver between personal and social aggrievement, which wavering is temporarily "solved" by the abrupt and bitter return to the mockeries of public auction: "Who list her hunt, I put him out of doubt, / As well as I may spend his time in vain."

Let me confess at once that these "slow readings" are by nature both ungainly and distorting. I do not for a minute mean to propose that the reader of the poem on the page or, in ordinary circumstances, "on the voice" will consciously pause to contemplate the blow-by-blow vicissitudes of the inner audience I have described: now he's got their attention, now he's losing it, etc. Nor even: now they're vividly invoked, now they're fading into something else, etc. Much less do I mean to suggest that Wyatt's compositional method involved the hypercalculation of local transitions. This is not, as I understand it, how poems get made. It's the speed and economy with which Wyatt limns the ever-changing social circumstance of lyric speech; it's the radical provisionality of speaking voice, the overlap and permeability and cross-fades of rhetorical propositions, that make his work so thrilling and so new and also so decisive for later lyricists like Sidney and Shakespeare. Instability is the method, mobility the key effect. "Intermittence" is Wyatt's genius.[4]

I won't dwell in comparable detail on the yet more complicated negotiations of voice in Wyatt's sestet, but it is worth noting one technique that has been added to the effects described above. *Noli me tangere*: the phrase is "spoken" in diamonds around the neck of the hind. "[F]or Caesars

I am." The diamonds purport to speak on behalf of the first-person hind, who speaks on behalf of "Caesar," who claims to own her. "Caesar" quotes the risen Christ. The poet quotes Petrarch quoting a white doe quoting the risen Christ. In Petrarch's shimmering vision, the paradox of freedom and prior possession, untouchability and stamp-of-ownership, invokes a coherent system of spiritual transcendence. In Wyatt's poem, Caesar's claims and God's claims are restored to their foundational irreconcilability. And more. If the poet, as is plausible for this era as for our own, expects to be "recognized" behind the lyric persona as Thomas Wyatt, lover of Anne Boleyn, he risks not only blasphemy but the very real and palpable wrath of Caesar. Let us call this "layered voicing" and note the extraordinary limberness it requires of poet and reader alike.

2. John Ashbery

And one is left sitting in the yard
To try to write poetry
Using what Wyatt and Surrey left around,
Took up and put down again
Like so much gorgeous raw material . . .[5]

No one has picked up Wyatt's gorgeous raw materials—the irreverence, the shifts in diction and implicit context, the teasing suggestions of person-behind-the-screen, the delirious juxtapositions of high and low—with more amplitude and resourcefulness than the American poet John Ashbery.

All things seem mention of themselves
And the names which stem from them branch out to
    other referents.
Hugely, spring exists again. The weigela does its dusty
    thing
In fire-hammered air. And garbage cans are heaved
    against
The railing as the tulips yawn and crack open and fall
    apart.

And today is Monday. Today's lunch is: Spanish omelet,
  lettuce and tomato salad.
Jello, milk and cookies. Tomorrow's: sloppy joe on
   bun,
Scalloped corn, stewed tomatoes, rice pudding and
   milk.

("Grand Galop")

From high theory (American infatuation with the French imports was at its
height in 1975 when this poem was published in *Self-Portrait in a Convex Mirror*) to the purest American demotic ("does its thing"), from semiotics to
sloppy joes, the poet invites his readers to join him in the gleeful festivity and
supple improvisation of a grand galop. Ashbery is not the only portal through
which the rhetorical experimentation of sixteenth-century England came to
twentieth-century America, far from it. But among writers of the late twentieth
century, his is at once the most consolidated and the most bountiful exploration of vocal gesture I know. His fascination with the push and pull of rhetorical expectation seems to know no limits. His work has wonderfully
enlarged (and challenged) our ability to think about the porous boundaries
between ornament and semantics, periphery and center, throwaway and philosophical core.

3. Ross Gay

On the surface, the title poem of Ross Gay's *Bringing the Shovel Down* would
seem to stake coherence on the assumption, or the built effect, of personal
voice.[6] "Because I love you," begins this poem,

> . . . and beneath the uncountable stars
> I have become the delicate piston threading itself through
>   your chest,
>
> I want to tell you a story I shouldn't but will . . .

Because I love you. The stakes are high at once, both intimate and mysterious:

Who is this you? Who is speaking to the you? What has either of them to do with me? Everything, says the poem, as it trawls through the vastness of the starry sky to the inwardness of the pulse in the breast with the hook that reels me in: a story. And, best of all, a forbidden story, which makes me co-conspirator in something that shouldn't, for reasons yet to be revealed, be told.

> "I want to tell you a story I shouldn't but will, and in the
> meantime neglect, Love . . ."

There it is again—that liberty taken, the intimate address, and this time it is not merely a thing the speaker claims to do or feel—love—but a thing—Love—he or she has become, the one whom he addresses, who is and is not me.

> . . . and in the meantime neglect, Love,
> the discordant melody spilling from my ears but attend,
>
> instead, to this tale, for a river burns inside my mouth
> and it wants both purgation and to eternally sip your
> thousand drippings

Ears do not spill melodies, they are instruments of apprehension. Mouths do not run with rivers. Rivers do not burn. Disciplined to the parameters of a consistent and obedient conceit, drippings may constitute the source of a river, but they may also, disturbingly, gather in a roasting pan. And there is nothing obedient or well-behaved about this cascading imagery. Enthralling, synesthetic, these extravagant sensory promptings conjure a speaker who is not entirely in control and an auditor—the "you," who is me—whose boundaries are not intact. The one who speaks and the one who listens interanimate. The story injects itself into the very veins:

> and in the story is a dog and unnamed it leads to less
> heartbreak,
> so name him Max, and in the story . . .

And there we have it, there with the speed of a by-the-way, we are warned.
The story is toxic and aimed at the heart.

>...and in the story are neighborhood kids

who spin a yarn about Max like I'm singing to you, except they tell a child,
>...and combining in their story the big kids make

the boy who shall remain unnamed believe Max to be sick and rabid,
and say his limp and regular smell of piss are just two signs,

but the worst of it, they say, is that he'll likely find you in the night,
and ... inside the boy's head grew a fire beneath the same stars

as you and I, Love, your leg between mine, the fine hairs
on your upper thigh nearly glistening in the night, and the boy,

the night, the incalculable mysteries as he sleeps with a stuffed animal
tucked beneath his chin and rolls tight against his brother

in their shared bed, who rolls away, and you know by now

And you know by now where the story is going and you shouldn't continue
to listen but you do.

>... and I shouldn't tell you, but I will,
the unnamed boy

on the third night of the dreams which harden his soft face
puts on pants and a sweatshirt and quietly takes the spade from the
den ...

And the poet, inch by inch and detail by detail, takes his story exactly where
we fear it will go:

>   . . . and Max whimpers,
>   and the boy sees a wolf where stands this ratty
>
>   and sad and groveling dog and beneath these very stars
>   the boy brings the shovel down
>
>   until Max's hind legs stop twitching and his left ear folds into itself,
>   and the unnamed boy stares at the rabid wolf whose wild eyes loll
>   white in his head,
>
>   taking slow steps backward through the wet grass and feels,
>   for the first time in days, the breath in his lungs, which is cool, . . .

And with something like redemption flooding over him, the boy returns in
the first light of morning to the bush where days ago the neighborhood kids
found him picking raspberries:

>   . . . where an occasional prick
>   leaves on his arm or leg a spot of blood the color of these raspberries
>
>   and tasting of salt, and filling his upturned shirt with them he beams
>   that he could pull from the earth that which might make you smile,
>
>   Love, which you'll find in the fridge, on the bottom shelf, behind the
>   milk,
>   in the bowl you made with your own lovely hands.

From the ominous title through every insinuating reiteration of the intimate address, the promised story contaminates the air with dread. And
because we love to be frightened, we are responsible for the story: the poem is
a moral entangling. In the category of voice—the simultaneous construction
of speaker and auditor—the poem is a veritable handbook of rhetorical technique. As an aging dog with its smell of piss infects the air, as malicious boys
infect the mind of one who is weaker, as you and I, Love, your leg between
mine, begin to lose our separate contours, so the story accumulates momentum and begins to colonize everything in its path. I cannot help but hear in

those terms of endearment—Love, Love, Darling, Love—the echoes of Rudyard Kipling: "In the sea, once upon a time, O my Best Beloved, there was a Whale . . ." The echo is not, I think, accidental. In the *Just So Stories*, storytelling at its most elemental (Once upon a time) mingles with the teasing authority of intimate address. The one who speaks is one who knows, the one who listens is a child, and the scene is one of instruction: How the Whale Got His Throat, How the Camel Got His Hump. The story (in the shadow of bedtime?) is one of origins, which in "Bringing the Shovel Down" becomes the origin of evil.

The essence of Gay's poem would seem to be momentum, narration moving relentlessly, heart-chillingly forward in a single rolling sentence. Yet in the course of this momentum it also builds a conspicuous formal coherence, at once aesthetically pleasurable and morally alarming. In the alternating registers of diction, from lofty to homely and back again, in the echoing images of what ought to be reassuring—lovers in bed, their legs intertwined; brother and brother in bed, a stuffed animal between them—the story enlarges and enlarges its embrace, until the darkness is all-encompassing. We are afforded no reprieve or moral insulation. The story that constitutes the subject of the poem becomes the story the poem itself enacts: neighborhood kids "spin a yarn . . . like I'm singing to you." They do it for the hell of it; they do it because they can; they do it because someone is willing to listen, and power, like fear, is a kind of drug. And the yarn they spin is as venerable as the one that is spun by fate.

A lesser poet might end with the death of the dog: helplessness done in by innocence. But Gay deepens our sense of inextricability by turning and turning his tale. In a false catharsis that, horribly, works as well as the true, the credulous child finds peace again; dawn brings him back to sweet berries; the blood on his arm is merely the price of the sweetness. And the berries, crossing the most porous of narrative membranes, are the same as those now waiting for "you" in the fridge. In honor of your rapt attention, the bowl in which they chill is "yours." That the intact gift of chilling fruit inverts, in its chilly doubleness, a famous William Carlos Williams poem[7] is only the final sign of your, of our, capitulation.

Significantly, this poem appears not once but twice in *Bringing the Shovel Down*; in the second instance it is titled simply "Again." The second poem conforms, line by line and turn by turn, to its original, except for a crucial difference, which changes everything:

and the boy sees a wolf where stands this ratty

and sad and groveling dog and beneath these very stars
Max raises his head to look at the unnamed boy

with one glaucous eye nearly glued shut
and the other wet from the cool breeze and wheezing

Max catches the gaze of the boy who sees,
at last, the raw skin on the dog's flanks, the quiver

of his spindly legs, and as Max bends his nose
to the franks the boy watches him struggle

to snatch the meat with his gums, and bringing the
    shovel down
he bends to lift the meat to Max's toothless mouth,

and rubs the length of his throat and chin,
Max arching his neck with his eyes closed, now,

and licking the boy's round face, until the boy unchains
    the dog,
and stands, taking slow steps backward . . .

. . . into the rest of the poem as originally written, which acts now as a blessing rather than a curse.[8]

It is no accident that the turning point in this second version is a reciprocal gaze, the gaze of recognition that is poetry's dearest fantasy. At its urgent best, the lyric recognizes, and grants its reader the gift of recognizing, a world that is larger than we are, ensoulments that are distinct from yet inextricably connected to our own. In its trajectory of emotion, its music, its ethics, its insinuating narrative, "Again" is as conspicuously manipulated as is the earlier "Bringing the Shovel Down": how could it be otherwise? Poetry's tools are technical. Its powers—of shared attention—rely upon the collaborative production of meaning, for better and for worse. It exposes to critical view both the dynamics of complicity and the possibilities of compassion.

4. Interlude: Poetic Method

The disclaimer built into my discussion of Wyatt merits further explanation, especially in the context of evaluative criticism.

I believe in "slow reading" as a durable source of insight and pleasure. I believe that detailed formal and semantic analysis is an invaluable tool for nuanced understanding of poetry. While I acknowledge and treasure other modes of response, I believe that the pleasures of analysis are not extraneous but integral to poetry. I know from personal experience that such analysis can teach a reader to admire the workings of poetry that may initially have left her cold. While I enjoy and even admire some poems that use themselves up on a first or second reading, I prefer poetry that gets richer over time, poetry whose effects are layered: some of them immediate, some slower to emerge, some even at odds with one another. I quite like poetry that makes me work, but I want it to make me want to work. I describe this to my students as my pig-and-truffle theory of poetry. More of this below.

So. Given my passionate advocacy of slow, close reading, why have I described it as "distorting?" I firmly believe that the methods and meanings unearthed by meticulous explication are constituent components of poetry (as indeed of other art forms) and not gratuitous add-ons. But. Meticulous explication does not and is not designed to capture the actual dynamics of ordinary reading or—and this is equally important—of poetic composition.

Pig-and-truffle. Years ago, the owner of a small French bistro in Palo Alto, California—let's call him Théo—used to reminisce about truffle hunting in his native Dordogne. Théo was wont to wax most eloquent on the virtues of truffle-hunting pigs: they were far more intelligent than dogs, he averred, far more sensitive, superior in every way. But, warned Théo, raising his right eyebrow, you cannot hoard all the truffles for yourself; you have to allow the pig to eat an occasional truffle or he will become "discouraged." I remember that last word in particular; it was carefully chosen.

So, I tell my students, you have to let the reader have a truffle now and then: some foothold, some ostensibly easy-of-access moment. The reader will put up with, will even relish, any number of demands: technical vocabularies, ephemeral cultural references, fragmentary and contradictory narratives, disruptions of syntax, unfamiliar place-names and dates that are clearly intended to resonate with historical significance. Many of these can be navigated by means of a simple Google search (reading has been mightily transformed); others can be part of the ordinary push-and-pull of rhetorical negotiation. Readers may even come to relish their own subversion: a grammatical clause that promises to continue in one direction but swerves into another, a historical or scientific or biographical detail that willfully obscures the distinction between "actual" and "fictional." But, barring artificial pressure, like preparation for a workshop, the reader wants encouragement along the way, some flash of recognition, however momentary, some sense of making sense: some truffle.

As to poetic composition: the process is as varied and variable, of course, as are the people who make poems. That said, I believe there are some commonalities:

1. No poem emerges as the product of unimpeded will. Its medium is a complex fabric of vested inheritance. Words bring with them any number of digressive possibilities: vestiges of historical change and metaphorical adoption, sonic resemblance to words that have utterly different meanings, registers of diction that invoke particular social and linguistic codes, and so forth. Words are wonderfully sullied in transmission: they've passed through many hands, many vocal chords by the time they come to us; they bear traces of them all. The poet can weight her words in a given direction, she can do her best to narrow the interpretive possibilities, she can modulate context and tonality, but she can never be entirely in control. Words fight back. Voicing meets—no—voicing *is produced by* resistance.

2. No poem emerges as the product of unimpeded will. It is worth belaboring the obvious here: language is not simply an assortment of words; it is at once a form of architecture and a series of momentums. Syntax is itself a contract of expectation. If I begin a sentence this way ... If I begin a sentence this way, I seem to promise that something will follow. I may decide to fulfill the expectation I have raised; I may subvert it; I may bait and switch. When the poet adopts the

momentums of syntax, as when she willy-nilly invokes the felt alliances and oppositions of grammar, she is already engaged in collaborative work.

3. No poem emerges as the product of unimpeded will. Poets love constraint. Think of it as a kind of bondage fetish. In addition to the social, linguistic, and generic dicta that every writer chooses to engage, if only oppositionally, poets seek out something extra, some added layer of tethering-to-the-arbitrary. We call this form. It may be involve meter and rhyme, a set rotation of end-words or a repetition of lines, a series of modal expectations (elegy, praise poem, epithalamion), or the systematic inclusions of chance (a roll of the dice, the workings of a Ouija board). It may be entirely nonce, devised for the occasion or the length of a sequence. Pieces of fancy turned into coercion.

4. To multiple business bound, then—to words, to syntax, to form in all its playfulness and stricture, and sometimes to the additional momentums of description or poetic figure or the lineaments of story—the poet takes on more than she can manage. Call it multitasking. Call it purposeful distraction. Call it whatever you will, but in the busyness of overcommitment, the poet finds that some things happen as though without her. Attending to the metrics, she must let syntax do part of the work on its own. Derailing an overly predictable rhyme, she finds that her pitch of diction has shifted. Correcting for a lapse into overly harsh or overly sentimental tonalities, she finds she needs the assistance of a new image or an interruptive second speaker. Conscious will is blessedly augmented and derailed. This is the phenomenon that used to be called the muse.

5. As the poet in the course of writing must devise some means for opening intention to surprise, that is, to discovery, so a poem must afford its reader both a welcome and a path forward. This is what I call rhetorical negotiation, which I think of as a form of hospitality. T. S. Eliot once praised the kind of poetry that "can communicate before it is understood." The construction and performance of voice is one of its surest means of doing exactly that. Poetry is perforce a collaborative medium.

So what about Augustine's "chair of lies"? How can lyric function, how ought it to function when the darker powers of rhetoric appear to have gained ascendancy? When, as the ancient philosophers feared, persuasion has forgotten its ties to truth? When even "facts" are manipulable? In the summer of 2019 I attended a poetry festival in Berlin,[9] a large one, featuring poets from South Africa, Slovenia, Turkey, Brazil, China, Iran, Great Britain, and a host of other countries. The theme of the conference was *Zeit für Sprache*, Time for Language, a phrase that might have been perfectly empty, as might the obligatory speeches, by arts leaders and the German minister for culture, with which the conference opened. "Opening remarks" are not often the occasion for penetrating thought. As these speeches proceeded, however, it became clear that the present conference had been conceived with real urgency, as a site of resistance to the current degradation of public discourse, with its descent into obfuscation and distrust. And in panel after panel, many of us tried to tackle just this issue: Is there a role for poetry in such an era? Are there forms of presence it can model and encourage? Can its aptitudes for sonic and semantic play constitute a positive ground for community? Can poetry resuscitate good-faith-in-words? In that context, let me adduce a final example of the work to be done by the flexible construction of poetic voice.

5. Kathleen Graber

Kathleen Graber's poetry has always been notable for its sheer capaciousness: its landscapes are urban and rural, domestic and industrial, exotic and just around the corner. Its language is borrowed from the ancients and from headlines in the daily news. Its structures of thought are informed by Walter Benjamin, Marcus Aurelius, Carl Linneaus, Darwin, Freud, and Augustine, by a dying father, a children's book, a helpful stranger in the post office. The range of thought and image and occasion and phrase is also, always, a range of feeling, and finds its unity in the supple deployment of poetic voice. The speaker is with us, palpable, grounded, inclusive. A pre-Socratic philosopher and a countertop oven and mass-distribution movies can cohabit in a single poem because the poet's mind treats each of them as a valued intimate, grants each of them the aura of individuation, and refuses both the snobberies and the sentimentalism that would make them alien to one another. This extraordinary democracy of vision does not sink to false homogenizing:

historical embeddedness, abstract thought, and material circumstance are never stripped of their proper dynamism in Graber's work.

In a longer chapter, I would wish to dwell on some of her more complicated longer poems, those best exemplifying her deployment of lyric voice as a through-line for what we might otherwise encounter as dissonant frames of cultural reference. But for present purposes, in the context of what-ails-us, let me adduce instead a poem of relative straightforwardness. It is one of a sequence of "America" poems in Graber's most recent book; the ostensible naïveté of their second-person address is an essential feature of their rhetorical and formal sophistication.

AMERICA [PEACHES]¹⁰

America, I know I could do better by you,
though I stoop conscientiously three times a day
to pick up my dog's waste from the grass
with black biodegradable bags. And lest you suspect
that this is more pretension than allegiance, know
my dog was the one at the shelter no one else
would take. He is fat & lazy & I could do better
by him as well . . .
                                            I confess
it would have been a moral error to embrace him
if I did not have the means to keep him fed. But
I am writing tonight because there is something wrong
with your peaches. The ones from the supermarket
are so soft & cheap—half the cost of the ones
sold at the local farm—but the flesh near the pit
is so bitter & green. It is a fruit like the mind
we are making together: both overripe & immature.
Trust me, I still have the simple tastes you gave me:
I am delighted by the common robins & cardinals,
the way they set the trees at dusk aflame. Thank you
for Tuesday's reliable trash collection. If you are
constellated somehow, a little bit inside
each of your people, I am sorry that there is more

& more of you lately I do not understand.
Sometimes I want simply to sit alone a long time
in silence. America, you must want this too.

The gentle humor ("Thank you / for Tuesday's reliable trash collection"), the confessed temptation to self-righteousness ("more pretension than allegiance"), and the palpable affection ("the common robins & cardinals, / the way they set the trees at dusk aflame") are part and parcel of what is, after all, a stern moral reckoning.

The question of *we* is a fraught one in contemporary American poetry: who am I to speak for "us"? Who am I to speak for or about others at all, particularly about their suffering? Yet what could be more urgent in a time like ours? And what is the alternative? Culpable indifference? An infinitely tender, infinitely tedious chart of the fluctuations in my own pulse rate? Whatever would pure inwardness look like anyway? Isn't language itself an instrument of life-with-others? Certainly there are dangers inherent in the address to broader issues: presumption, for example, and preachiness. But neither could be further from the meticulous engagements of Kathleen Graber's poetry. Ardent and witty, affirming and subversive, loving and filled-with-sorrow at the same time, Graber's America poems make me feel honored to be part of the "we" she takes to task.

> Sometimes I say *I*, as though someone
> might still believe there could be a coherent, distinct self in here.
> Sometimes I forget that I cannot say *I*, or I assume that you know
>   that
>
> when I say *I*, I mean *we*. Or that I at least want to mean *we*, even
>   when
> grammar or the simple ethics of the situation seems to demand *you*
>   or,
> worse yet, *them*.
>   As in today: Two women—blood on their faces & hands,
>
> their scarves—stepping arm-in-arm, over the bodies fallen around
>   them,

after cars painted to look like ambulances explode on a street.

("Self-Portrait with *The Sleeping Man*")[11]

Graber's subjects are the mutual dependencies, the mutual failings, the mutual forms of sustenance that make us human; these constitute the very fibers of her consciousness. And so, while never abandoning the modesty and penetration of the personal voice, she is able to address large subjects. The self is always a self among others.

5. Lyric Address

In a handful of examples, I have tried to suggest both the formal powers of lyric address and the analytic opportunities to be gained when we renew our focus on lyric voicing as a rhetorical instrument. Does any of this pertain to the public role of poetry as conceived by the organizers of poesiefestival berlin 2019? Can poetry serve, however incrementally, as antidote to the willful corruption and emptying out of public discourse? Do such lenses help us understand how this might be so? Can we speak to one another?

Among the most durable arguments on behalf of literature in general is that which calls attention to the ability of novels and poems and memoirs to constitute a bridge between self and others. You may come from a different part of the world than I do; you may adhere to a different faith; you may be of a different race or gender or ethnicity; the material circumstances of your life may be utterly foreign to me; but if I can hear, truly hear, something of your story or your voice, my field of recognition might be enlarged. The relative intimacy and compression of the lyric make it particularly apt at inducing what I feel to be recognition—the encounter with a speaking presence distinct from my own. Recognition: sensing kinship-in-difference, which is quite the opposite of *reducing* difference to likeness.

But what about the "vocal construction" of which I have made so much in earlier sections of this chapter? The fact that the "speaking presence" encountered in a lyric poem, whether its contours and circumstances are purely fictive or intimately based on authorial experience, is always and forever a thing that has been made from words? Intermittent or continuous, sympathetic or sinister, coherent or riddled with contradiction, the not-me I posit within or behind the lyric voice is irreducibly a poetic effect, and therein lies its power. In order to exist, it requires my—the reader's—imaginative collaboration. Even its most conspicuous manipulations, its feints and pivots and internal contradictions, teach me to be more adept at the give-and-take that makes for meaning. Good faith, in the public realm as in the private, is a two-part invention. Poetic voice is virtual. The dynamic of which it is a part and which it generates is real.

Notes

1. Linda Gregerson, "Open Voicing: Wyatt and Shakespeare," *The Oxford Handbook of Shakespeare's Poetry*, ed. Jonathan Post (Oxford: Oxford University Press, 2013), 151–67.

2. Wyatt's original is poem 190 from Petrarch's *Rime sparse*:

> *Una candida cerva sopra l'erba*
> *verde m'apparve con duo corna d'oro,*
> *fra due riviere all'ombra d'un alloro,*
> *levando 'l sole a la stagione acerba.*
>
> *Era sua vista sì dolce superba*
> *ch' i' i' lasciai per seguirla ogni lavoro,*
> *come l'avaro che'n cercar tesoro*
> *con diletto l'affanno disacerba.*
>
> *"Nessun mi tocchi," al bel collo d'intorno*
> *scritto avea di diamanti et di topazi.*
> *"Libera farmi al mio Cesare parve."*
>
> *Et era 'l sol già vòlto al mezzo giorno,*
> *gli occhi miei stanchi di mirar, non sazi,*
> *quand'io caddi ne l'acqua et elle sparve.*

And here is Robert Durling's translation:

A white doe on the green grass appeared to me, with two golden horns, between two rivers, in the shade of a laurel, when the sun was rising in the unripe season.

Her look was so sweet and proud that to follow her I left every task, like the miser who as he seeks treasure sweetens his trouble with delight.

"Let no one touch me," she bore written with diamonds and topazes around her lovely neck. "It has pleased my Caesar to make me free."

And the sun had already turned at midday; my eyes were tired by looking but not sated, when I fell into the water, and she disappeared.

From *Petrarch's Lyric Poems: The "Rime sparse" and Other Lyrics*, trans. and ed. Robert M. Durling (Cambridge, MA: Harvard University Press, 1976). All citations of Petrarch, in English and Italian, derive from this dual-language edition.

3. For this and subsequent citations of Wyatt's poems, I have relied upon *Sir Thomas Wyatt: The Complete Poems*, ed. R. A. Rebholz (New Haven, CT: Yale University Press, 1978).

4. For a reading of the poem under discussion here that fully acknowledges its complexity but argues for "consistency in the poet's complex stance," see Richard Strier, "Paleness versus Eloquence: The Ideologies of Style in the English Renaissance," *Explorations in Renaissance Culture* 45, no. 2 (November 2019): 91–120, https://brill.com/view/journals/erc/45/2/article-p91_91.xml.

5. John Ashbery, "Grand Galop," *Self-Portrait in a Convex Mirror* (New York: Viking Press, 1975), 14–21, passage cited 19.

6. Ross Gay, *Bringing the Shovel Down* (Pittsburgh: University of Pittsburgh Press, 2011), 7–9.

7. "This Is Just to Say"

> I have eaten
> the plums
> that were in
> the icebox
>
> and which
> you were probably
> saving
> for breakfast
> Forgive me
> they were delicious
> so sweet
> and so cold

William Carlos Williams, *The Collected Poems: Volume 1, 1909–1939* (New York: New Directions, 1991).

8. Gay, *Bringing the Shovel Down*, 58–61.
9. 20th poesiefestival berlin, director Thomas Wohlfahrt, June 14–20, 2019.
10. Kathleen Graber, *The River Twice* (Princeton, NJ: Princeton University Press, 2019).
11. Ibid., 7–9.

CHAPTER 2

The Extravagance of Elizabeth Bishop

STEPHEN YENSER

WHEN I BLUR my metaphysical vision and slip into vatic mode, two writers, Elizabeth Bishop and James Merrill, rise above the other summits in the mountain range of American poetry during the second half of the twentieth century and stand out as the most variously absorbing and memorable, the most diversely accomplished, and the most perdurable poets of the era. So I have thought that it might be illuminating to see Bishop's work—especially some of it that is less well known, since I have written elsewhere about other poems—in the light of Merrill's reactions to it, while at the same time indicating more precisely the distinctive qualities that they have in common. I suspect that Merrill at least would not be displeased with the approach. A generation older, Bishop influenced his work, they hosted each other and exchanged letters and cards, and he wrote an intricately witty poem dedicated to her, in addition to several eulogistic prose pieces, part of a chapter in a critical book by his friend David Kalstone (who died before completing it), and an homage in his posthumous volume *A Scattering of Salts* (1995). "Of all the splendid and curious works belonging to my time," Merrill once offered, Bishop's "are the poems that I love best and tire of least."

Bishop has often been understood as the "ordinary woman" that Merrill acutely observed she had spent her life "impersonating"—in spite of his point, that she was mimicking that figure, that she was in fact exceptional, even extravagant. I mean the latter word in the venerable sense indicating errancy, wandering, deviation, exploration. The Transcendentalists were fond of it. Thoreau, providing etymological source and apt example at once, "fear[ed] lest [his] expression may not be *extra-vagant* enough, may not wander far enough beyond the narrow limits of [his] daily experience, so as to be adequate" to its occasion. Emerson, who could well have been thinking of his fellow Concordian, alerted us that "rare and extravagant spirits come by [only] as of intervals." Othello was to the common Venetian "an extravagant and wheeling stranger / Of here and everywhere." Bishop, like Merrill an itinerant soul who spent much time here and everywhere, also went to curious places in her poetry. Though intimately bound to the Western tradition, she is venturesome, if rarely ostentatious—inventive and surprising. (Consider the conjoined mirroring sonnets that constitute "The Map," the first poem in her first book; her appraisal of Ezra Pound that takes its form from "The House That Jack Built"; her villanelle "One Art" with its riskily innovative approximations and intrusions; and the singular prose pieces that she published in two of her volumes.)

If extravagance is one of Bishop's virtues, a complementary modesty is of course another and the more apparent. Something of this paradox informs a verse that Merrill wrote when he was asked for an essay about her work.

HER CRAFT

> Elizabeth Bishop—swan boat or
> Amazon steamer? Neither: a Dream Boat.
> Among topheavy wrecks, she stays afloat.
> Mine's this white hanky waving from the shore
> —In lieu of the requested "essay." (Faute
> De pire, if I may say so. Less is more.)

Though he wrote it in 1977, he did not collect it in any of his volumes. He had already dedicated to her the rich forty-line ars poetica entitled "The Victor Dog" included in *Braving the Elements* (1972), and after her death in 1979 he would publish several prose encomia as well. Suitably unpretentious, in view of its trope and its brevity, this tribute would have seemed too ephemeral, perhaps too campy—rather in the vein of Bishop's own "Exchanging Hats," published in 1957 but uncollected in her lifetime. Another of Merrill's favorite writers, Italo Calvino, in his *Six Memos for the Next Millennium*, sets out a half dozen "values, qualities, or peculiarities of literature that are very close to [his] heart," and among them is a virtue that shades off into modesty and that "Her Craft" imputes to Bishop: "lightness," which Calvino also calls "weightless gravity" (*la gravità senza peso*).

Like Calvino's clarifying phrase, Merrill's title "Her Craft" emphasizes buoyancy. In context, the "craft" is a small boat or trading vessel, as distinct from a steamer or a "topheavy wreck." (It is surely relevant that Bishop's longtime friend and admirer Robert Lowell, whose work Merrill appreciated much less than hers, published in 1973 the "one poem" *History*, many years in the making, comprising 368 "sonnets," which its author feared "failed to avoid . . . gigantism.") But the term "craft" also carries ample ballast, dating as it does in English to the sententia that opens *The Parliament of Fowls*, a rendition by way of the Latin maxim "ars longa, vita brevis" of a declaration probably original with Hippocrates. Chaucer's incisive decasyllabic version— "the lyf so short, the craft so longe to lerne"—pertains explicitly to skill in "love" but applies to all craft or art.

"Weightless gravity." Bishop's own magical phrase, ostensibly for droplets of fog precipitated on a window, is "heavy with light" ("The End of March"). The same quality suffuses her elegant translation of Octavio Paz's "Objetos y apariciones," an ekphrastic tribute to Joseph Cornell's boxes, in which the objects become apparitions whose "bodies weigh less than light, / lasting as long as this phrase lasts" (a pair of lines that deserve to last as long as Chaucer's). A great admirer of Cornell's work, Bishop aspired to this virtue in her own. Merrill rings changes on Bishop's legerity in the elegiac "Overdue Pilgrimage to Nova Scotia" (*A Scattering of Salts*, 1995), one of his many variations on the sonnet sequence. Her "art," he notes, "Refused to tip the scale of being human / By adding unearned weight," and therefore it is fitting that the village's memorial for Bishop includes among its exhibits ("All circa 1915") some "Small-as-life desks." As their car goes through the edge of a storm, and a "shower of self-belittling brilliants falls" on its windshield, he and his companion (along with the reader) must think of her trim, quiet poems, delicately cut, radiant, yet unassuming. By poem's end, he and his companion outpace a thunderstorm—that meteorological condition so loved by the proverbial Romantic poet—and, still "snug and dry" in their vehicle, briefly weather instead the "pent-up fury" of a "car-wash," with its "streaming, / Foaming 'emotions'—impersonal, cathartic, / Closer to both art and what we are / Than the gush of nothings one outpours to people" on extreme occasions in daily life. However dolorous those occasions might be, craft transmutes and leavens the emotions.

Merrill takes up this theme in another, earlier poem dedicated to Bishop, "The Victor Dog," in which the iconic canine listening to "His Master's Voice" on the vinyl record company's label comes to epitomize the artist, as he "ponders the Schumann Concerto's tall willow hit / By lightning, and stays put." Again,

> When he surmises
> Through one of Bach's eternal boxwood mazes
> The oboe pungent as a bitch in heat,
>
> Or when the calypso decants its raw bay rum
> Or the moon in *Wozzeck* reddens ripe for murder,
> He doesn't sneeze or howl; just listens harder.
> Adamant needles bear down on him from
>
> Whirlings of outer space, too black, too near—
> But he was taught as a puppy not to flinch,
> Much less to imitate his bête noire Blanche
> Who barked, fat foolish creature, at King Lear.

Strong feeling in dire situations is one thing; passion under the shaping pressure of craft is another. Yeats had the same quality in mind in "Lapis Lazuli" when he praised the poets who "are always gay," who, "If worthy their prominent part in the play" of life (which Yeats too had linked in passing to *Lear*), "Do not break up their lines to weep." Merrill addresses the matter frequently, often fleetingly, as in the audaciously camouflaged pun at the end of "Pledge," a poem commemorating the breakup of the marriage of a pair of friends. His final stanza quotes the toast he composes for them:

> "You who have drained dry
> Your golden goblet are about to learn
> As in my turn
> Have I—

How life, unsweetened, fizzing up again
Fills the heart.
I drink to you apart
In that champagne."

As Merrill hinted in an interview with Helen Vendler, the pain the poet suffers in "life" ("The life" that art asks of us, he says wryly in "The Victor Dog," "is a dog's life") becomes a "sham pain" in art. (In a certain phase in his life, we might note, the champagne cocktail, which blends bitters with sugar, was one of Merrill's favorite drinks.)

My point is what I take to be Merrill's: the craft turns common feeling into uncommon forms and in the process often renders the craftsman self-effacing. I imagine that Proust had that process in mind when he remarked of something he had written: "Il est trop honnête d'être sincere." For the writer, accuracy trumps ego; exactitude prevails over self-expression.

A corollary of the proposition that, in Marianne Moore's "Silence," "deepest feeling always shows itself in silence; not in silence, / but restraint," is that attention to detail is a virtue. Attention, restraint—"patience, patience" as Paul Valéry counseled, because each atom of silence harbors the possibility of a ripe fruit. Merrill did not read much literary criticism, but one book he admired, perhaps surprisingly, was Hugh Kenner's *The Pound Era*, and surely one reason for his approval was Kenner's enthusiasm for narrow focus. "God is concentration," Kenner speculated, and "a work of art is someone's act of attention, evoking ours." Paraphrasing Pound, Kenner noted that if in the context of poetry the term "technique" sometimes provokes condescension, it is because some minds are "too trivial to believe that any subject could be worth the labor of exact presentation." A quite different sort of critic, Yvor Winters, agreed, pointing out in *The Function of Criticism* that "the learned but non-poetic critic . . . usually considers the exact evaluation of detail as somehow trivial," whereas in fact "the proof of a structure is in the quality of the details which it produces."

Bishop, reflecting on her paragon Charles Darwin, admires "the lonely young man, his eyes fixed on facts and minute details, sinking or sliding giddily off into the unknown," who practices "a self-forgetful, perfectly useless concentration." It is but a step to the preoccupation of her "Sandpiper," a prototypical poet and a "student of Blake" (who found eternity in a grain of sand)—or to the ideal immured poet of "The End of March," who would withdraw to an isolated house where she could "look through binoculars, / read boring books, old long, long books, and write down useless notes." "Exactitude" (*esattezza*)—along with *leggerezza*—Calvino avers, is one of his desiderata. He puts it the other way around: "the worst blight in modern writing . . . is vagueness." Bishop, for her part, in a draft beginning "Writing poetry is an unnatural act," when naming the three qualities she admires in her favorite poems, specifies "*Accuracy*" first. She finds it in Marianne Moore's "A Grave," where "The firs stand in procession, each with an emerald turkey-foot at the top."

Her own precise, lucid details or "self-belittling brilliants," in Merrill's metaphor, are the basis of her "craft," the implicit subject of "12 O'Clock News," a piece with a comparatively low profile, even now that she has gained a wide readership among the cognoscenti and even though it was published in the acclaimed volume *Geography III*, only ten titles long. A self-explicating allegory or catenation of conceits, "12 O'Clock News" interprets in its body, which comprises a newscaster's report on an alien scene (that is, the various paraphernalia on the poet's desk), meanwhile glossing in italics in its left margin (à la Coleridge in "The Rime of the Ancient Mariner") each item as the poet herself sees it. Merrill responds to it all in a letter to her:

> How I love the array on *your* worktable. It's simply uncanny what you do with tone in that poem—the newscaster's idiom grows into the saddest, truest analogue of that strange, remote "involvement" even I have felt, those few nights I've ever been sober + lonely long enough to work late. That snow-covered peak—"White is their color, and behold my head!" *This* may be the saddest poem you've ever written.

This gnomic passage makes an interesting focal point for a discussion of Bishop's craft for several reasons, the least evident of which might be that Merrill, himself a precisionist, refers casually, twice, to what many readers would consider a prose poem as a "poem." More evident is his attention to the "tone," the nuanced command of which is Bishop's métier.

————

Surprisingly little is written these days about tone in recent poetry—so little that some enterprising critic could make a significant contribution by analyzing the rhetoric of that staple element. Recent fiction is a different matter; the novelist's tones are often remarked upon. Whether or not my dark suspicion is true—that contemporary fiction writers, less beset by notions of "the post-avant" such as conceptual poetry and flarf, have given their readers more to work with—Bishop's masterfully detailed handling of tone accounts in part for her singularity, her strangeness, even as it allows her to be "self-forgetful."

Merrill's paragraph quoted above assumes that Bishop, for whom George Herbert was a guiding light, means to recall the latter's poem "The Forerunners." Like Merrill, Bishop was intimate with Metaphysical poetry, which after T. S. Eliot's lauding of it earlier in the twentieth century has reverted to the realm of the esoteric among later American poets. "The Forerunners" opens with lines that might momentarily puzzle some readers of this millennium:

> The Harbingers are come. See, see their mark,
> White is their colour, and behold my head.
> But must they have my Braine? must they dispark
> Those sparkling notions, which therein were bred?
> Must Dulnesse turn me to a Clod?

Forerunners preceded an entourage in order to select and mark with chalk above the doorway the next house in which the royal personage would stay the night. In Herbert's figure of speech, the white hairs on his temples are the marks that presage the arrival of his Lord at the poet's death and make him wonder whether he will have to surrender even his wit for the comfort of his guest. Bishop, Merrill notices, adapts Herbert's figure, itself an extravagance, near the end of "12 O'Clock News" when she refers implicitly to her own head as "the country's snow-covered mountain peak."

That allusion comes in the final paragraph of Bishop's peculiar prose poem—but the tonal chord it strikes permeates the whole. Indeed, both tenor and vehicle of the concluding metaphor are foreshadowed by the opening paragraph:

As you all know, tonight is the night of the full
moon, half the world over. But here the moon
gooseneck   seems to hang motionless in the sky. It gives very
lamp   little light; it could be dead. Visibility is poor.
Nevertheless, we shall try to give you some idea of
the lay of the land and the present situation.

If we think between her lines of Herbert's poem, we already find Bishop
worrying about the effect of age on her own "Braine," including her vision
and by extension her general acuity, though what the newscaster, the speaker
in the prose narrative, sees is a scene apparently relayed to him by an "aerial
reconnaissance" team. (In the absence of gender markers, I assume this
speaker to be male, perhaps because it is easier for me to differentiate the
newscaster that way—almost as easy as to imagine her "Crusoe," as bright as
the newscaster is benighted, a man. Bishop's delicate probing of the gender
boundary in both of these monologues is an aspect of her craft that deserves
more attention than it will get here. In this instance, her strategic first-person
plural allows us ample fudge room.)

The distinctive if muted "sadness" that Merrill singles out in his letter will
manifest itself increasingly. In the second paragraph—*"typewriter"*—the
speaker, unaware of the poet's marginal note and assessing the topographical
conditions of the "tiny principality" that the aerial reconnaissance team has
photographed, tells the audience about "small, peculiarly shaped terraces" on
the "southern glacis" of the "escarpment that rises abruptly from the central
plain." On them (he infers), "the welfare" of this "small, backward country"
(as he soon calls it) depends. "What endless labor [the terraces] represent!"
he muses. An exorbitant metaphor, itself indicative of Bishop's debt to the
Metaphysical poets, this rendering of the typewriter keys takes a moment for
us to weigh out, to realize that it is neither simply the elaborate, now nearly
antique mechanism that the poet has in mind, nor even it including the letters its keys bear—and by extension the English alphabet (not to mention the
numbers, punctuation marks, and other signs)—but writing *itself*, which
dates back at least to Paleolithic caves forty thousand years ago and provides
the drive behind the evolution of mind proper. "Endless labor" indeed. Like
so much of her work, this prose poem focuses on a narrow, provincial situation (based though it is on an allegedly exotic vignette), yet opens up, at the

slightest pressure, to encompass our entire history. It is at the point of this realization—whenever it comes in the course of the particular reader's experience, for the slow dawning is part of the experience's weirdness—that we see that the poet is not identical with the speaker, who cannot make the extrapolation we just have.

Such hardly noticeable complication of tone and theme by means of obsessive attention to detail is at the core of Bishop's craft. The local tone itself aspires to be flat, almost objective, to the extent that it is the newscaster's, though an innate sympathy with the underdog colors his account and leads him to choose the counterbalancing modifiers in "endless labor" and "tiny principality"—and even provokes him (here the mask slips a bit to give us a glimpse of the poet who wrote "At the Fishhouses") to a rare simile: the terracing "gleams faintly in the dim light, like fish scales."

So the prose poem has begun to resonate with the discrepancy in the points of view, the newscaster's and the poet's, which discrepancy bears directly on the tone of the whole. In the following paragraph, the newscaster discovers in the landscape a "landslide . . . almost white, calcareous, and shaly" ("*pile of mss.*," the scholium tells us), and he reassures us that "There are believed to have been no casualties." Ah, *believed* to have been . . . But this is the poet who wrote this book's "One Art," and we know that her "one" art is love and loss, which is to say life, or (for the writer) writing. In short, the manuscripts have been caused precisely by (and doubtless have caused) "casualties." Whatever the newscaster—the detached critic, let's say—might think, the "situation" being fleshed out is painful for the principals. But—and this is crucial—the feelings of "dread" have made for this work, which represents a transfiguring "gaiety," in Yeats's term.

So the "uncanny" tone includes notes of confession, resignation (how hard it is to write poems worthy of their tradition and their language), and even failure, but also aspiration, indispensable to anyone bound to such a vocation—as we recall when the speaker describes a "large rectangular 'field,' hitherto unknown to us, obviously man-made. It is dark-speckled. An airstrip? A cemetery?" Well, it is a "*typed sheet*," from the poet's perspective, though the "field" might well be for her precisely either a point of departure for an imaginative flight or the site for the burial of an inspiration. Similarly, the power of writing takes the shape for the newscaster of a "mysterious, oddly shaped, black structure" (an "*ink-bottle*"), either some "terrifying 'secret weapon'" or "a *numen*, a great altar" honoring one of the gods that the supposedly primitive indigenous people ("afflicted by superstition and helplessness") might "regard as a 'savior,' one last hope of rescue from their grave difficulties." The pathos of that condition—which is the poet's normal state, after all, but which as Bishop's wizard phrasing implies is easily overstated, and thus subject to belittling irony (writing as salvation indeed!)—is what Merrill means by an uncanny tone, one of a specially inflected "sadness."

From the reconnaissance crew's "superior vantage, we can see clearly into a sort of dugout, possibly a shell crater, a 'nest' of soldiers . . . heaped together, wearing the camouflage 'battle dress' intended for 'winter warfare.' They are in hideously contorted positions, all dead," the deluded speaker confidently reports. But his purportedly "superior vantage" gives way to the poet's better point of view, as the marginalium reveals that the prospect actually shows, rather than uniformed corpses, an "*ashtray*" full of stubbed-out cigarettes. Meanwhile, undeterred, the naïve newscaster deduces, on the basis of the white camouflage, that the soldiers *must* have intended an assault "on the country's one snow-covered mountain peak."

This "peak" is wisely not interpreted in the margin (imagine the damaging aesthetic effect), so the reader must speculate. As Merrill knew well, Bishop, whose hair had whitened, was a chain smoker. Left to our own devices now, we must evaluate the newscaster's concluding, climactic, self-satisfied claim about the infantry and the world they inhabit:

> The fact that these poor soldiers are wearing them *here*, on the plain,
> gives further proof, if proof were necessary, either of the childishness and
> hopeless impracticality of this inscrutable people, our opponents, or of
> the sad corruption of their leaders.

How ridiculously the newscaster—like the soldiers he has invented—has gone astray, we think. How distorted his vision of this world. "Visibility is poor" understates the case. *We* know that this piece is "really" Bishop's wry self-portrait in situ, a caricature of the poet, influenced by her cherished Metaphysical mode, at the expense of the cocksure critic in the person of the newscaster. To the sophisticated reader, it is all an entertaining (or at least engaging) extravagance.

Yet Merrill was nothing if not sophisticated, and he found "12 O'Clock News" extraordinarily "sad." So might Robert Lowell have done. Lowell, quoted on the endpapers of *Questions of Travel*, praises Bishop's signature "tone, a tone of large, grave tenderness and sorrowing amusement." In this case the complex tonal chord owes its bittersweetness partly to the perspective of the newscaster, who, however superficially errant, is also, ironically, spot on. Having earned the means, largely by way of the craftily devised persona, Bishop can introduce her "dread" or her fears, which haunt many a writer, that her vocation entails "childishness and hopeless impracticality"— such as the contrivances of this very prose poem, which finally allow her to present herself as her own "opponent," if therefore also "inscrutable." She opposes herself not only in the sense that her addictions—smoking and more notoriously drinking—undermine her health but also in the sense that her alienation from her society (arguably the result of another addiction, to writing, refracted here in the reporter's misunderstanding) can only contribute to its deterioration. In the prose poem's intricately ominous terms, the newscaster's ignorant misconstruing of the situation is culpable—his naïveté makes him his own unacknowledged enemy—and from Bishop's vantage, the poet's "impracticality" and "childishness" implicate her as well.

We recall that "12 O'Clock News" opens on a provocative note, all too easily skimmed over: "As you all know, tonight is the night of the full moon, half the world over. But here . . ." But—"But"? And *where*? And what is the nature of "our" moon tonight? And what to make of "all" and "full" and "half"? The details are vital. Any "full moon" shows us exactly half of it, for one thing. As the questions in those basic but vertiginous questions from the primer quoted in the epigraph to *Geography III* ("*What Is a Map?*" and so on) would suggest, the appropriate, perhaps the inevitable attitude is interrogative—"dubious," to lift a key adjective from "The End of March." One thought we might have is that the poet and the newscaster are alter egos—or different phases or faces of the moon. The poet must be her own if sometimes dim critic, after all. She is altogether involved in the ramifications of her thoughts, regardless of her attempt to achieve a "superior vantage."

To be human is to be "involved," complicit in the pervasive "corruption." According to Bishop's biographer Brett Millier, the cover of a notebook the poet kept when she was a student at Vassar bore a quotation from one of her favorite poets, Gerard Manley Hopkins. The line is the most straightforward in his uniquely lavish—not to say extravagant—draft entitled "On the Portrait of Two Beautiful Young People": "Enough: Corruption was the world's first woe."

———————

That Vassar notebook contains sketches of characters for a novel based on Bishop's childhood. The novel never materialized, but the subject fueled much of *Questions of Travel*, most notably "In the Village," a short story. Merrill would never have called *it* a "poem," but one could be excused for thinking of it as a prose poem, notwithstanding its length (thirty small pages)—especially since the so-called prose poem has the existential status of the camelopard.

A swatch of writing is a "prose poem," after all, only by a fiat sanctioned by the tradition in French literature. No one can distinguish between the prose poem and flash fiction or even plain old short fiction or brief meditation. The only (but indelible) line that one can draw between poetry and prose is the line itself: continual reminder of the power of exactitude, and dependable enabler of the virtue of lightness, it is part and parcel of the one genre, and the other does not have it. The poet, whether Dickinson or Whitman, controls the margins, whereas the prose writer is in the indifferent hands of the typesetter. The fact that prose can rhyme and can even be metered does not alter the case; poetry has one material means, lineation, which prose lacks. Which is of course not to say that poetry is a superior medium, though it is the older one and the one more connected to music—connected by the line, which is a means and a unit of measure. Nor is it an inferior medium, *pace* Plato. "Poetry" is not by nature an evaluative classification (there are indisputably hideous poems), though both the commercial world and the world of nineteenth-century French literature have appropriated it because of honorific connotations.

Still, if one were looking perversely for a piece of writing in English to exemplify prose poetry, one might nominate "12 O'Clock News." Another candidate would be "In the Village," an exquisite product, or *process*, to be strictly accurate, that has been somewhat overlooked precisely because it is a story included (exceptionally if not extravagantly) in a collection of poems, *Questions of Travel*. Other nominees to represent the fictive hybrid genre (in addition to those soi-disant) might include gems quarried from sources as heterogeneous as James Joyce's *Finnegans Wake*, Sir Thomas Browne's *Hydrotaphia*, Thoreau's *Walden*, Gertrude Stein's *Tender Buttons*, Sybille Bedford's *A Legacy*, Ralph Ellison's *Invisible Man*, and William Gass's "In the Heart of the Heart of the Country." Yeats outrageously included Walter Pater's description of the *Mona Lisa* in his Oxford poetry anthology, and other editors have excerpted Djuna Barnes's *Nightwood*. By the same token, we have to sympathize with Robert Lowell's surrender to the temptation to convert Bishop's story by means of lineation into a poem he called "The Scream." The result of his attempt, alas, is a good example of a hideous poem—with a title that seems to testify to the excruciating experience of its metamorphosis—but his apparently irresistible temptation to versify it suggests the rare nature of "In the Village." (Merrill's unthinking labeling of "12 O'Clock News" as a poem betrays a similar motivation.) None of her contemporaries and no one since has published anything much like it. (Compare Lowell's "91 Revere Street" in *Life Studies*, which provided Bishop with precedent, as she notes in a letter to him. An eccentric, polished piece of prose in its own right, it would never be regarded as a prose poem. Merrill's own "Prose of Departure," modeled on Matsuo Bashō's *haibun* or travel sketches with haiku embedded, exemplifies in its own way the compulsion to reconcile prose and poetry, and as a consequence, like "In the Village," gets less critical commentary than it warrants.)

Again her handling of tone is "uncanny," in Merrill's mot juste, and all the other secondary features we might (tenuously) associate with poetry are here in "In the Village": euphony, breathtaking metaphors, unforgettable images, figures of compression, figures of repetition, delicacy of transition, density of motif, not to mention scattered rhymes and metrical riffs. There are instances of sensitive "line breaks" to boot, thanks to what we have to call the paragraphing, and then there are techniques we might associate primarily with the fiction writer such as refracted narrative, prolepsis, delayed revelation, juggling of tenses, and tactical suppression of proper names. Everywhere the craft is evident—no, all but invisible: the light touch, the transparent care for detail.

Now for a necessary and thereafter dispensable summary, which perforce ignores what was specified in the preceding paragraph. Our narrator, adopting for the most part the point of view that she had as a girl about six years old, relates a few days in her life of that period. She lives with her grandparents in a Nova Scotia village, where her grandmother's sisters also reside. The girl's father has died, and her mother, psychologically frail, who has been institutionalized in Boston, has recuperated sufficiently to try out life in the village, and so she must have mourning clothes made for her by the local dressmaker, Miss Gurley. Not far from the girl's home is the shop of the blacksmith, Nate, who is close to the girl and who makes rings for her from heated nails, and whose daily chores are often heard in the background.

One of the girl's duties is to take the cow Nelly to pasture, and we follow them on a typical day as they go through the village with its familiar shops and residents to the rented field and then return home. One day her mother has a yen for humbugs, "a kind of candy" she hasn't had in years, and the child is sent on an errand to buy some at Mealy's shop in the village. It is a hopeful episode, because her mother's request indicates a potential return to normality for the family. On a subsequent night, a fire breaks out in a barn down the road, and the village mobilizes to help. The atmosphere in the child's home is especially tense because the turmoil disturbs the mother, though it turns out that she does not break down and scream, as happens in the worst crises.

Before long, however, she does lose her grip, and her condition demands that she return to the sanitarium. The child's routine now includes a weekly trip through the village to the post office, where with the aid of Mr. Johnson the postmaster she mails to her mother a package of gifts and books. Each week she returns across the bridge over the river and past the blacksmith's shop, where she visits with Nate as he shapes horseshoes.

The preceding bare-bones summary excludes the gradations of tone from the comic to the despondent, the manipulation of the point of view, the rhetorical finesse, and the restraint that extends down through the story's important omissions—which is to say all of the patiently calculated and unaccountably inspired detail that fleshes it out into the masterpiece it is, this story that could have been entitled (had Bishop had a tin ear) "Portrait of the Artist as a Girl."

This story's parallel to the poet's work space in "12 O'Clock News," the locus of the craftsman, belongs to the dressmaker Miss Gurley:

Her house is littered with scraps of cloth and tissue-paper patterns, yellow, pinked, with holes in the shapes of A, B, C, and D in them, and numbers, and threads everywhere like a fine vegetation. She has a bosom full of needles with threads ready to pull out and make nests with. She sleeps in her thimble. A gray kitten once lay on the treadle of her sewing machine, where she rocked it as she sewed, like a baby in a cradle, but it got hanged on the belt. Or did she make that up? But another gray-and-white one lies now by the arm of the machine, in imminent danger of being sewn into a turban. There is a table covered with laces and braids, embroidery silks, and cards of buttons of all colors—big ones for winter coats, small pearls, little glass delicious ones to suck.

Tone: here its essential component is in the paragraph's shortest sentence: "She sleeps in her thimble." For a moment, the claim is startling, astonishing, even, as it seems to come from nowhere. But then we understand that it displays the child's imagination in its purest form, which is, however, operative everywhere, as in her earlier simile, "threads everywhere like a fine vegetation," and her not quite realized metaphor involving a pin cushion: "a bosom full of needles ready to pull out and make nests with." For the writer herself to make nests with, of course. And so it is that the prose inches us into the child's sensibility, and further prepares us for the full immersion by the image of the "nests," where one might sleep, before plunging us in with that coup of a declaration: "She sleeps in her thimble." The quasi-oneiric tone helps the girl slip into the memory of Miss Gurley's tale of the kitten who slept "like a baby in a cradle" on the sewing machine's "treadle." In this dreamy aura we hear subliminally the grating slant rhyme of "treadle" with "cradle." Once the mother returned to the institution, she must have seemed as inexplicably snatched away as the kitten.

Miss Gurley is making a dress for the girl's mother, and that connection between the two women, reinforced as early in this paragraph as the reference to the dressmaker's "bosom," continues through the reference to making "nests," and culminates imperceptibly but undeniably in the reference to her "buttons . . . delicious to suck." The child's mother has abandoned her, even as she has lost her mind, and the dressmaker provides a surrogate—and more important a model. The two aspects—mother and maker—merge in a wonderful passage in which we learn that her mother too embroidered ("'She did beautiful work,' says my grandmother"). Among her mother's possessions is "a case of little embroidery tools":

> I abscond with a little ivory stick with a sharp point. To keep it forever I
> bury it under a bleeding heart by the crab-apple tree, but it is never found
> again.

"To keep it forever I bury it": read psychologically or aesthetically, there is but "one art" indeed, that of love and loss. Rarely has "a sharp point" been both lost and made so vividly.

Miss Gurley has her own disconcerting stories to tell ("Or did she make that up?") or hide, and those pinked letters—"A, B, C, and D"—point to the writer's craft, both the alphabet and the poetic "patterns" (cf. the conventional notation for, say, the villanelle's scheme—A^1, b, A^2 / a, b, A^1, and so on—that we can find in Bishop's worksheets for "One Art") that the girl would grow up to work with, as do the "numbers" (the old word for meter), while this very text, an "embroidery," is shot through with "fine threads" of imagery and sound. In *Six Memos for the Next Millennium*, Calvino calls this aspect of art "multiplicity" (*moltiplicità*). Multiplicity, like its complement "exactitude," produces a "network of relationships" that enables a work to grow "denser and denser from the inside through its own organic vitality," by means of fractal and synecdoche, and thus to represent in small the "web" of connections that the world is.

Bishop's web or embroidery makes use for example of the colorful "cards" on the dressmaker's table. They connect with the "bundle of postcards" in the grandparents' home, a source of enchantment to the girl. Some of the postcards "are plain, or photographs, but some have lines of metallic crystals on them—how beautiful!—silver, gold, red, and green." Again: "Some cards, instead of lines around the buildings, have words written in their skies with the same stuff, crumbling, dazzling and crumbling, raining down a little on the people who sometimes stand about below: pictures of Pentecost? What are the messages? I cannot tell." She is too young to make sense of them. But we can begin to do so. At Pentecost, the Holy Spirit descended in tongues of flame upon the disciples, and in the girl's story the night of the fire precipitates the recurrence of her mother's "possession." Equally to the "sharp point," in writing "In the Village" Bishop discovered exactly what "messages" her childhood relayed to her, the chief of which is that the world we know is a fabric of relationships, such that even seeming polarities like the terrible and the beautiful, the dark and the light, partake of one another. Bishop chose her epitaph from the concluding lines of "The Bight," subtitled "On my birthday": "All the untidy activity continues, / awful but cheerful." That last line, an adonic, is the epitaph.

So Miss Gurley is one of two chief models for our nascent poet. The other, associated like the postcard images with fire, is Nate the blacksmith, the local avatar of Hephaestus, as Miss Gurley is of Penelope—"Nate, wearing a long black leather apron over his trousers and bare chest, sweating hard, a black leather cap on top of dry, thick, black-and-gray curls, a black sooty face; iron filings, whiskers, and gold teeth, all together, and a smell of red-hot metal and horses' hoofs." Here is Nate's work space:

> In the blacksmith's shop things hang up in the shadows and shadows
> hang up in the things, and there are black and glistening piles of dust
> in each corner. A tub of night-black water stands by the forge. The
> horseshoes sail through the dark like bloody little moons and follow
> each other like bloody little moons to drown in the black water, hissing,
> protesting.

Like the Pentecostal symbol, the first sentence's imagery ties together the physical and the spiritual, at the same time that the whole passage rhymes Nate dramatically but surreptitiously with Miss Gurley.

One hardly needs to introduce the pertinent lines from Bishop's "Sestina" (*Questions of Travel*) to reinforce the fit between the two makers—or rather three, since the poet is everywhere here—but let us reason not the "need" in view of the magical transformation. In the conspicuous absence of the mother, and under the sign of an unnamed sorrow embodied in an "almanac" hanging "half-open" on the wall, "the grandmother" and "the child" in "Sestina" keep company in the kitchen, making tea and drawing respectively:

>   . . . secretly, while the grandmother
> busies herself about the stove,
> the little moons fall down like tears
> from between the pages of the almanac
> into the flower bed the child

has carefully placed in front of the house.

We probably would not overlook the relationship between the ostensibly contrary figures of blacksmith and dressmaker, but the passage immediately following the description of the blacksmith's shop, as thrillingly tight as you can get in prose, obviates that possibility:

> Outside, along the matted eaves, painstakingly, sweetly, wasps go over and over a honeysuckle vine.
> Inside, the bellows creak. Nate does wonders with both hands; with one hand. The attendant horse stamps his foot and nods his head as if agreeing to a peace treaty.

The wasps go over and over the vine like seamstresses making their stitches; the stinging wasps weave through the sweet honeysuckle; the outside and the inside interlace or weld as they do so often in Bishop's text of a world. On the one hand, Nate works magic, and on the other, the dressmaker does as well, and they both use both hands, and those hands are now the poet's. Bishop's story is a melancholy one, because it (like many of her poems, from "Filling Station" to "The Moose") is in part about the loss of her mother, and it is a sweet one, because it constitutes fruitful response. "In the Village," "awful but cheerful," is "painstakingly, sweetly" written. Sappho's adjective "sweetbitter" is her signature tone.

Meanwhile, who among us does not identify with the "attendant horse" in Nate's shop?

Bishop has Marvell's paradoxical virtues as Vita Sackville-West perceived them. A poem—or a story like this one (if there are any)—can be "spilling and voluptuous as a horn of plenty" and yet "hard and tight as a knot"— florabundant yet exact, tight but complex or contradictory (or "self-interfering," in Kenner's phrase taken from Buckminster Fuller)—and in this instance the miracle repeats itself on a small scale. If we step way back, we see that "In the Village" begins with one enduring sound and ends with another. The opening paragraph, the first of thirteen unnumbered sections (separated by what used to be called an extra lead), is a tour de force:

> A scream, the echo of a scream, hangs over that Nova Scotian village.
> No one hears it; it hangs there forever, a slight stain in those pure blue

skies, skies that travellers compare to those of Switzerland, too dark, too blue, so that they seem to keep on darkening a little more around the horizon—or is it around the rims of the eyes?—the color of the cloud of bloom on the elm trees, the violet on the fields of oats; something darkening over the woods and waters as well as the sky. The scream hangs like that, unheard, in memory—in the past, in the present, and those years between. It was not even loud to begin with, perhaps. It just came there to live, forever—not loud, just alive forever. Its pitch would be the pitch of my village. Flick the lightning rod on top of the church steeple with your fingernail and you will hear it.

This paragraph represents and forecasts the music of the whole, which relies on reverberation, on the varied repetition "over and over" (to lift a phrase from the passage on the wasps) of related motifs, on the weaving together of them. The introductory fragment contains the technique in small: "A scream, the echo of a scream." The preposition "over" appears at the beginning and in the middle of the paragraph, the verb "hangs" recurs throughout, "darkening" repeats, and so does "forever." At paragraph's close, the pair of sentences following the second "forever" make a little coda—or another one of those miniature prose poems, as Bishop puns on "pitch" brilliantly to join the sonic, the visual (in two ways, since "pitch" indicates steepness, while it connotes darkness, especially in conjunction with "lightning"), and the tactile—or an epitome of this exceptionally sensuous story about the nature of art. One understands why Lowell felt compelled to put this perfectly extravagant story into verse.

The corresponding images at the story's conclusion are more drawn out and integrally involved with their brief narrative. I'll reluctantly quote only the last third of the final section, which turns to the sound of Nate shaping a horseshoe on his forge:

Now there is no scream. Once there was one and it settled slowly down
to earth one hot summer afternoon; or did it float up, into that dark, too
dark, blue sky? But surely it has gone away, forever.
Clang.
It sounds like a bell buoy out at sea.
It is the elements speaking: earth, air, fire, water.

> All those other things—clothes, crumbling postcards, broken china;
> things damaged and lost, sickened or destroyed; even the frail almost-lost
> scream—are they too frail for us to hear their voices long, too mortal?
> Nate!
> Oh, beautiful sound, strike again!

Regardless and indeed partly because of the first sentence, the "scream" goes on, even as the word "forever" repeats from that first section, though it is "frail" and "almost lost." Move into its vicinity, and you will hear it "again." We can hear it now, though it has merged with the sound of the hammer on the forge, the fiery *"Clang"* that speaks for all "the elements"—the air (where the scream hangs forever), the earth ("Flop, flop, down over the dirt sidewalk" go Nelly's hooves), and the water ("*Slp*, [the river] says," "an unexpected gurgle")—and serves like a bell buoy as a warning and a sign to facilitate navigation.

More forcefully than Miss Gurley, Nate anticipates the craftsman, the artist, the poet. Another of the poet's forerunners here, though unnamed, is the alchemist. Throughout the story Bishop describes and effortlessly demonstrates transformation, a facility shown off at the outset of the fifth section.

> Mysteriously enough, poor Miss Gurley—I know she is poor—gives
> me a five-cent piece. She leans over and drops it in the pocket of the
> red-and-white dress that she has made herself. It is very tiny, very shiny.
> King George's beard is like a little silver flame. Because they look like
> herring- or maybe salmon-scales, five-cent pieces are called "fish-scales."
> One heard of people's rings being found inside fish, or their long-lost
> jackknives. What if one could scrape a salmon and find a little picture of
> King George on every scale?
> I put my five-cent piece in my mouth for greater safety on the way home,
> and swallow it. Months later, as far as I know, it is still in me, transmuting
> all its precious metals into my growing teeth and hair.

One of the alchemist's objects is of course the transmutation of baser metals into gold, a pure metal Nate has already been linked to by his "gold teeth." The alchemist also framed his quest as an attempt to discover the essence of all things—or the quintessence, the fifth essence, since it underlay the four elements, earth, water, air, and fire. It is perhaps fortuitous that the ancient philosophy shadows this story's fifth section, and that the girl is given "five big pennies" to buy the humbugs for her mother, and that Bishop's subject is "a five-cent piece." But it is plainly a piece about aesthetic alchemy that involves intensely all five senses.

Some "people's rings" crop up here partly because early in the story Nate "instantly" makes the girl a "ring" out of a heated nail, partly because the girl finds in the mother's sewing kit "Two pale, smooth wooden hoops . . . pressed together in the linen," and partly because the story, as we have seen, makes its own ring. The "jackknives" come in to make the transition to the imaginary scraping with a knife of the salmon scales. I suspect that the paragraph ends with the phrase "every scale" because Bishop's densely interrelated world involves forms that reproduce themselves on every scale: the coin, a "fish-scale," swallowed by the salmon, reappears as the fish armored in scales. ("Scale" also has an interesting subsidiary role in "Crusoe in England," when Bishop lets her speaker mediate, unintentionally, between topography and music. Having conjured a backdrop of a landscape of volcanoes so miniaturized that he can imagine he had "become a giant," he recollects his "home-made flute": "I think it had the weirdest scale on earth.")

Alchemist, blacksmith, seamstress—they are intervolved, so chiasmus is a fitting figure: "In the blacksmith's shop things hang up in the shadows and shadows hang up in the things." That rhetorical flourish might recall another matter left hanging: the kitten possibly "hanged" in the belt on Miss Gurley's sewing machine in section five. That grotesque possibility is a discordant note, partially retracted immediately: "Or did she make that up?" But it hangs there, a bizarre loose end. The scream hangs there throughout, light and omnipresent as air. Not long ago, one could read criticism in which Bishop was disparaged (as was Merrill) for being a "doily-maker," not to mention a belated colonialist because of her alleged disregard of historical facts, though that particular criticism was anticipated by "Filling Station" and should have been precluded by "Brazil, January 1, 1502."

In fact, violence and terror are never far beneath or above the surface in

Bishop's work, and the recognition of their presence is as indispensable as her legerity to her characteristic sublime. We hear "the scream" that begins "In the Village" just once in section two, in a simple yet pivotal moment, and nothing is made of it at that time, though the inner and the outer, the terrible and the beautiful, and the present and the past converge:

> *Clang.*
> The pure note: pure and angelic.
> The dress was all wrong. She screamed.
> The child vanishes.

That's it. One scream, at the heart of the emotional trauma in the poem, and it suffices. It was adumbrated at the outset and is heard here, and for the rest of the story, as we read in section seven, "We are waiting for a scream. But it is not screamed again, and the red sun sets in silence." That's it—the suspended scream, the missing mother—and it is at this juncture that the tense changes. To this point, the narrative has been in the past tense, right through "screamed." But then at the same time that "the child vanishes" and gives way to the adult writer, we step, extravagantly, into the present tense, never to return to the past that preceded the scream.

The world has changed forever—as it has in "In the Waiting Room," when the speaker, a child of almost seven years old, having accompanied her aunt to the dentist, hears her cry out:

> Suddenly, from inside,
> came an *oh!* of pain
> —Aunt Consuelo's voice—
> Not very loud or long.

Like the scream in the story, the cry is a linchpin in Bishop's structure. Again, she does not initially dwell on the moment, but within a few lines we begin gradually to infer that somehow the aunt's cry has also provoked a cry from the child, who, internalizing a form of the pain of the other, nearly faints under the pressure of a revelation she cannot comprehend but that the reader gathers is an intimation of the effects of the passage of time: mortality and death.

Surely one of the reasons that Merrill admired Bishop is this ability to temper a climactic moment. His narrator in *The (Diblos) Notebook*, a writer, urges himself to follow the example of Racine in *Phèdre*, "where the overlay of prismatic verse deflects a brutal, horrible action." (The novel ultimately has its climactic counterpart.) Unlike their contemporaries, Lowell, Jarrell, Berryman, and other "confessional" poets of the 1960s, Merrill and Bishop, in the interest of lightness and restraint, specialized in deflection and refraction, but in much of their best work anguish is implicit—as the scream is in the air in Bishop's image, "unheard, in memory," and "not even loud to begin with, perhaps," but always present. "Flick the lightning rod on top of the church steeple with your fingernail and you will hear it."

The scale implied in that last sentence of the opening paragraph of "In the Village" recalls the scale that prevails throughout "12 O'Clock News" (the poet's desk lamp is the speaker's moon) and the first part of "Crusoe in England." The latter follows "In the Waiting Room" in *Geography III* and picks up the motif of the concealed interior. "Crusoe in England" opens with an explicit reprisal, this time hyperbolic, of Aunt Consuelo's cry: "Another volcano has erupted." There are no fireworks in the present in this poem, where the speaker lives among "fifty-two / miserable small volcanoes," but the latent energy gets its due when Crusoe notes that they stand, "naked and leaden, with their heads blown off." This is for the most part a subdued, thoughtful monologue, full of "a deep affection for / the smallest of my island industries" and modest expressions of "a miserable philosophy," and such passages contrast vividly with its reflective tones, but it deals with bedrock issues. These issues are overlain by wit, as when Crusoe tells us with some bilingual equivocation that he "christened" one volcano "*Mont d'Espoir* or *Mount Despair*," but—or rather therefore—Bishop can address fundamentals. She never feels compelled to say as directly as Coleridge (another of her luminaries), in his poem "Constancy to an Ideal Object," that "like strangers shelt'ring from a storm, / Hope and Despair meet in the porch of Death." Suffering from addiction like Coleridge, she was familiar with that porch. (What one wouldn't give to know what thoughts she and her dear friend Lowell must have exchanged about his poem featuring Coleridge, "To Delmore Schwartz.") An *isolato* at heart ("When you write my epitaph, you must say I was the loneliest person who ever lived," she advised Lowell), she experienced Crusoe's alienation and perhaps even some of his nightmares:

Dreams were the worst. Of course I dreamed of food
and love, but they were pleasant rather
than otherwise. But then I'd dream of things
like slitting a baby's throat, mistaking it
for a baby goat.

Did she endure any of Merrill's feelings of guilt about being childless? We know something of how passionate her love life was—and look how she renders it here (in conjunction with the nulliparous condition, since in this context we have to note the overtones of "baby" and "carry"):

Friday was nice.
Friday was nice, and we were friends.
If only he had been a woman!
I wanted to propagate my kind,
and so did he, I think, poor boy.
He'd pet the baby goats sometimes,
and race around with them, or carry one around.
—Pretty to watch; he had a pretty body.

And then one day they came and took us off.

Bishop once offered that her favorite pentameter line was "I hate to see that evenin' sun go down," and I like to think that the blues song is in her mind when she writes the last line quoted. It stands alone—this, the eleventh section, the only section in the poem that amounts to only one line—as alone as Crusoe. "And then one day they came and took us off." "They" might as well be the Fates, since love's loss always comes in one form or another, but the event is recorded as a simple matter of fact. No need to emphasize the loss of Eden. The extent of this loss registers with us in the stillness after the poem's end, when Crusoe recurs to Friday: "—And Friday, my dear Friday, died of measles / seventeen years ago come March." Merrill, who adored this poem, deferentially suggested in a letter that she might elaborate on the relationship between the two men—might, for instance, have them figure out how to converse. For once, Merrill, one of the most sensitive of readers and reticent of writers (his extraordinary fluency notwithstanding), was wrong, and Bishop, master of lightness and restraint, was silent in response and let the passage stand.

Bishop's dry offhandedness affects the whole of some of the "minor" poems, as "Chemin de Fer" has been called, not without reason. Here the speaker relates taking a walk along a railroad track into an "impoverished" countryside and coming to "the little pond / where the dirty hermit lives" with a "pet hen" just as he "shot off his shotgun" and "screamed" that "'Love should be put into action.'" A nicely put together poem of five quatrains of trimeter lines, it seems inconsequential until one puts some pressure on the details, at which point the shotgun blast corresponds to the mother's scream, the aunt's cry of pain, and the volcanoes that blew their heads off. The speaker was "Alone," we learn with the first word, and walking "with a pounding heart" on "ties" that "were too close together / or maybe too far apart." The "ties" are nominally railroad ties, but if we imagine that romantic bonds are the actual issue, the entire wasteland of a landscape, the "impoverished" scenery and the pond that "lie[s] like an old tear," makes perfect sense. The poem slowly reveals itself as a self-portrait and the "dirty old hermit" as a caricature. As for the hermit's shotgun blast: isn't this marvelously disguised but egregious, desperate self-abuse? Could it also suggest suicidal thoughts? The speaker at the poem's opening is perilously walking down those railroad tracks. Crusoe's volcanoes, which have blown or have had their heads blown off and which are "naked," presumably like the shipwrecked man himself in the beginning, surely do so, since he tells us of his despondency: "Just when I thought I couldn't stand it / another minute longer, Friday came."

Another lighter venture among the uncollected poems, "Trouvée" is also a set of quatrains in which a hen has a central role. The *donnée* is even simpler than that in "Chemin de Fer":

Oh, why should a *hen*
have been run over
on West Fourth Street
in the middle of the summer?

As she is wont to do, Bishop thickens the plot subtly in the second stanza with a couple of further questions, more plangent than that opening one: "How did she get here? / Where was she going?" Of whom could those questions not be meaningfully asked? The writing responds to the call:

Her wing feathers spread
flat, flat in the tar,
all dirtied, and thin
as tissue paper.

Here the poet's ear is engaged—note the emphatic spondee in the second line—and in the service of an image at once accurate, grisly, and delicate. But the tone remains casual through the next stanza and then darkens and complicates at the end, where the poet in a splendid stroke sends the speaker "back / to look again":

I hadn't dreamed it:
there is a hen

turned into a quaint
old country saying
scribbled in chalk
(except for the beak).

She went back "to look again," because that is what good poets do. Revision, Merrill attests, is the one dependable pleasure. That last line—a frisson less graphic than but in the mode of Donne's "A bracelet of bright hair about the bone," it makes its own bracelet with its parentheses, a device used as effectively by no other poet—pointedly leaves the "beak" intact. Eliot commended Webster and by extension other writers of the seventeenth century for discerning "the skull beneath the skin."

Even after looking again, good poets also scribble things in chalk. (Bishop thought highly of Wallace Stevens, whose "Connoisseur of Chaos" endorses poetic propositions as "things chalked / On the sidewalk so that the pensive man may see.") Poets also fiddle with old country sayings. "Why did the chicken cross the road?" The title itself underwrites the whimsical identification of the poet with the hen. It is not perfectly clear to this reader why "Chemin de Fer" has a French title, but "Trouvée," in addition to meaning "found," refers to an orphan, a "foundling," as we say similarly in English, a definition that can only bring the hen and this poet, brought up from a young age without a mother and father, significantly closer. Bishop lived for a time on West Fourth Street, where she could find, all about her, things "awful but cheerful."

Merrill consciously echoes Bishop's line in an interview when he explains his own dualistic sensibility as "the ability to see both ways at once," which "isn't merely an idiosyncrasy but corresponds to how the world needs to be seen: cheerful *and* awful, opaque *and* transparent. The plus and minus signs of a vast evolving formula." Midway through his career, speaking from the point of view of a burning "Log" breaking up and turning to ash in a fireplace or a campfire, he concludes with a couplet that poses a rhetorical question: "Dear light along the way to nothingness, / What could be made of you but light, and this?" "This" is the poetry, exactingly crafted in Merrill's case as in Bishop's right down to the details of meter and punctuation, and light as the ghost of a box kite in Bishop's "The End of March," instinct with a grave consciousness of "nothingness" and a sense of humor alike, that comports with a world at odds with itself and yet shot through with gratifying relationship. Bishop's "Five Flights Up," the short poem that ends *Geography III*, set on a morning called with etymological scruple "ponderous, meticulous," contrasts in its last two lines the nature of the bird and dog next door with the poet's emotional state:

—Yesterday brought to today so lightly!
(A yesterday I find almost impossible to lift.)

Confirming the importance of its "almost," the discreet, powerful parentheses raise the burden of the concluding heptameter just off the page.

CHAPTER 3

James Merrill, Off the Gold Standard

LANGDON HAMMER

THAT JAMES MERRILL is an important poet might seem to be a settled fact. He won virtually every major prize an American poet could win, including two National Book Awards. His poetry was featured for decades in *Poetry* and the *New Yorker*, and championed by Harold Bloom and Helen Vendler. The publication of his occult trilogy, *The Changing Light at Sandover* (1982), was a sensation; so ambitious was it in its scope, and so outlandish in its means (much of it was written with a Ouija board), national newspapers and magazines weighed in, calling it "an event of importance in our culture"[1] and "the greatest long poem [. . .] an American has yet produced."[2] Since his death in 1995, his collected poems and other writings have appeared in uniform authoritative editions from Alfred A. Knopf, publisher of Langston Hughes and Wallace Stevens.[3] He is the subject of a critical biography and numerous academic monographs, book chapters, and articles. His wit, elegance, and prodigious verse technique are noted whenever he is mentioned.

But few reputations in American poetry of the late twentieth century are settled, and Merrill's is no exception. Despite the honors and attention just described, he hardly figures in some accounts of his era. Rather than securing his standing, the official consecration he enjoyed can make him look like a Fireside Poet for our day. To judge by anecdote, he is not much read by younger poets today, unless they see themselves as rhyming formalists. Ever fewer readers are equipped or inclined to appreciate his mastery of rhyme and meter, or the extraordinary variety of verse forms he worked in, all of which were stamped with his sense of style. In our current "post-lyric" moment, when the expressive first person has been subject to sweeping critique,[4] his mode of lyric autobiography, for all of its novelty and sophistication, will be dismissed by some as naïve and irrelevant.

Add to these changes in ideology and taste certain complaints that dogged Merrill throughout his writing life. There have always been readers who found his poetry mannered to the point of pretension and obscurity.[5] Others have complained that it is merely ornamental, a poetry of decor for decor's sake (even his friend Richard Howard called him "the most glamour-clogged" poet in American history).[6] Related to those complaints are charges that his work is cold, lacking in strong feelings, apolitical, and elitist, being too far removed from real life and ordinary experience. Some of these objections secretly (or not so secretly) convey aversion to his homosexuality, resentment at his class background and personal wealth, or both feelings mixed together. Perhaps it is natural to suspect that, as the son of a famous financier, he bought his success. "Not only does money talk, it also sometimes writes poetry."[7]

Merrill knew how to shrug off ad hominem criticism. But just as often, if only to prove someone wrong, he took a negative review as a prod to change, deepen, and enlarge his work.[8] Over time, this meant opening his poetry to strong feelings, politics, pop culture, and everyday life, if never quite to plain speech and simple self-disclosure. Sick with AIDS and close to death in the early 1990s, he looked back on his life as a long process of "becoming human."[9] It is not a bad way to describe the history of his work. By dint of effort over four decades, he made his poetry more urgent, moving, and complexly textured, as he interrogated the social privilege he began with, recognizing his common humanity and vulnerability without ever renouncing the refinement and virtuosity that privilege had nurtured in him.

Two late poems, "Family Week at Oracle Ranch" and "Self-Portrait in a Tyvek™ Windbreaker," are powerful examples of that theme. In the first, Merrill describes the therapy he participates in while supporting his lover at an addiction recovery center. In group meetings, Merrill is required like everyone else at the center to use "Just seven words—AFRAID, / HURT, LONELY, etc." (654)—to express himself. Ken, with a name as simple and common as those seven adjectives, sympathizes with Merrill in the child-like idiom of the place: "'When / James told the group he worried about dying / Without his lover beside him, I felt SAD.'" Merrill continues: "Thank you for sharing, Ken, // I keep from saying; it would come out snide" (655). This is a complicated moment. Merrill rejects Ken's formulaic sympathy with his snide miming of the banal discourse of the day ("Thank you for sharing"). But he also stops short of doing so and withdraws the joke. Meanwhile, he has slipped into the poem, in Ken's mouth, a disarmingly plain statement of his fear of dying alone.

In "Self-Portrait," Merrill's conflicted attitude toward plain speech and common life is again front and center. Here he describes himself wearing a windbreaker made of a synthetic, "Unrippable" (669), "airless" (673) material, Tyvek, on which a map of the world is printed. The jacket is a symbol of the world system (call it late capitalism, postmodernity, or globalization) in which people are trapped in an international consumer economy that is fast destroying nature. There is no place to stand outside this social order, and no one inside it is innocent or safe. The "figleaf's lesson" is that "Styles betray / Some guilty knowledge" (672), whether we are talking about styles of leisure wear or poetry. "As I leave the gym a smiling-as-if-I-should-know-her / Teenager [. . .] wearing 'our' / Windbreaker" greets Merrill familiarly. Although he would prefer not to, he submits to her tainted, ordinary solidarity, and returns "her wave / Like an accomplice" (671).

"Becoming human" in scenes like these does not involve a sentimental affirmation of the universal, or a dream of personal redemption. It is a tragicomic realism that comes down to the double recognition that we are all alone, and all together. This is the complex point of view in Merrill's poems in which AIDS is the explicit or (more often) implicit subject. On the one hand, Merrill was silent in his poetry about his illness and the physical and psychological suffering his condition caused him. On the other hand, he wrote about the disease, and what it was like to have it, subtly and variously throughout the eight years he lived with the diagnosis. His way of talking and not talking about AIDS was a refusal either to single himself out or to identify with the political community of people with AIDS. With a characteristic doubleness, the strategy involved denial and courage.

Above all, it expressed his determination to confront his mortality on his own terms. Melodrama and panic were threats that realism and discretion defended against. By keeping silent in the way that he did, and bringing the discipline of elegance to bear on the appalling facts of disease, he enlarged his poetry's frame of reference and made it about more than his own case. That capacity to write simultaneously from inside and outside his own experience is on view when he writes about the illness and death of close friends and the approach of his own death in "Investiture at Cecconi's," "Prose of Departure," "Farewell Performance," "b o d y," "Tony: Ending the Life," the companion poems "A Downward Look" and "An Upward Look" (the poems that open and close his final book of poems), "Oranges," and "Days of 1994." In "Christmas Tree," written in the last weeks of his life, only Merrill's irrepressible wit and the technical challenge of a dramatic monologue cast in a clever verse form (the poem is in the shape of a tree) keep the pathos of a dying man's last Christmas under the emotional control he needed to articulate and share it.

Anyone who finds Merrill's poetry lacking in strong feeling should read those poems. Anyone who finds his work apolitical should read—well, the list would be surprisingly long. A short list that suggests the range of his political engagements would include "Domino" (about whiteness and the way aesthetic refinement is implicated in structures of social and racial domination), "Page from the Koran" (protesting the readiness of every society to sacrifice human lives in the name of supreme fictions), the antic "Graffito," which leaves no "ism" intact, "Icecap" (a good candidate for the first poem anyone wrote about climate change), and "Little Fallacy," which tenderly entertains and dismisses the fantasy that poetry might intervene in a world at war. Any list of Merrill's political poems would also have to include *The Changing Light at Sandover*. The Ouija board trilogy asks whether we will come to our senses or destroy the world through nuclear war, unchecked population growth, environmental degradation, or another failure of rational choice. It is also true that, as the work of a gay poet forced to contend with a society hostile to gay people, all of his poems are to some degree political. In short, that Merrill is a poet primarily of the private life is a misreading, albeit one he himself promoted.

In my biography of Merrill, I develop these and other arguments on behalf of the deep interest and permanent value of his work. But the negative reactions Merrill's poetry elicited, early and late, need to be acknowledged— because there are grounds for those reactions, and paying attention to them brings forward curious but essential characteristics of his work that we have to deny or downplay if we are only determined to defend it.

Take "Christmas Tree." The poem is almost overwhelmingly moving, yet it revolves around the type of cute conceit that could be the basis of a *New Yorker* cartoon. The idea is that a Christmas tree is speaking, and so its days are numbered. The tree knows "it will only be a matter of weeks" before it is stripped and put out on "the cold street," its "chemicals plowed back into the Earth for lives to come" (866). This is a bearable way for Merrill to speak about what is just ahead for him (bearable for both Merrill and the reader, whom he wants to entertain and enliven, not impose upon). But it is also a gimmick, and the tone of it is teasingly coy. The title of the next poem Merrill wrote, also about his imminent death, and published posthumously in the *New Yorker*, is "Koi."

The artificiality of the conceit is compounded by the verse form—a shape poem. Through the mock-innocence of that choice, Merrill gestures touchingly toward the simple joys of childhood. But a further dimension is added to the gesture by the fact that the tree shape is asymmetrical, being oddly cropped on the left side of the page. We don't see the tree straight on and whole, but obliquely, from another room with a wall partially intervening in our view. In short, Merrill can't resist complicating the picture. He is incapable, as if constitutionally, of the simplicity of feeling and statement he wistfully evokes in the glow of that farther room, where we hear a mother's loving voice (*"Holding up wonderfully!"*) and infer her children beside her, gathered around the tree.

"For honestly, / It did help to be wound in jewels," the tree reflects, commenting by implication on Merrill's deathbed addiction to decoration. Ornament is cheering, consoling, and protective, a compensation; and this is the case even when the jewels in question are merely baubles and trinkets. Value then becomes a matter of style and point of view, determined by nothing more than a personal assertion. "Purple and silver chains" and "eaves-dripping tinsel" cast a "shining spell," creating the illusion of something truly precious. The effect paradoxically depends on the thinness of the illusion, the fact that it is so easy to see through. Then the force of personal assertion comes to the fore. The smaller, the more arbitrary the object of worship, the greater the faith. And yes, that modifier is actually "eavesdripping." Merrill is inviting us to see how the tinsel imitates icicles hanging from the roof of a house. But the point of the word is nothing more than the fun of inventing it: it is a tiny, all but gratuitous flourish. The tree's cheerful decorations, its "Amulets" and "milagros," like the word "eavesdripping" itself (866), are dollhouse-size props for a knowingly wishful, whimsically subjective faith.

That faith is a species of camp. Camp's first principle—that only the frivolous is truly serious—is a key to the tonal complexity of much of Merrill's work, which introduces pathos where we do not expect it and evacuates it where we do. His poetics of artifice expresses a queer sensibility's deep alienation from the dominant order of sex and gender, which claims to define what is real, natural, whole, and normal. The other room that we see into in "Christmas Tree" is bright with "Faces love lit" and full of "Gifts underfoot." The children who will unwrap those gifts on Christmas morning, a boy and girl, are a miniature model of the gender binary. Their noticeably gendered names, "BUD and BEA," suggest budding and being (866). They connect the simplicity and innocence that Merrill cannot have, and that he eschews, with the organic, and with natural reproduction. This is not to say he feels much about them, however. These children are not even worthy objects of resentment, being nothing more than puns.

"Christmas Tree" is characteristic of the way Merrill's poetry welcomes eddies and distractions, toys and "eavesdripping tinsel," at the cost of clarity, unity, and dignity of effect. Johnson's complaint about Shakespeare's love of wordplay ("A quibble is the golden apple for which he will always turn aside from his career, or stoop from his elevation"[10]) applies to Merrill in spades. "The Broken Home" is a series of seven sonnets in which Merrill defines his mature point of view against the examples that his parents set. At one point, he mentions his father's Irish setter. Then, in the last line, he imagines watching "a red setter stretch and sink in cloud" (200). Often anthologized, the poem is his best known; it is as emotionally charged as anything he wrote; and it ends in an awful, groan-inducing pun. There is no particular point to the joke except to mock solemnity and to evoke the sunset, the oldest, stalest trope of closure, in a fresh and funny way.

Despite his reputation for refinement and good manners, Merrill was an inveterate punster, in thrall to "the lowest form of humor."[11] It is "as though one had done an unseemly thing in adult society, like slipping a hand up the hostess's dress," he remarks in an essay on Francis Ponge in which he reflects on the nature of puns, pointing out that wordplay can be a way of expressing sexual desire and aggression, and that playing with words is held to be immature behavior. "The pun's objet trouvé aspect cheapens it further," he adds. Readers usually want a human maker, not the verbal medium, to be the source of meaning. Merrill protests that bias: "A Freudian slip is taken seriously: it betrays its maker's hidden wish. The pun (or rhyme, for that matter) 'merely' betrays the hidden wish of words" (*Prose*, 210). That slipped-in parenthesis slyly opens up the point to include not only the pun but the full array of devices and effects that fascinated Merrill, from rhyme and meter to the Ouija board.

The pun's dubious reputation "betrays also a historical dilemma," Merrill continues, complicating his claims about wordplay by historicizing them. The problem for literature after modernism—that is, for writers of his generation—was, he explains, how "to create works whose resonance lasted more than a season." The rupture in cultural continuity and consensus that produced modernism left literature with a crisis of value. Literary language was in danger of becoming a paper currency with nothing to back it up. Merrill comments:

A culture without Greek or Latin or Anglo-Saxon goes off the gold standard. How to draw upon the treasure? At once representing and parodying our vital wealth, the lightweight crackle of wordplay would retain no little transactional power in the right hands. But was it— had the gold itself been—moral? Didn't all that smack of ill-gotten gains? Even today, how many poets choose the holy poverty of some secondhand diction, pure dull content in translation from a never-to-be-known original. "There is no wing like meaning," Stevens said. Two are required to get off the ground. (210)

The "gold standard" is Merrill's metaphor for the cultural capital embodied in literary tradition and the institutions that support it—which are compactly suggested here by Greek, Latin, and Anglo-Saxon, languages of origin for English and the foundational curriculum for elite education in the West. Without classics, he suggests, producing a classic literature, meaning one capable of lasting "more than a season," is increasingly difficult, if not impossible, and he laments that fact. Yet he also knows that cultural "treasure" smacks "of ill-gotten gains" as much as other treasure does. Cultural capital is a form of capital, and his question, "was it—had the gold itself been—moral?," is rhetorical: the answer is no. Rather than enlarge on that thought, he pivots to distinguish himself from poets who choose "the holy poverty" of a diction that is felt to be "moral" because it is stripped down and plain, free of wordplay. There is no meaning, he suggests, until there are two meanings.

If he lamented the loss of the gold standard, Merrill strongly resisted modernism's bids to reestablish it in the form of an idealized literary tradition, as Pound does in Canto I, which is his translation into Anglo-Saxon alliterative verse of a Renaissance Latin translation of Homer's Greek. Merrill made a point of not reading *The Cantos* until he was almost fifty. Eliot was much harder to ignore, but Merrill gave the impression of wishing he could. "The day I went up to the Parthenon," he relates in "The Thousand and Second Night," "Its humane splendor made me think *So what?*," and he rhymes "T. S. Eliot" with "*So what?*" (179). "The Thousand and Second Night" is a long, arch, daringly digressive poem in which Merrill writes his own version of the modern poetic quest sequence, challenging Yeats and Eliot. Merrill wrote the poem in 1962, when Eliot's reputation and influence were still very high. Eliot, the reinventor of tradition and its self-proclaimed inheritor, was for Merrill a cultural monument as exalted and annoying as the Parthenon.

On the Acropolis, it was the Erechtheum, the Porch of the Maidens, that attracted Merrill. "I *know* [it] was designed and built in a fortnight by a Japanese," he wrote in a letter to a friend. "It says everything the Parthenon doesn't say, that is, a good deal more than the P. actually says."[12] The Erechtheum is a case of Merrill's aesthetic preference for what is typically the subordinate term across a series of asymmetrical pairs: feminine (not masculine), fancy (not plain), surface (not depth), art (not nature). For Merrill, the two terms in each pair were always in competition and not simple alternatives. Thus, his preference for the weaker position was a strong move, confronting and challenging the dominant and what it stood for. The Erechtheum says not merely "everything the Parthenon doesn't say," but "a great deal more" than the Parthenon "actually says."

Merrill wanted something similar: he wanted to write major poetry from a minority position. Nowhere is this ambivalence more evident than in *The*

Changing Light at Sandover, his most controversial, most difficult to assess work. At the start of this chapter, I quoted critics who made grand claims for the poem. Its conspicuous ambition demanded that response. But not all readers gave in. About *Scripts for the Pageant,* the third section of the trilogy, Denis Donoghue wrote disapprovingly: "Its subject is nothing less than the meaning of life, but the poem degrades the theme and makes a poor show of itself with camp silliness and giggling." *The Book of Ephraim,* the first section of the trilogy, he continued, "was apparently undaunted by the epigraph from Dante with which it began"—a limpid tercet from the *Paradiso.* "Now, five hundred pages later, the work has dwindled so far into mannerism that I would choose for a motto Mademoiselle de Nazianzi's swoon in Ronald Firbank [. . .]: 'Help me, heaven, to be decorative and to do right!'"[13] It is tempting to dismiss this response as hopelessly prim, if not homophobic. But Donoghue's remarks usefully highlight Merrill's perversity and impudence. It was not just the Firbankian frivolity of *Sandover* that provoked Donoghue, but the pairing of it with Dante; not just the poem's tone, but its epic scale ("Now, five hundred pages later . . .").

Like wordplay, "representing and parodying our vital wealth," *Sandover* both mocks and models itself on solid gold classics. The mockery is significant. The poem is subversive of some of the core ideologies of Western culture. Being based on channeled speech, it rejects the Romantic ideal of originality in at least two ways at once (there are two writers on the Ouija board, and the words they produce come from neither of them). It repudiates Christianity wholesale, as when W. H. Auden, speaking through the Ouija board, posthumously recants his Anglican faith and curses "THE DREARY DREARY DEAD BANG WRONG / CHURCH" (128). It hilariously hollows out the biological basis of patriarchy via a system of reincarnation over which homosexuals preside, while souls change sexes and races from one life to the next. The poem insists that the truth-claims of science are beautiful metaphors.

Yet *Sandover* is not all ludic carnival. It is not the case that, as one critic maintains, the long poem's "grand strategy" is to deflate "what Yeats called 'monuments of unaging intellect' to the camp status of, say, a Flash Gordon cartoon, a Busby Berkeley spectacle, or a Bellini opera."[14] Merrill grasped the historicity of every worldview, his own no less than Dante's. But he wanted to do more than "baffle and disperse the windy platitudes of the Western humanist tradition."[15] His frankly visionary ambitions in *Sandover* make him an inheritor of Dante—and of Milton, Blake, Hugo, Mallarmé, Yeats, and other occultists and visionaries. Merrill believed that, in the words of Heinrich Zimmer (the Jungian Indologist),[16] "The powers have to be consulted again directly—again, again, and again. Our primary task is to learn, not so much what they are said to have said, as how to approach them, evoke fresh speech from them, and understand that speech" (*Sandover*, 62).

The crucial and unlikely fact is that, for Merrill, evoking "fresh speech" from "the powers" involved a Ouija board and a good deal of "camp silliness and giggling," not to mention a dose of New Age philosophy and science fiction cosmology. Zimmer's remarks, quoted in *The Book of Ephraim*, continue: "In the face of that assignment," that is, in view of the obligation to consult the powers directly, "we must all remain dilettantes, whether we like it or not." Zimmer's "dilettantes" operate as amateurs outside of formal institutions and without agreed-upon protocols; otherwise, they can only repeat what has already been said, not "evoke fresh speech." The pose of the dilettante or amateur was key for Merrill, in *Sandover* and throughout his work. Like the calculated flimsiness of his homemade Ouija board, it countered the seriousness and monumentality of modernism as embodied by Eliot and the Eliot-influenced New Criticism, at the same that it rejected the professionalism of creative writing programs, which increasingly influenced poetry culture over the span of Merrill's career.

The twist—of which Merrill was fully aware, but just as powerless to resist—is that his dilettantism produced a distended work that suffers from the same gigantism that he had deplored in the great modernists. The irony is apparent not merely in the five hundred–plus pages that affronted Donoghue but in the tradition *Sandover* constructs, which is homosexual and willfully eccentric but overlaps enough with canonical precedent to assert a naked claim to authority and permanence. Section Q of *Ephraim* consists of "a partial smattering" of quotations. The passage from Zimmer appears there alongside jokes, a haiku by Li Po, a Ouija transcript, images from Proust, stanzas from *The Faerie Queene*, a quatrain from Auden, and other odds and ends. Although full of significance when we take the time to contemplate them, these quotations are invested with the arbitrary aura of whim, like the amulets and *milagros* that will later decorate Merrill's "Christmas Tree." So far, so good. But as the poem progresses, it increasingly aligns itself with conventional external authority. *Sandover* culminates in a coda in which Merrill reads the completed poem to an assembly in the spirit world that mixes great authors (Dante, Pope, Jane Austen, even Eliot) and Merrill's friends. Some of those friends are well-known artists (the Dutch poet Hans Lodeizen, the experimental filmmaker Maya Deren) while others are not, being interesting and notable only insofar as Merrill found them so. The scene does not deconsecrate the canon in favor of Merrill's personal affections; it folds the personal into the canonical. This is the direction the trilogy takes in *Mirabell: Books of Number* and particularly *Scripts for the Pageant*. The growing self-enclosure and self-approval are features of the genre (how can you undertake a spiritual quest without some vanity and pretension?).[17] They enact a queer person's revenge against social stigma (I am better than the society that hates me, and I have friends in high places who agree). But as Merrill's poem grows simultaneously grander and cozier, the combination is hard to take. By the end of *Sandover*, the Erechtheum is bigger than the Parthenon.

Underlying and expressed in all the features that make Merrill's poetry tricky to evaluate—for instance, the decorative manner, excesses of metaphor, tonal instability, whimsical subjectivity, devotion to wordplay, and, in *Sandover*, the convoluted, outsize ambition—is a basic ambivalence about normative values, literary and otherwise. The ambivalence can be explained biographically by his social positioning as a rich, white homosexual, a member of a dominated fraction within the dominant class. But we can also see it as a sign of the "historical dilemma" that he sketches in the essay on Ponge. Merrill's desire both to dismantle and claim tradition, "representing and parodying our vital wealth," expresses an ambivalence about normative values that characterized American poetry as a whole during an era when literature had gone "off the gold standard," and it was becoming very hard to say what literary value consisted in, and should consist in; an era when at first the contents and then the form and function of literary tradition became a focus for sophisticated analysis and public debate. To borrow a slogan from the Ouija board spirits, it is "NO ACCIDENT" (196, 199) that *The Changing Light at Sandover* appeared in 1983, the same year that the academic journal *Critical Inquiry* devoted an issue to the subject of canon formation, and "the canon" became an inescapable term for anyone with a stake in literature and the history of poetry in particular.[18]

––––––––––

It is possible not to pay very much attention to Merrill's puns. They are not the first feature of his work to strike you if you approach him as a love poet, the role in which he most liked to present himself, and the role he established first. We don't have to make allowances for "The Black Swan" to feel that this poem, written during Merrill's junior year at college, belongs with the rest and perhaps even the best of his love poems. Its manner is stagey. The scene is idealized, and thus somewhat unreal. But unreality is essential to the strangeness of the vision of the black swan—which remains haunting even once the child's cry, "I love the black swan" (3), has been decoded as Merrill's declaration of love for Kimon Friar, his first lover and an influential mentor, who assigned him the task of writing the poem and then published it in a chapbook called *The Black Swan* (1946). The unreality is unavoidable because the child has discovered in himself a passion that, although entirely real, has no natural place in the world. The lake on which the black swan moves can only be a symbolic space. It is a preliminary version of the Other World that Merrill would discover on the Ouija board. The abstraction—Love—strikes him like a sword.

Merrill's greatest love poem is "Days of 1964," a curious homage to and imitation of Constantine Cavafy's "Days of . . ." poems—curious, because the fiction in Cavafy's erotic poems is that they were composed in distant retrospect, and Merrill was writing about an affair he was in the middle of. Perhaps he holds his lover at a distance in order to balance the boldness and intimacy of a poem that is openly about sexual desire and fantasy, money, and emotional exposure. When he wrote it, Merrill had recently moved to Athens, where he spent at least half of every year until 1979. The move marked a development in his poetry. There is fluency and vitality in "Days of 1964," in contrast to the airless atmosphere of an early poem like "The Black Swan." The later poem happens very much in this world (granted that "this world" means Greece, which for Merrill was another world in relation to his life in the United States). The change is evident in the poem's brilliant description of Athens and in vignettes involving Merrill, his housekeeper, and his lover. One day he meets the housekeeper Kleo on her way to what he presumes is a rendezvous, on the basis of her makeup. "*Eat me, pay me*," her painted face seems to say. Merrill calls it "the erotic mask / Worn the world over by illusion / To weddings of itself and simple need" (221). From there, the poem builds to a remembered moment of transformation. Merrill says to his lover: "Where I hid my face, your touch, quick, merciful, / Blindfolded me. A god breathed from my lips." He adds, thinking of Kleo's mask, "If that was illusion, I wanted it to last long" (221).

The beloved in "Days of 1964" returns in later poems. Eventually, Merrill tells us his first name, Strato; in the last poem about him, "The House Fly," from many years later, Merrill gives his full name. Strato becomes progressively more real over time. In another sense, however, he becomes ever more stylized, a literary character in Merrill's ongoing lyric autobiography. It would be a mistake to overemphasize the developing actuality of Merrill's love poetry, and of his work generally. The real people in "Days of 1964" are not so deeply different in quality from the symbolic figures in "The Black Swan." We see this when the images of blindfolding and the breathing god suddenly turn the poem into a retelling of the Eros and Psyche story. In Merrill's poetry, the abstract and symbolic are not incompatible with intense personal feeling; just the opposite. "A Renewal" describes a conversation in which Merrill tells a lover he wants to end their relationship. He is calm and reasonable. Then, after a moment's reflection, "Love buries itself in me, up to the hilt" (66).

This talent for "seeing double" ("To a Butterfly," 161), for moving back and forth between real and symbolic, concrete and abstract, actual and virtual, memoir and myth, drives Merrill's poetry from beginning to end. In "The Broken Home," his battling, tipsy parents are both their quite specific selves *and* "Father Time and Mother Earth, / A marriage on the rocks" (198). "You don't see eternity *except* in the grain of sand, or history except at the family dinner table," Merrill remarked, commenting on that passage (*Prose*, 114). So even when a Merrill poem doesn't conspicuously involve wordplay, the same imagination is at work. Doubleness is what Merrill loved in the pun, and the principle he insists on in his addendum to Stevens's aphorism: "'There is no wing like meaning,'" but "Two are required to get off the ground."

Variously through pun, metaphor, and myth, then, Merrill's poetry continually insists upon, and trusts in the sufficiency of, its own "poeticity"— to take a term from Roman Jakobson referring to the moment in a "verbal work" when "the word is felt as a word and not as a mere representation of the object being named or an outburst of emotion."[19] Merrill, the dilettante, would object to Jakobson's scientific-sounding word. His preferred term would be "style," with its suggestion of dandyism. Style, like homosexuality as Merrill lived it, was nothing more—or less—than a personal preference. Promoting style as a good above all others, or at least as a principle adequate unto itself, was Merrill's way of placing himself in a literary field subdivided among competing poetries that purported to transcend mere style by grounding themselves in authenticity or craft ("the raw and the cooked"), Deep Images, a specific political program, or the deconstruction of lyric transparency, among other legitimation strategies.[20] Reacting to these positions as rhetorical moves that try to disguise their contingency, Merrill grounded his own poetry in its poeticity, which is to say his insistence that we remember that it is nothing more than words.

Given this emphasis on words themselves, it was tempting for Merrill to propose language as a substitute ground for metaphysics. He sometimes moves in that direction, as when in *Sandover* he celebrates the "flesh made word" (31) and the spirits speak of "THE LIFE RAFT LANGUAGE" (119). But he stops short, even in *Sandover*, of propounding a postmodern religion based on language as a unitary and universal structure with redemptive potential. "Lost in Translation," which is in my view his very best poem, speaks to this issue. A poem of personal memory and a searching philosophical meditation that takes the nature of language as its subject, it explores two models for how consciousness and language work. The first model says that the mind uses language to put experience together like the pieces of a jigsaw puzzle, arriving over time at a representation in which word links up with world, and "nothing's lost" (367). The second model says that making sense of experience is like translating a text. This model foregrounds the plurality of languages, the gaps between them, and the gaps between word and world.

The first model is quasi-theological; the second emphatically secular. Both appealed to Merrill, but there is no question in "Lost in Translation" that poetry is on the side of the second. The poem's title plays on the cliché commonly attributed to Frost: poetry is what gets lost in translation. When translation is the model, there is no such thing as language, only languages, meaning multiple systems of representation, none of which takes priority over the others. In this situation, there is no original, no principle of equivalence, no gold standard. Rather, "all is translation / And every bit of us is lost in it," Merrill concludes. Except he doesn't conclude; he immediately adds, "or found" (367). The special power and exhilaration of this poem lie in Merrill's ability to keep reversing positions by turning around whatever he has just said. This involves repeatedly flipping figure and ground, so that what had seemed literal turns out to be figurative, and vice versa. It also means that the assertion "all is translation" is not an abstract principle to be extracted like a moral, but merely an offhand expression, a way of speaking, even while it suggests a whole worldview.

The depth of thought in "Lost in Translation" is masked by the surface manner of the dilettante. Casualness was necessary for Merrill to keep toying with words, day after day, in a compositional practice that, when we study his notebooks and worksheets, looks like arduous discipline. I'm referring to the dozens of drafts behind every stanza, the pages of anagrams, doodles, and musings, and the diaries that Merrill wrote in everywhere he went—in short, the archival evidence of his obsessive daily writing practice. The point of this way of working was to "KEEP MEANING SPINNING LIKE A COIN" (*Sandover*, 492) and prevent thought from freezing up in "monolithic Truths" ("Lost in Translation," 367). Sharp reversals of the literal and figurative result, in Merrill's poetry, in a vision of the relation between world and word that is bracingly fluid and volatile, and always in need of restatement. Jakobson, in his definition of "poeticity," explains the idea precisely:

> [B]esides the direct awareness of the identity between the sign and object (*A* is *A1*), there is a necessity for the direct awareness of the inadequacy of that identity (*A* is not *A1*). The reason this antinomy is essential is that without contradiction there is no mobility of concepts, no mobility of signs, and the relationship between concept and sign becomes automatized. Activity comes to a halt, and the awareness of reality dies out.[21]

Even or perhaps especially in its seemingly unreal effects, in what is most artificial and crafted about it, Merrill's poetry is meant to keep the mind's "activity" alive, and enhance our awareness of reality. "For Proust" is a statement of this aim from early in Merrill's career. The poem follows Proust, the dilettante Merrill took for his hero, as he goes out into the crowded social world ("Jean takes your elbow, Jacques your coat") and then returns to the solitude of the room where he writes: now "What happened is becoming literature" (140). The poem is set up in quatrains rhymed *abba* with an odd twist: the *a* rhyme is conventional in form (*hotel* / *personnel*), but the internal *b* rhyme consists of the same word used twice. Sometimes these repetitions pair abstract and concrete senses of the word. Sometimes Merrill varies the part of speech, or he draws out some nuance via the repetition. But usually the nuance is slight, and it is not meant to impress us with cleverness. These choices combine to keep the reader from settling into a pattern. The device is a version of the French practice of rime riche, appropriate in a poem honoring Proust. Usually, English requires more distance between words before they count as rhyming. So the device makes rhyme just a little bit strange. This goes with the way Merrill makes us look twice at the words he repeats. The repetition in each case is a moment of denaturalization that makes us aware of Merrill's language, as if to say: when life is becoming literature, reality submits to artifice, "*A1*" returns as "*A*," and "the word is felt as a word."

The last line of "For Proust" is one of the most memorable in Merrill's work. When Proust's night is over, and his writing is done, "The world will have put on a thin gold mask" (141). The image sums up Merrill's ambivalence about literary value, and the peculiar challenge of fixing the value of his work. It says that the world transformed in Proust's novel will be like the world transformed at dawn. On the one hand, the image gestures toward finality. The future perfect tense ("The world will have . . .") projects a day to come in which the work has been perfected, in the sense of completed and fixed in form; it throws Proust's writing forward in time, toward a new day, which is surely the canonical future Merrill hopes for, silently, for his own work. This is Merrill wishing for a literature that will last "more than a season," the Merrill who wants to create enduring works of art—like the golden "mask of Agamemnon" excavated at Mycenae, which he might be thinking of here;[22] "treasure" in the shape of a man's face to be recovered someday from a tomb. This is the Merrill who walked off with so many golden poetry prizes.

On the other hand, that "thin gold mask"[23] evokes the most evanescent of effects: how sunrise brings the world freshly into view. If literature works that way, it renews how we see things, and it elevates their value, but only momentarily and artificially, as a function of our own subjectivity; the world isn't changed—only how it looks. For the gold has nothing behind it.

It is "thin," not an illusion precisely but a trick of sunlight playing on the surface of things, bound to change again shortly, and purely a matter of perception. It is the same way with the flickering, improbable, metamorphic spirits in *The Changing Light at Sandover*, who are only made of words and about whose reality Merrill was (naturally) "always of two minds" (*Prose*, 143).

The "thin gold mask" is finally only a dignified form of "eavesdripping tinsel." The Merrill who imagined it is the poet who wound the world in "jewels," hoping that the magic they cast would "last long," or at least long enough to hold off the darkness of disease, broken promises and broken homes, human destructiveness, "greed and savagery" ("Self-Portrait in a Tyvek™ Windbreaker," 670), and simple mortality, of which his poetry never stopped being aware. This is writing "off the gold standard." It is a nice irony that, if it lasts, the qualities that disqualify Merrill's poetry from classic status will have to be part of the reason why.

Notes

1. Michael Harrington, "Paradise or Disintegration," *Commonweal*, November 4, 1983.
2. David Lehman, "Merrill's Celestial Comedy," *Newsweek*, February 28, 1983.
3. I quote from these editions, each of which was edited by J. D. McClatchy and Stephen Yenser and published by Alfred A. Knopf. They include, in order of publication: *Collected Poems* (2001), *Collected Prose* (2004), *Collected Novels and Plays* (2005), and *The Changing Light at Sandover* (2006).
4. A critique of the Romantic lyric was central to Language poetry beginning in the 1970s, and recently to Documentary poetry and Conceptual writing, while the critical movement known as historical poetics has argued that the lyric speaker is the construction of a reading practice. See, for instance, Virginia Jackson and Yopie Prins, eds., *The Lyric Theory Reader: A Critical Anthology* (Baltimore: Johns Hopkins University Press, 2013). On the racialization of the form, see Kamran Javadizadeh, "The Atlantic Ocean Breaking on Our Heads: Claudia Rankine, Robert Lowell, and the Whiteness of the Lyric Subject," *PMLA* 134, no. 3 (2019): 475–90.
5. The theme is first sounded by W. L. Frederici, "Lit. Review," *The Lawrence*, January 15, 1943.
6. Richard Howard, review of *Nights and Days*, by James Merrill, *Poetry* 108 (August 1966): 329. See also Mary Karr, "Against Decoration," *Parnassus: Poetry in Review* 16, no. 2 (1991): 277.

7. Alfred Corn, "Make Song of Them," *The Smart Set*, June 1, 2015, https://www.thesmartset.com/make-song-of-them/.

8. This trait is evident early and late in his career, when we see him responding directly to critiques of his work. The most striking example is the way *The Book of Ephraim* emerged from his meditation on a negative review of *Braving the Elements* and the controversy surrounding his winning of the Bollingen Prize. I describe this in *James Merrill: Life and Art* (New York: Alfred A. Knopf, 2015), 529–33, 560–61.

9. Hammer, *James Merrill*, xviii–xix.

10. Samuel Johnson, "Preface to Shakespeare," in *Selected Poetry and Prose*, ed. Frank Brady and William K. Wimsatt (Berkeley: University of California Press, 1978), 309.

11. James Merrill, "Object Lessons," in *Collected Prose*, 210.

12. James Merrill to Daryl Hine, letter, May 22, 1962 (Special Collections, Olin Library, Washington University in St. Louis).

13. Denis Donoghue, "What the Ouija Board Said," *New York Times Book Review*, June 15, 1980. Donoghue made it clear that he hadn't been reading Firbank himself; he found the quotation in Auden.

14. Walter B. Kalaidjian, *Languages of Liberation: The Social Text in Contemporary American Poetry* (New York: Columbia University Press, 1989), 96–97.

15. Kalaidjian, *Languages of Liberation*, 98.

16. See Stephen Yenser's comments on Zimmer in his annotated edition of *The Book of Ephraim* (New York: Alfred A. Knopf, 2018), 166.

17. Timothy Materer, in *James Merrill's Apocalypse* (Ithaca, NY: Cornell University Press, 2000), argues that the poem's elitism is a generic feature of apocalyptic narrative.

18. There had been some prominent treatments of the topic, such as Leslie A. Fiedler and Houston A. Baker Jr., eds., *English Literature: Opening Up the Canon; Selected Papers from the English Institute, 1979* (Baltimore: Johns Hopkins University Press, 1981). But it's in *Critical Inquiry*, volume 10 (1983), that canon formation comes to the fore as an indispensable term in literary criticism. That issue of the magazine was the basis for *Canons* (Chicago: University of Chicago Press, 1984); both the magazine and the book were edited by Robert von Hallberg. Included in both was "The Ideology of Canon Formation: T. S. Eliot and Cleanth Brooks" by John Guillory, the seed essay that grew into Guillory's definitive study, *Cultural Capital: The Problem of Literary Canon Formation* (Chicago: University of Chicago Press, 1993).

19. Roman Jakobson, "What Is Poetry?," in *Selected Writings*, vol. 3: *Poetry of Grammar and Grammar of Poetry*, by Roman Jakobson, ed. Stephen Rudy (The Hague: Mouton, 1981), 750.

20. For a discussion of how a putative amateurism functioned for Merrill as a way of placing himself in the field of postwar American poetry, see my essay "The

Biographical Container," *Yale Review* 104, no. 3 (July 2016): 19–39.

21. Jakobson, "What Is Poetry?," 750.

22. Stephen Yenser proposes this reference in *The Consuming Myth: The Work of James Merrill* (Cambridge, MA: Harvard University Press, 1987), 81.

23. While he was a fellow at the James Merrill House in Stonington, Connecticut, Walt Hunter picked up Merrill's copy of Elinor Wylie's poetry and opened it to "Sunset on a Spire," which ends: "All that I / Could ever ask / Wears that sky / Like a thin gold mask." I'm grateful to Hunter for pointing out to me this source for Merrill's line. Wylie was the favorite poet of the teenage Merrill. That she was a "poetess" who wrote of love in rhyme and meter appealed to him when he was reading Proust for the first time and coincidentally discovering his own homosexuality. Wylie and Proust merge in "For Proust," underlining Merrill's preference for a "weak," feminine stance (the Erechtheum again) as he positioned himself in the field of modern literature.

CHAPTER 4

Why the Poetry of C. D. Wright Is Likely to Last a Long Time (with Attention to Why Poetry Lasts, More Generally)

STEPHANIE BURT

IN ORDER TO explain why it seems to me that the poetry of C. D. Wright will last, why I think the future will go on cherishing and examining and even imitating it, I'll have to start far away from Wright's own poetry, with the history of poetry in general. Poems, poets, books of poetry can get noticed when they do one thing exceptionally well: so well that readers with a few minutes to spare, and many other poems they could have chosen, pick *this* poem out of a magazine, or off the internet, or from a friend's notebook, and copy it over or read it aloud or forward it to the rest of their friends. Books and bodies of poetry with slightly longer shelf lives than the average do at least one thing so well that they rise above the others, or shine in the dark: when a significant poem, or poet, gets popular suddenly, it's often not hard to say why. Taking only the period 1870–1920, Algernon Charles Swinburne; A. E. Housman; Paul Laurence Dunbar, the early W. B. Yeats, Wilfred Owen, and Edna St. Vincent Millay come to mind.

Each of these poets had, and still has, what gossip columnists, academic advisers, and entertainment critics today call an elevator pitch—a very short, very clear way to explain what made so many people want to read their books. Some of these pitches (as with Owen and Millay) connect the poet in obvious ways to current events, to the tenor of their times; others connect the poetry indirectly, or by opposition, to the very same times. *A Shropshire Lad* says explicitly, and correctly, that its troubled lads and wayward shepherd demonstrate emotions and situations that do not change very much, if at all, when society changes: "Others, I am not the first, / Have willed more mischief than they durst" (see generally poems 12, 30, and 31). Housman's first book of poems almost insists that we read it, as tens or hundreds of thousands of people have already read it, as a sweetly sour escape from whatever problems seem brand new, high-tech, specific to our own time.

Or at least that was how it could be read, back then; if *A Shropshire Lad* does *not* last—if it ends up, in 2050, as a book that only specialists in late Victorian poetry read—the critics of 2050 will conclude that whatever it did for the common reader in 1897 and 1957 it cannot do any more. They will also have to conclude that it does not, at the moment, in 2050, do anything else; new aspects of the work have not emerged to replace the aspects that it has lost. If those critics want to revive it—as John Donne, to pick a well-known example, has been revived—they will have to argue for it either on the basis of its historical interest ("people used to like this a lot; you'll learn history if you learn why") or on the basis of some other aspect that, once you look for it, becomes something you (you future reader; you, in 2050) can see. The former tack produces scholarly discussion; the latter, when it works, gives new readers—new amateur readers; new readers who choose to read this and not that in their free time—to old poems.

And for the latter to work—with Housman or with Elizabeth Barrett Browning or with Paul Laurence Dunbar or with Arnaut Daniel or with any poet who has been gone for more than a couple of years, who has fallen out of favor with their initial audience for whatever reason—the poetry has to present new reasons for new readers to like it; it must, that is, have more than one string to its bow (if we imagine that poems are premodern weapons), or more than one cuisine into which it fits (if we imagine poems as food), or more than one way to score, pass, or defend (if we imagine poems as basketball players). Poems and poets that can do only one thing quite well, that reward only one sort of reading, are like the hit songs that climb pop charts and then go away; their fans run out of reasons to *keep* listening to them, and no new reasons, later on, emerge.

Poems that stick around (and some of Housman's, and some of Owen's, and even some of Millay's, belong to this category) are poems that give many readers, and many kinds of readers, multiple reasons to reread them. Philip Larkin complained, in "Continuing to Live," that it was hardly worth it to seek out one's own particular identity, "the blind impress / All our behavings bear" (I'll come back to that "our"), much less to embody that identity in memorably worked language, since the resulting discovery or conclusion "applied only to one man once / And that man dying." Like many of Larkin's most quotable poems, "Continuing to Live" could be read as a search for universals, for an "our" that far exceeds "my," for a conclusion that—like many of Larkin's conclusions—appears to apply to many, many people, over a vast reach of time and space (the musings on love in "Faith Healing," for example, or the conclusions about our religious feelings in "Church Going").

Yet that search for universals, and for their elegant embodiment, seems to me an incomplete, and often misleading, way to think about literary history. Larkin survives not because so many readers get the same thing from him but because many readers get, from his poetry and even from individual poems, many different things; the poems "apply" (to use Larkin's word) in one way to the morose, in another to readers who treasure closure and elegance, in another to readers in search of England and Englishness in its sad postimperial modes, in yet another to those who want sarcastic jokes. I do not mean to discount Larkin's ear, nor his gifts with the arrangement of words (do not mean to discount, that is, what a Kantian reader might say just *is* what makes the poems good); rather, the ear, the sense of arrangement, is what makes the versatility, the way of embodying so many reactions, so many readings, possible. Worse poets are not able to say, consistently and memorably, nearly so much, even when they say and show (as Larkin's nearest contemporaries in form and manner, from Kingsley Amis to Elizabeth Jennings, show) *something* of interest, in an elegant way.

I've been discussing poets' reputations with crowds, with generations, with a literary reading public, but I could say almost the same thing about individual poems and poets who stay with you as an individual reader: you—yes, you, Marcia or Pat or Berto or Kofi or Miyako or Paul or Paula—might get excited about a poet for one reason on first reading, but if you are likely to go back to the book, to keep on reading or teaching or recommending it year after year, it will have to divulge something new, something of language or style or emotion or wisdom that did not pop out the first time.

According to this model of why poets last, great poems do not stand out for their universality, for saying or doing one thing that matters for some critic's time-bound notion of "everybody," but for a depth best conceived as versatility: they do a lot of things, which means more people will care for one of the things. Different readers care for different things, and those differences in turn generate argument around the poems, which in turn helps them last. That versatility might be conceived as resilience (read the same poem several times, and it's different each time: we never look into the same poem twice, as Lionel Trilling did not quite say) or as multiple overlapping appeal (as in David Kellogg's still too little read stunt essay of 2001, explaining John Ashbery's multiple appeals to multiple audiences while copping its language from Watson and Crick's 1953 report on DNA).

The most notorious negative review in American poetry, Louis Simpson's 1963 attack on Gwendolyn Brooks, stands out in this light not just as a symptomatic white reader's failure to understand race, but also as a way to show why versatility and depth make intelligible criteria for discussion of poetic value, while universality will not. Simpson claimed that Brooks, like any Black poet, could not help but write about being Black, which in turn kept her poems from being universal. The demand for universality in poetry, lyric, and otherwise—inasmuch as it is anything other than a cover for white resentment (though here, as often, it includes that too)—keeps coming up in part because it misunderstands the wish for durability, the (well-supported) belief that something has to distinguish the poems that can last; and those poems do last not because they say one thing that can be understood by "everyone," but because they can say and do many things, for many (overlapping but noncoextensive) sets of readers.

Brooks—and Housman—furnish good examples. The same Housman quatrains that served his fans, in 1899, as a familiar example of English pastoral, an object of nostalgia, may now please readers (some of them far from England) who hear their elegance as foreign, who did not grow up with those place-names, those trees, those forms. Brooks's poems—the same poems—speak in one way (as I learned by teaching in New Zealand) to pakeha- and Maori-identified readers quite unfamiliar with Black Chicago, in another way to white Americans, in another way to the Black Chicagoans who were Brooks's first and last audience, and in yet another way to Black Americans far removed in location and social class from the South Side.

And, of course, Brooks's best poems ("kitchenette building," say, and "Boy Breaking Glass") could not do any of those things if readers could not find in them the sonic balances and intricacies that make them worth hearing, rehearing, rereading. Those balances also support the emotional lives of Brooks's characters, which cannot be explained *without* reference to race, but which cannot be exhausted by that (nor by any) single topic. Brooks's poems, like John Milton's, take on many subjects for many audiences, some of which, and some of whom, were (in the early 1960s) specifically African American. For example, "kitchenette building" speaks of urban poverty, and of familial resentment, and of how childhood hopes dry out amid the practicalities of adulthood, and of American hypocrisy around class mobility; it also speaks of the emotional overtones of the basic Lakoffian metaphors "dry" and "wet," and it speaks to the history of the sonnet, with its thump of a finished couplet, but in order to hear all seven effects you may have to read the sonnet seven times—or to have seven readers discuss the poem. If it did not achieve something aesthetically interesting, something linguistically noteworthy, around each of those topics, it would not be the anthology piece that it has rightly become.

In general: poets who stick around do more than one thing, which means that they can also work on multiple readers, for multiple reasons. They are versatile: both of their time and not of it, interesting for reasons of diction or sound or line shape and, also, interesting for reasons of substance, for the claims they make about the world; interesting to readers who want to scrutinize one phrase forever, and to readers who take poetry in at great gulps. Poets who stick around are not—to borrow a word from the TV chef Alton Brown—unitaskers; and Brown, as his fans know, refuses to keep even the most elegant unitasker in his versatile, efficiency-driven kitchen.[1] It's easy to find one reason why one person might like a sonnet by Barnabe Barnes; if you can find one hundred reasons why one, or one hundred, people might like the same sonnet, you are more likely to be reading Hopkins, or Shakespeare—and you, as Larkin, and Shakespeare, and Langston Hughes, knew, may as well be different people at different times: one man [*sic*] in his [*sic*] time plays many parts.

And that is why the poetry of C. D. Wright seems especially likely to last.

More than any other American poet of her generation, Wright meant various things to various people, or to the same people in different poems: she was not only recognizable but at the same time versatile, variously emotionally engaging, both among her poems and between them. Wright, who died suddenly in early 2016, wrote—depending on how you count them and on how you define "poetry"—either seventeen, fourteen, thirteen, or eleven books of poetry. Each one added to her repertoire of modes, lines, claims, and gestures, and the best poems (including the prose poems, lyric essays, multimedia documentary elements, and lyric sequences) in each did many things at once.

A more conventional introduction to Wright—I've written several such essays myself at this point, as have other critics—would proceed chronologically through her career, from Fayetteville, Arkansas, to San Francisco to Mexico to Providence to the later poems of travel through Georgia, Louisiana, Mexico again, and back to Providence, or through the goals and outlines of her book-length poems, from the book-length elegiac sequence *Translation of the Gospel Back into Tongues* (1981) through the abject sexuality of *Just Whistle* (1992), the disoriented travelogue *Deepstep Come Shining* (1998), the capacious documentary project *One Big Self: Prisoners of Louisiana* (2003, rev. 2013), and the memoir-essay-prose poem *One with Others* (2012). These sorts of introductions, while helpful, tend to scant her short poems, and her late poems, and they describe her thematic goals so thoroughly that they may not leave time for the virtues of her style— the virtues by which all poems, if they last, must last.

I hope instead to describe these virtues, to show how many of them she had, and how they overlap within single poems. These virtues, taken together, will point not only to Wright's idiosyncratic set of powers but also to one thing that unifies many of her gifts, something that distinguishes her from other celebrated—and, I suspect, less durable—"experimental," disjunctive, or nonpropositional poets, and connects her to Housman, and to Brooks: Wright is, through all her changes, a predominantly lyric poet, in the strong sense of "lyric" put forward most recently and comprehensively by Jonathan Culler. She brings many new things, together, to old lyric goals; it is as lyric in that capacious sense that her poems—which resemble neither songs, nor conventional confessional first-person verse—will endure.

First, work from Wright's last book (in press when she died), *ShallCross*. Here is a short one entitled "Poem of a Forest of Clouds Sweeping By":

your life blew past as a shift off a line
but then turned and turned again
O Archangel of the Mirror
what would you have done
it's been said that over the years
the house sustained the smell
of fresh-cooked trout and the rest
as we well know is still journeying[2]

Short and stichic (like all the poems in the first part of *ShallCross*), "Poem of a Forest . . ." also becomes generically recognizable: it is a memorial poem, addressed (as Culler says all lyric is in some sense addressed) to someone who cannot hear or respond, in this case to someone dead, to someone who died fast, or died too young. Wright pursues rapidity, ephemerality, the ashes-to-ashes contrast of a durable phrase that sticks in the mind with a life that "blew past" and is gone (though really the life lasted longer than the phrase; the apparent contrast in felt duration is the opposite of the real one). The seasons turn and turn again, and we do not; "turn, turn, turn," as Pete Seeger and then the Byrds put it (a poet of Wright's generation would certainly have the Byrds' version of Ecclesiastes in mind). The wind is the inspiration, the absent soul, now gone (as in Hadrian's *animula*) who knows where; "the house," like an improvised sepulcher, like the deserted houses in Frost, reflects one absence, but also the absence of everyone, eventually: we are all on the same journey to death.

That is to say that Wright has made vivid and colloquial—and also removed the normal grammatical linking parts and connections from—a very traditional kind of lyric; she writes, here, a monody, as she writes, elsewhere, aubades, erotic lyrics of invitation, even the inscriptional, location-specific, not-quite-lyric verse of antiquity (as in her *Ozark Odes*). She remakes these ancient (Cullerian) genres. She also makes them casual, and Southern, or Arkansan, or rural, as a matter of diction and cadence but also as a matter of sense impression: clotheslines (unstable ones), gossip ("it's been said"), foodways (trout, perhaps). This combination of linguistic density (she is never verbose and no raconteur; she respects a reader's time), indirection or parataxis, and Southern, Arkansan, or rural properties was something Wright could have seen, from time to time, in equally strange but far less technically assured Southern precursors (especially Besmilr Brigham, whose work she tried to revive); but executed over and over, with confidence, the combination is hers.

So is the sense—arrived at through parataxis, through Southernisms, as well as through the (also Cullerian) vocative—that when we read her poems we see a face. The face in question (addressed as a "forest of clouds," of which more soon) is the face of an absent figure, but also a face in a mirror: that archangel, that messenger (Greek *anggelos*), arrives instead of a ghost and appears not as the dead friend's face, but as our own. We look into a mirror, looking for lost loved ones, and instead we see ourselves. That is, again, an effect proper to lyric, which presents at once the face of a particular other person and our own face, our own feelings, made newly clear.

But it is, also, an effect made new by Wright's own poetry, with its frequent debts to modern photography, to portraits, to landscapes, to figure studies, to documentary and journalistic work: Wright's first three book-length works (*Just Whistle, Deepstep Come Shining,* and *One Big Self: Prisoners of Louisiana*) all began in collaborations with the photographer Deborah Luster. Wright's thinking about her own art drank deeply and frequently from the well of art photography; her poems likened themselves to art photographers' light-mediated versions of landscapes, or interiors, or—as here—of a face.

Whose face? Wright's husband, who survives her, was the considerable poet and translator Forrest Gander (himself a regular collaborator with Southern photographers, including Sally Mann). Is it Forrest who is sweeping by? Or is it another intimate partner, one who has died, one who once shared a clouded, familiar house? Wright's early poetry mourned the prolific, self-destructive, charismatic Arkansas poet Frank Stanford (1948–1978)—they had been lovers toward the end of his brief life—and his death, which she rarely discussed directly, colored the reception of her later work: Stanford is the star not only of the Gothic Americana in *Translation of the Gospel Back into Tongues* (1981) but of the poems in *String Light* (1991), which tell Stanford's life story. In one of the first we literally see his face—we see him as he is born, in "King's Daughters, Home for Unwed Mothers, 1948" (the title of the poem): his mother "is up on her elbows, bangs wet in her eyes. The head / of the unborn is visible at the opening. The head / crowns. Many helping hands are on her."[3] From this vivid, lineated present-tense description, Wright opens out, once the child gets born, into a vast list presented as a prose block: "Volumes of letters, morning glories on a string trellis, the job at the Maybelline factory, the job at the weapons plant, the hummingbird hive . . ." (*SA* 64). The parents, after this proleptic explosion of information, of noun phrases from Stanford's future life, "will never know / That they will outlive him. They will never know. / Whether he will do things they never dreamed." (*SA* 65).

This sense of a life partly told, of a biography—usually, in the early work, Stanford's—sliced into small segments and rearranged into lyric shapes, became one of Wright's special achievements. Usually the life—here, clearly Stanford's—deserved, and received, honor: Wright really believed, and tried to put into her phrasing, the Whitmanian claim that all lives deserve honor, especially those (obscure or notorious) that have not received it through institutional channels. (Like Whitman, though in rhythms unlike his, she wanted to make those honors sound American, informal, acoustically distinct from European and English forms.)

We get that sense of a biography fractured, and of a life honored, again in "Forest of Clouds," separated from any certainty about whose life we hear or smell. Stanford was always "journeying"—he worked as a land surveyor— and his fast life certainly "blew past." Yet Wright's memory of what "the house sustained," of feminized labor in word and action—"sweeping," drying clothes, cooking—suggests that a woman is mourned: and some of Wright's elegiac verse and lyric prose looks for a feminist mode of mourning, a way to recognize the persistence in repetitive tasks, the devotion to one locality, the ambition and lack of ambition, the friendly righteousness, of the women (mostly older women) whom Wright has known. The book-length poem, or poetic essay, *One with Others* constitutes such a tribute, honoring a teacher Wright names V, who stood up against Jim Crow. Here is a representative passage from *One with Others*, the whole of page 33:

V's bush was sweet-betsy. I broke off a twig in her oldest daughter's yard. Over the coming months, I break it over and over for a quick hit of camphor.

And offshore Camille brought rain that September. The year they put the kids under arrest and put them in the swimming pool.

King called "it" a disease, segregation. [Sounds contagious.]
It's cradle work is what it is. It begins before the quickening.

When V ended up in Kentucky after her expulsion from Big Tree, she
kept a retired fighting cock. It was her only pleasure, Helmet. No one
else could get near him.[4]

Here is the feminist strain in Wright's achievement, honoring V's fight; here,
too, the gospel strain, the "journey" of spirituals and other old songs.

Wright's work more generally strives to fit—as few professedly
experimental, unconventional poets (at least until the 2010s) wanted to fit—
what the cultural critic Craig Werner has identified as the gospel strain in
American music, the moves (Werner means both emotional moves, attitudes,
and particular timbres and chord changes) that say we're all in this together;
things can get better; the Lord is on our side; look to the future. (Among the
other poets who have combined avant-garde, antisemantic techniques with
this strain, the only notable success so far may be Fred Moten, whose other
ambitions run in different, and not necessarily lyric, directions.) Werner's
persuasive read on American culture through pop music, entitled *A Change
Is Gonna Come*, contrasts the gospel strain in African American and African
American–derived music to the jazz strain (favoring individuality, the
present, and cerebral experiment) and to blues (the body; the past; lament).

You can find all three strains in Wright, in her titles, with their analogies
to kinds of nonclassical music: "More Blues and the Abstract Truth" (the
earlier title of a jazz album by Oliver Nelson); "Song of the Gourd"; "Like
Having a Light at Your Back You Can't See but You Can Still Feel" (a light
that could be, but turns out not to be, the Lord's). (I have argued elsewhere
that Terrance Hayes also includes all three of Werner's strains; few other
poets do.) You can find, if you look for it in Wright, the gospel strain uncut:
she really writes to provide backbone, shared fortitude, inspiration:
"Comrades, be not in mourning for your being // to express happiness and
expel scorpions is the best job on earth."[5] You can also find odd concatenations
of words that no one has ever assembled before, parts of Wright that Werner
would liken to jazz. And you can find the gritty commonality, the sexualized
embodiment, of the blues.

One of the best (and longest) academic pieces on Wright so far, Lynn

Keller's chapter on Wright in *Thinking Poetry*, looks at Wright's long poem *Just Whistle* (1992) (which includes bluesy ballad stanzas) and concludes that this poem, as much as any long poem of our era, tries to bring bodily perceptions, arousal and proprioception and kinesthesia, onto the page. It's sexy, at times, but also (as Keller writes) demystifying. It is also confusing. Keller cites Elizabeth Grosz: "[L]ocating the center of consciousness in or close to the notably concretized perceptions of the pantied body [note: pantied, as in panties, not painted] dramatically exaggerates the difficulty of distinguishing literal from figurative."[6] *Just Whistle* is abject, slippery, literally visceral (it imagines the interior of its female bodies, their viscera).

Just Whistle isn't the place to start reading Wright, unless you have a particular line in nonlinear, post-avant-garde folk/blues-inflected depictions of embodiment; it seems a bit academic, a bit extreme, now, and it's one of the books that future readers will discover after they discover that they like Wright, which they will more likely do through *One Big Self*, with its documentary fragments and its many quoted voices. (Wright published two books with that title, but their texts are substantially identical: the first, glossier and larger, included the photographs by Deborah Luster that came into being alongside the poem.) Readers may also discover Wright through the essayistic *One with Others*, or through Wright's shorter poems, some of which also carry a visceral, erotic charge. Some of the erotic poems in her *Ozark Odes* are positively classical in their compression and their honesty as to how male and female bodies work:

> Where the sharp rock on shore
> give way to the hairy rock in the shallows,
> we enlisted in the rise and fall of love.
> His seed broadcast like short, sweet grass.
> Nothing came up there. (*SA* 96)

"Broadcast" returns to the word's agricultural origins; come is both salty and sweet, with a pun on the word ("nothing came up") and a pun on the idea of love as a contest, sowing the defeated ground with salt. The same sequence holds other samples of female embodiment, other glimpses of what has not quite been put into well-made poems before—"I can still see Cuddihy's sisters / trimming the red tufts / under one another's arms." (*SA* 97). Wright later wrote poems of intimate domesticity, some devoted to the real life she shared with Forrest Gander, others to same-sex companions, in the set of short works she called "Girl Friend Poems," as in "Cervical Jazz: A Girl Friend Poem," which ends:

> The blind street
>
> bowl of paperwhites . . .
>
> Holiness only in living;
> this the tablecloth knows;
>
> the pillowcase makes it so. (*SA* 192)

That pillowcase gives the girl friend a place to lie down; it also matches the tablecloth as a site that makes appetite holy, a place where desires ("make it so") come true. (From the next "girl friend poem" in the completed sequence: "From the jagged shade of her pillowcase / she turned // from her own honey spot she turned"; *L* 189).

Wright's poems of proprioception, of the erotic, of the intimate female body, will give some readers a way in. Other readers will see them as special cases, not so much of the love poem, or the erotic poem, in the late twentieth century (though that too), but of the embodied sensory poem, the poem that not only mentions but tries to emulate in its pace, its associations, its gritty word-hoard, in the experience of its reading, something of scent, touch, taste, kinesthesia, hot and cold, pain and stimulation, all the senses that (unlike sight) take place on the surface of the body. "Don't go boring your nose in the fork of a tree not even present," Wright warns in "Like Peaches," hoping to protect the nose, the "lingering smell / protected by a succulent seal" (the word "succulent" means, here, both "delicious" and "retaining moisture") (*SA* 152).

Critics have seen Wright's evocations of the five or seven or nine senses (including proprioception, temperature, and so on) in terms of the erotic, or in terms of gender, and those critics were not wrong. They were, however, noticing only some parts of Wright's larger achievement in matching her language to the embodied senses, to auditory and tactile life. "A lid slams down / On a pounded piano / As the words sink into me" (the powerful word here is *pounded*, the piano misplayed, its force measured in pounds) (*S* 134). Later in the same poem—which incorporates an elegy to the singer-songwriter Vic Chesnutt—

My disappointment sits

Under the Tree of Disappointment

In a dirty skirt in a ruff

Of dirt the color of dirt

If a hand and it could be my hand

Moves over the bark it touches

Where an arrow passed through the trunk

The mind wills it into reverse (*S* 138)

The gritty or dirty hand, which cannot unbury the head or reverse time's arrow, runs over the tree bark and feels the metaphors fail: dirt is like death is like nothing except itself.

That's how Wright uses the senses, makes her poetry visceral, in pursuit of grief. Just as often, though, her engagement with all the senses makes her (as she put it) "intent on seizing happiness"; she is "trying to invent a new way of moving under my dress," a way analogous (in the same poem) to the movement of a fluid meniscus ("when we cut below the silver skin of the surface the center retains its fluidity"), to tacitly sexual contact ("the thigh keeps quiet under nylon") (*L* 172).

These kinds of immediate, often pleasurable, sense experiences—contact with other human bodies, but also with air, soil, food—generally appear in Wright's short poems as positives, as experiences that she and her characters have, that she shares with you; if, as Stevens claimed, "the greatest poverty is not to live / In a physical world," Wright's phrases are a remedy for poverty,

one few other poets provide. The characters in *One Big Self*, however—
Wright's most celebrated book-length poem, and likely her best—are poor,
both literally and in Stevens's sense of physical deprivation: they are "prisoners of Louisiana," and Wright's physicality in that poem, when she writes in
propria persona, considers how lucky she is, how lucky most of us are, what
kinds of experiences most of us take for granted, what prisoners do not have:

> If you were me:
> If you wanted blueberries you could have a big bowl. Two dozen bushes
> right on your hill. And thornless raspberries at the bottom. Walk
> barefooted: there's no glass. If you want to kiss your kid you can . . .

> If I were you:
> Screw up today, and it's solitary, Sister Woman, the padded dress with the
> food log to gnaw upon. This is where you enter the eye of the fart. The air
> is foul. The dirt is gumbo. Avoid all physical contact. Come nightfall the
> bugs will carry you off. You don't have a clue, do you. (*SA* 217)

Few of us do. "The food log" is a real, repellent, nutritive mass provided to
prisoners who—as further punishment—are denied cafeteria food; it is also
one more negative sense experience—the prisoners in solitary are parodies
of beavers in their dams, the dirt from poorly maintained cells a parody both
of real dirt and of thick, dark soup.

Here Wright sounds like herself: dense, rich with spondees, at times
recognizably Southern, attentive to the senses, more likely than other poets
to use sentence fragments, the vocative and the imperative. She also tried,
at times, not to sound like herself, to let into her poems the voices of the
other people she knew, especially when they were people (like those prisoners) rarely seen and even less often heard: Wright's long sets of short lines
and sentence fragments integrated their own voices (literally, from interviews) with hers: she became a master at the respectful use of heard or
overheard speech, and at the use of awkward, incomplete bits of conversation:

> She is so sweet you wouldn't believe she had did
>   all the things they say she did

That one, she's got a gaggle of tricks up her you-know-what

Drawn on a wall in solitary by a young one
   mom love god

   before he had a face on him

Don't blink don't miss nothing: It's *your* furlough

The Asian lady beetle won't reproduce indoors (*SA* 215)

These lists may feel like bits of transcribed interviews, or like the unassembled pieces of a big jigsaw puzzle: we put them together, or else leave them in a heap. Their unsorted secondhand experience may bring to mind familiar modernist heaps of fragments, shored against particular poets' ruins, but they are also a heap of imagined democracy: Wright cannot put the quotations into an order until the people who uttered them can come together in freedom and agree on an order for them. Her documentary disorder, in other words, reflects a disordered, unjust criminal justice system, without any claim that she knows how to fix it all.

It also reflects the value that Wright—for all that she learned from avant-garde organization and disorganization—continued to place on the individual human voice. Voices that are not Wright's turn up in long concatenations, and in prose blocks, where they do some of the work once reserved for verse in lyric, embodying and making transferable something of the experience of another (necessarily imagined) human being; in *One Big Self* we find the poet attempting over and over (with her photographer companion) to get to know someone else, to record their voice, not just her own. In the same passages we also find the poet's own distinctive sounds, her dialect, her phrases, addressed to the experience she wants to share with that Other, the experience she wishes they could have. Her long poly-vocal homage, report, ode, and jeremiad on the prisoners of Louisiana, in other words, does something that poets, novelists, literary essayists, and journalists have long wanted to do, and had trouble doing, something that the philosopher Emmanuel Levinas is read (perhaps misread) as recommending: they acknowledge another person, as if to her face, as an unknowable other, distinct from the speaking self, and then try to make a connection anyway.

Nor are Wright's writings on prisoners unique in this ambition: some of the same ambitions extend, in her "Retablo" series and in the poems of *Rising, Falling, Hovering*, to Mexico. Her poems are heterogeneous, populous, generous, as few poets' long poems have been; they incorporate ambitions central to lyric poetry, ambitions to present and yet get beyond the self, as few long poems in our time have tried to do. To see the conjunction of powers in Wright's verse, and to see how it stands apart from that of her peers, is also to see how those powers coexist with, and draw strength from, the goals that Culler and others identify as lyric; the projection of something like a voice that is not exactly a voice (though Wright might say, as Culler would not say, that it was a representation of a voice); the sense that poems try to do something that is literally impossible, to resurrect the dead, to go back in time, to make a meeting of minds.

Wright's goals—though also experimental, disjunctive, documentary, multimedia—are usually lyric goals. And those goals explain why some of her signature poems, those that will come up first, I think, when future readers discover her, are poems that foreground portraiture (like "King's Daughters, Home for Unwed Mothers, 1948" or "Forest of Clouds") or else poems that foreground self-portraiture, poems that say, with Whitman or with the biblical Isaac, "here I am," poems that project a self or soul. Wright took seriously the idea that poetry was a way to meet strangers on disarming and intimate terms, that it not only presented the self to the self but allowed the self to encounter readers as others.

No wonder, then, that Wright sought, and sometimes found, analogies and kinds of poems that let her foreground that kind of introduction. She found them in imagined scripts for films, and in depictions of travel, as if we could literally go to meet her (especially in her early book *Further Adventures with You*). She found them in newspaper personal ads, as in "Personals," from *String Light* ("Some nights I sleep with my dress on," it begins); that poem is probably the best way to introduce undergraduates to Wright, and I have seen it directly imitated in recent first books. Later, Wright found a way to renew, and to render demotic and tactile and also comic, the lyric introduction by imitating the signatures in high school yearbooks: that is what she did in "Autographs," from her great and still underrated collection of short poems, *Tremble*. I will conclude, instead, with a later poem of crackling, disarming, ambitious self-portraiture, one that also takes up the Whitmanian goal of intimate prophecy, using her own admittedly unusual temperament to inspire others, to imagine a unity in idiosyncrasy, even to save the republic.

Most of *Rising, Falling, Hovering* (2008) consists of long-lined, multipage poems with multiple subjects, from her son's misadventures in Mexico to the war in Iraq: it's one of her best books, but may not be in toto the best place to start. The leadoff poem, however—a kind of more public, more Whitmanian, equally sensory, less comic sequel to "Personal"—makes a great place to start: it has the very American title "Re: Happiness, in pursuit thereof."

> I am located at the corner of Waterway
> and Bluff. I need your help. You will find me
> to the left of the graveyard, where the trees
> grow especially talkative at night,
> where fog and alcohol rub off the edge.
> We burn to make one another sing;
> to stay the lake that it not boil, earth
> not rock. We are running on Aztec time,
> fifth and final cycle. Eyes switch on/off.[7]

I have not said much about rhythm, because discussions of rhythm in free verse get technical, and inconclusive, and debatable, fast, but one of the things these lines show—one more of the things that Wright did especially well—is the distinctive twang of her not-quite-blank verse; the lines work hard *not* to resolve into pentameter, though they enter it anyway at one point ("where fog and alcohol rub off the edge") before leaping back into spondees as if startled. These kinds of rhythms, which she accomplished consistently, help her sound urgent and intimate, and American, and sometimes Ozark, too. Here they work in tandem with aspects of Wright that I have already pointed out: the way she uses multiple senses, for example, the way she presents a vivid life without telling a whole story, the way she takes in both the blues imperative (the embodied, repeated lament) and the gospel impulse to lift us up and bring us together: the burning, singing readers who respond to her call do not only sing for the joy of it—we sing to honor her seaside locality, and to honor the Earth, to "be balm or chamomile," and to honor Wright's sense of America, whether or not it can be saved.

I have shown, I hope, how Wright incorporates biography, and elegy, and also the erotic, while writing a poetry of parts and fragments; I have shown how she uses familiar kinds, both those from literary history and those (like the personal ad) from outside it. I have shown how her rhythms stand out, and how she uses all the senses (especially those not often heard from in most poems): that sensory attention, that immediacy, alongside her fragment-heavy, part-heavy organization, will strike many readers right away. I have tried to show how other people, their faces and voices, come into some of her poems, and why they still sound like her. I have shown how she sounds like her version of Arkansas, and how she revivifies that very traditional goal of lyric poetry, to present a face, and how she introduces herself in democratic fashion to us, asking us to join her, without telling us what to do.

Those introductions—unavoidable in her poems of self-portraiture ("Personals," "Autographs," "Re: Happiness," and others), sporadically apparent when she works in other genres—also point to the last of the many virtues that her versatile poems incorporate: they do not merely introduce us to some personality, some imagined self, but introduce many of us to one we would like to get to know. The persona Wright's poems construct and present is not only eclectic, folksy, energetic, attentive, and Southern (to name other obvious attributes): it is also, for many readers, the kind of person we would like to take up as a friend. Allen Grossman suggested that poems in general, or perhaps post-Romantic lyric in general, could become a reader's "hermeneutic friend," an intimate ally and listener despite its status as a complete set of words: Keats's urn, of course, was "a friend to Man," and could remain so as much else about human beings changed. The friendship that Wright's poems offer partakes of that (fairly abstract) kind of friendship proper to lyric as a literary kind, but it is also something more specific, something that Wright's poems share, for example, with Frank O'Hara's: here (so many readers think while rereading many of her poems) is the voice of a person I wish I could have as a friend. The person the poem projects is a person who, were she someone we could literally get to know, we would want to know.

That virtue is obviously not a necessary one for the survival of any particular body of work. Nor is it the same virtue as the one by which poems let us see ourselves in them. (One could argue that Byron and Dryden possess neither.) Indeed, inasmuch as poems (especially twentieth-century poems; think of Plath, or the early Louise Glück, or late Lowell) give voice to the otherwise unutterable, shameful, or baffling parts of ourselves, we may see in them the parts of ourselves that we would not want to discover in our friends! The poem may ask, with Wright and her older friend V in *One with Others*: "Everybody has a problem. What's yours" (*O* 29). (Note how much less interesting the line would be were it punctuated conventionally.) But a Wright poem, or a Wright essay, may not set out to share your problems so much as to give you a model for moving past them, a companion you wish you could hear and meet beyond the page. It's easiest to see and hear those effects when Wright is at her most domestic, most intimate, but they show up in her poems of observed rural poverty too, as in the English version of the bilingual "Handfishing Retablo #1": "Stuffed bear in the raked dirt / Smoke coming out of its butt . . . There is something worth knowing if / There is some one thing important for us / To know" (*SA* 34). Because the poems stay so colloquial, because they stop (as if to hear us) so often, because they touch base with the senses and with their locality so often, too, while working to offer grounded advice, because they incorporate humor alongside moral concern, because they share so many small pleasures that have not been shared in poems before, the poems are companionable: they give friendly support.

And this effect—the poem as friend, as a way to imagine someone we would want as a companion, ally, partner, in real life—is one readers often seek and critics rarely discuss; Wright seems to have been conscious of the way that her idiosyncrasies could make her poems feel like friends, like allies, like companions, as most other poets and poems do not. Starting from *Further Adventures with You* and proceeding all the way through *ShallCross*, the poems even set out (as George Herbert, Samuel Johnson, and indeed Gwendolyn Brooks also did) to offer support, courage, wisdom, general advice: "'Follow me,' the voice, the long, longed-for voice stops / the writing hand. 'I have your shoes.' . . . Every thing matters; no one a means, every one an end" (*L* 278).

All these are virtues that occur together—all her poems have several of them! Other poems have other virtues still. The poems share some of those virtues with literary writing that is not poetry (the travelogue noticings in

Deepstep Come Shining, for example, which readers often liken to James Agee). They share others with arts (especially photography) that exist without words. And you do not need to be looking for any one of those powers—you do not even need to notice it—to care about others: a reader who cherishes *Rising, Falling, Hovering* for its political engagement, who reads it alongside Muriel Rukeyser or Carolyn Forché for its reaction to the moments of newsworthy rupture, "When everyone drops their reserve // Everyone is thinking about the end of things" (65), will not be the same reader who likes *Rising* for its mysteriously visceral religious feeling ("We are back from the ark, almost. // Is it always this dark?" [79]), nor will she be the same reader who likes the same book for its curiously long and disconnected lines (reminiscent of the early D. A. Powell). But all three readers have good reasons to like the book. The variety of potential, and as of 2017 the variety of actual, readers who have loved and learned from Wright suggests quite strongly that days to come will find readers who feel the same way.

I have tried to show, first, that poets whose work lasts a long time are poets who show not universality but versatility, poets whose work can be loved by many readers for many reasons, because it can do many things. I have then tried to show that Wright is one of these poets, that she does many things: not that she does all these things, together, every time she writes a poem, but that she does several of these things in any given poem, things you might not think could be put together at all. Some of these conjunctions (as her critics note) speak to her unusual early adulthood, her unusual set of influences. Others do not—as in "King's Daughters," she did things that her influences could not have let anyone predict, things that no older poet ever dreamed. I have, finally, tried to show that many (not all) of these things, these effects, partake in the larger cluster of effects, with their long history, that Jonathan Culler and others have defended under the transhistorical (or at least longue durée) label of "lyric."

Some of Wright's effects have already entered American poetry through her: younger poets often imitate her collage effects, her quick documentaries, though they cannot usually take up her phrase-by-phrase attention to all the senses. Some of those younger poets have avant-garde pedigrees; others combine Wright's influences with those of clearer poets devoted to realism. (A partial list of notable younger poets influenced by Wright in some way, as of 2017, would have to include Rosa Alcalá, Christina Davis, Sina Queyras,

Atsuro Riley, Carmen Giménez Smith, Juliana Spahr, Brenda Shaughnessy, Brian Teare, and Monica Youn; most of these poets were *not* her students at Brown.) She is "experimental" and casual, quick like a watercolor and intense like oils, bluesy and soaring, authoritative and friendly, often at once. Any reader will find, in Wright, idiosyncratic diction, warmth, informality, and the continued presence of her Ozark origins; what else you find depends on what pages you open first, and on what you want to find. But there is a great deal you can find, much of it lyric in the deepest sense, and much of it—for the reasons I have tried to give—likely to last.

Notes

1. "The 'Unitasker' Kitchen Gadgets Alton Brown Loves to Loathe," NPR, December 23, 2015, http://www.npr.org/sections/thesalt/2015/12/23/460833325/ the-unitasker-kitchen-gadgets-alton-brown-loves-to-loathe.

2. C. D. Wright, *ShallCross* (Port Townsend, WA: Copper Canyon, 2017), 52; hereafter abbreviated as *S*.

3. C. D. Wright, *Steal Away* (Port Townsend, WA: Copper Canyon, 2002), 64; hereafter abbreviated as *SA*.

4. C. D. Wright, *One with Others* (Port Townsend, WA: Copper Canyon, 2010), 33; hereafter abbreviated as *O*.

5. C. D. Wright, *Like Something Flying Backwards* (Port Townsend, WA: Copper Canyon, 2007), 286; hereafter abbreviated as *L*.

6. Lynn Keller, *Thinking Poetry: Readings in Contemporary Women's Exploratory Poetics* (Iowa City: University of Iowa Press, 2010), 115.

7. C. D. Wright, *Rising, Falling, Hovering* (Port Townsend, WA: Copper Canyon, 2008), 3.

CHAPTER 5

Miłosz's *"Ars Poetica?"*

ROBERT FAGGEN

IN A 2009 column in the *New York Times*, poetry critic David Orr poked fun at what he considered the pomposity of Czesław Miłosz and his American devotees. Citing Miłosz's famous poem "Dedication," "What is poetry that does not save / Nations or people? / A connivance with official lies, / A song of drunkards whose throats will be cut in a moment? / Readings for sophomore girls,"[1] Orr concluded that in addition to being sexist, the lines were simply drivel and given more credit for the situation in which they were written than for the quality of the poetry itself.[2] This poem is far more complex than those lines, but Orr's criticism does raise for me the question of the value of the poet whose moral preoccupations may be inseparable from aesthetic concerns. It is one of the most naked, direct moments in Miłosz's poetry, but it also reflects a tendency that runs throughout: the relentless self-criticism of a scrupulous conscience. Miłosz most disliked even positive criticism that viewed his work as that of a moralist. But he also often trenchantly raised the question in his poetry and his criticism of whether the moral or the ethical could or should truly be excluded from evaluation. I would argue that some of the power of his poetry comes from a willingness to be highly skeptical and sometimes fiercely critical of the ethos fueling the aesthetic, particularly in the poem *"Ars Poetica?"* What I find exciting and powerful in Miłosz is the challenge he often poses to poetry itself, while ultimately affirming its value. He viewed poetry as a means to rescue a conception of reality in which beauty is not necessarily truth.

Miłosz made striking evaluative statements in his critical essays and interviews as well as in his poetry. Speaking of Philip Larkin, he criticized the English poet for being "hateful" (he was referring specifically to the poem "Aubade"). While recognizing Larkin's skill, he nevertheless found the poetry troubling because of the view of people and religion that might be presented in many of the poems. Miłosz admired greatly Eliot's attempt to revivify the imagination, particularly "the imagination's ability to conceive of a religious ordering of space. . . . Eliot did not join the adherents of art for art's sake." But Eliot was by choice in Miłosz's view an obscure poet, whose "digressions, such as those in *Four Quartets*, are indecipherable without resort to the often-dubious assistance of his commentators." Miłosz added: "It is easy to see that such a poetics, applied to the communication of indefinable states, of thought-feelings or moods, created exceptionally difficult conditions for a poet who was inclined to meditation and who had the temperament, perhaps, of a seventeenth-century Anglican priest."[3] Nevertheless, he acknowledges in the "compactness and energy of every line he [Eliot] wrote . . . he had no rival in the English language."[4]

Miłosz was far more critical of the obscurities of Robert Frost, who he believed dissembled. "His readers valued him, however, for his idyllic mood, which was only a disguise. Beneath it was concealed a grim, hopeless vision of man's fate."[5] Elaborating on that point, Miłosz asserts that Frost's poetry is "not lyrical but tragic, for his narrative poems about the ties between people are mini-tragedies; or else it is descriptive, or, more accurately, moralistic. I feel that it is cold."[6] Miłosz was concerned about two matters in Frost: his relationship to his reader and his vision of the way the world works. Miłosz's criticism of Robinson Jeffers reveals a much more complex relationship between himself and the poet of "inhumanism." Miłosz speculates that Jeffers "needed to see himself as being elevated above everything alive, contemplating vain passions and vain hopes, thereby rising above time as well."[7] He admits, however, that he recognizes some of this in himself. "I was sufficiently like him to re-create his thoughts from within and to feel what had given rise to them. But I did not like my own regal soarings above the Earth. That had been forced upon me and deserved to be called by its name, exile."[8] In addition to three published essays about Jeffers, Miłosz wrote a stunning poem, "To Robinson Jeffers," that forcefully encapsulates his views. On the one hand, Miłosz rejected Jeffers's worldview, seeing it not as truth but as truth derived from Nietzsche and biology textbooks. On the other hand, he seemed to forgive Jeffers as embodying or expressing something that was an inevitable part of his life and background. It is a great instance of one poet taking issue with another great poet, a kind of Dantean encounter in Hell or Purgatory. Miłosz's take on Jeffers is exciting in the way Miłosz really does attempt to enter the American poet's imagination, but especially because his admiration is represented as criticism.

But perhaps most striking is Miłosz's criticism of confessional poetry in "*Ars Poetica?*," which fascinates me not only because its author self-consciously tries to disavow the poem's own status as a poem and work of art—"What I am saying here is not, I agree, poetry"—but also because he fails to do so. The title questions whether the rules or boundaries of poetic art can be defined—a Horatian "art of poetry"—and it also questions the value of poetry itself. The former is understandable, but the latter would seem disingenuous except that the author puts his own authority forward at the outset and also makes a compelling case for the limits of poetic art. When Miłosz says, "[So] you may think I am only joking / or that I've devised yet one more means / of praising Art with the help of irony,"[9] he is obviously aware that his own skepticism about the value of art actually approaches the confessional morbidity that he distrusts. More important, he revisits the problem of honesty in confession. Miłosz never excluded "*Ars Poetica?*" from editions of his work, and he often read it in public. Is this really a study in irony after all—a clever poetic achievement not in spite of but actually because of its doubts about art? I would argue that what makes the work powerful is Miłosz's strong distaste for a certain kind of poetry. Behind that distaste is a deep skepticism about human nature. Ultimately, Miłosz does indicate conditions in which poetry might be worthwhile, conditions that are defined in terms of ethical psychology. The meaning of a poem is what it does. But the meaning and the motive, over which the author seems to have little control, are of greater significance than the quality of expression. Ugly feelings and cruel thoughts beautifully or powerfully expressed do not improve upon silence.

"*Ars Poetica?*" is as rhetorical as it is didactic; it has some of the more intimate and confessional qualities of poems written "to" other authors or thinkers, such as "To Raja Rao," "To Albert Einstein," "To Robinson Jeffers," and "To Robert Lowell." Miłosz speaks as though he were trying to justify his aesthetic choices to someone challenging them or to someone uncomprehending. No doubt "*Ars Poetica?*" also serves as a way of expressing criticism of a particular kind of poetry. Writing the poem in Berkeley in 1968, Miłosz had in mind the vogue of confessional poetry written by Allen Ginsberg—particularly "Howl" and "Kaddish"—Anne Sexton (who had won a Pulitzer Prize the previous year), Sylvia Plath, John Berryman, and, of course, Robert Lowell. Confessional poetry—so much admired and also ridiculed—seems to have had justification on ethical and psychological grounds: it enables authors and readers to bear guilt and suffering more easily and lifts taboos on highly personal and shameful subjects. Many of the poets who became known as "confessional" disavowed the idea that their poetry was truly autobiographical or directly personal. If the aim was aesthetic, then confessional poetry became a way of using what was publicly taboo to engage the reader by shock. In the cases of the authors I have mentioned, the subject matter of the poetry was made authentic by an author's horrifying biography: insanity, addiction, and, ultimately, suicide. To be a poet meant living the life of mental illness and writing about it but in a way far different from Christopher Smart. "Much madness" was not, as Dickinson suggested, "divinest sense." It had something to do with the ugliness of personal relations. Dickinson, a very great poet, gained even more credibility after death by being strange and not publishing her work. But postwar confessional poets gained credibility by disturbing behavior; suicide became the ultimate cultural mark of poetic authenticity and sincerity. Lowell became legendary for his bouts with insanity; nothing I have ever heard from those who witnessed them indicates that Miłosz was generally wrong in his assessment that Lowell indulged and nurtured his persona as a madman within and without the poetry. That aside, anyone who reads Miłosz knows that there is much in his own work that is strongly confessional and suggestive of great personal despair and even insanity. But Miłosz is suggesting that exposing and glorifying "sublime agonies" in poetry is ugly aesthetically and ethically. Miłosz's struggles to be honest and also to be "decent" would enable understanding of himself and others but without revelations of the most lurid secrets. His contempt for Lowell, whose conversion to Catholicism as well as his political engagement must have intrigued the émigré from Poland, eased remarkably—in a later confessional poem, "To Robert Lowell." In apologizing to Lowell, already long dead, Miłosz admits his own lurking insanity without revealing too many details:

Insanity, I knew, was insinuating itself
In a thin thread into my very being
And only waited for my permission
To carry me into its murky regions.[10]

If Miłosz does not give insanity permission to flourish, he does not claim this control as virtue but partly the result of "anger" and "vanity, unjustifiable." His frailty, he confesses, was his "émigré's envy"; now he seeks understanding across what separates them. This barrier is not death but the accidents of culture: "gestures, conventions, idioms, mores." What binds them is much deeper and more human than those mores.

For Miłosz, as for Dostoevsky, confession became a poetic and moral problem. Where does the irony stop? When has one achieved honesty? In 1968, Miłosz's children were still relatively young. The serious mental illness that afflicted his family had not been fully realized, and his later experience and understanding of mental illness no doubt modified his views about the ability of individuals to control themselves. He says nothing about that very personal experience in his poem to Lowell. He treads carefully, trying to avoid too much revelation that would in some way justify or glorify his frailty.

But I doubt that Miłosz ever lost his sense that a poem should be a revelation, especially one of a hard-won and limited wisdom. While he himself is fascinated with the psychology of confession, his way of coping with personal revelation does not presume that one's very personal difficulties or, more significantly, debilitating psychological experiences are fundamentally interesting or worthy of poetry. In "Dedication," he had expressed dissatisfaction with poetry "that does not save / Nations or people." In particular, he suggested two forms of failure: "connivance with official lies"—that is, some version of propaganda—or merely something for schoolgirls, an earlier twentieth-century version of sentimental pop music. Miłosz wanted poetry to change lives, but in the face of political atrocities, he envisioned that in large-scale terms. Saint Francis's more modest advice, "Do not change the world, change worlds," by which I believe he meant the lives of individuals, probably seemed insufficient to Miłosz at the time.

What, then, does Miłosz offer other than another version of Martin Luther, throwing ink at the devil, who could so easily undermine his faith and his willingness to write poetry? I use this analogy because it suggests, among other things, the moment in *The Brothers Karamazov* when Ivan confronts the devil (and also invokes that story of Luther). Miłosz wishes to challenge the notion that evil can or should be the inspiration for good art. At the same time, he raises problems of Dostoevsky's poetics: what can we say about the different and contradictory impulses that haunt us every minute? Polyphony of voices may be compelling. But at some point, we should perhaps turn down or turn off the excessive and inharmonious. *"Ars Poetica?"* begins and ends with a justification of spaciousness on the grounds that multiplicity and fracture may be a greater reality than an ideal of formal unity. What in Miłosz produces the need for this justification?

> I have always aspired to a more spacious form
> that would be free from the claims of poetry or prose
> and would let us understand each other without exposing
> the author or reader to sublime agonies.[11]

Miłosz begins with an apology, or, at least, an explanation of his sense of poetic form, one that violates traditional boundaries of form, including the obvious boundary between poetry and prose. His goal seems to be an openness between author and reader, but an openness that does not expose too much. We return, thus, to fundamental questions about decorum, about unity and form, as well as a basic metaphor of the poem and the self as a civil space. Ethics and aesthetics are both implied in the word. Decorum has been in question since Aristotle and Horace: what was right or proper in a poetic work as well as appropriate social behavior within set situations. Presumably, the more expansive the form, Miłosz suggests, the more slippery the notions of decorum. In Christianity, the problem of decorum is a struggle between the sacred and profane.

Miłosz then provides a rich and memorable little allegory of poetry's potential indecency. Poetry may be revelation and self-revelation. It reveals something unknown, though potentially bestial and dangerous. In poetry, "a thing is brought forth which we did not know we had in us." There is in the act of creation division, self-division. I think this is striking for the way it suggests a criticism of certain ideas about artistic creation: that something is better than nothing, that speech is greater than silence, which could be looked upon as a challenge to creation in general. In creating poetry out of personal experience, it is "as if a tiger had sprung out / and stood in the light, lashing his tail."[12]

The image is seductive and also dangerous. We can become entranced by this icon of power and beauty and turn it into a graven image. Miłosz seems to be providing some criticism of the Horatian idea of *ut pictura poesis*; it may involve too much amour propre. Part of the power rests in the element of surprise. Another part arises from the suggestion that poetry springs formed and uncontrolled from the mind.

The creator is surprised by his creation, an alienated image of the self, a modern version of the story of Athena sprung fully armed from the head of Zeus. But this strange beast confounds wisdom. We are aware of Milton's transformation of the story that depicts Sin leaping out of the head of Satan, who is surprised by sin, preceding the incest that results in the birth of Death. And Milton's Satan represents "the triumph of the ego" in its grandest form, and a heroic image of the modern thinker and poet as defiant romantic rebel. The image also suggests Captain Ahab's gnostic invocation to fire: "Light though thou be, thou leapest out of darkness. But I am darkness leaping out of light, leaping out of thee!," which embraces the conflict of light and dark as well as the circular ouroboros of creation or, perhaps, the vicious circle of self-obsession. And, of course, the tiger suggests Blake's "Tyger" and its formulation of theodicy and artistic creation: "In what furnace was thy brain?" Miłosz suggests that this tiger may have been framed not by "immortal hand or eye" but the sick brains of poets. Of what are such creations "mimetic" except the personal neuroses or demons of the poet? Perhaps worse, they express something terrible about creation and matter.

I somehow doubt that Miłosz ever abandoned his view that poetry should not be confused with the expression of personal perversity and mental illness or, simply, too much reality. I will return to his assertion that poetry is "dictated by a daimonion."[13] In the first part of a poem from *Provinces* entitled "To My Daimonion," the poet seems at odds with this inspiration. Seeking to encounter again an old woman, he speculates on her thoughts. But he is interrupted: "And you, daimonion, / Just at this moment interfere, interrupt us, averse to / Surnames and family names' actualities, / Too prosaic and ridiculous, no doubt." The "daimonion" may inspire poetry but also interfere with its excesses should it become too realistic. If Miłosz had adhered to his proscription at the end of "*Ars Poetica?*" that poems should be written only rarely and under great duress, then either he was under great duress for most of his life, or he did not follow or believe his own wisdom. He once said:

> Literature is born out of a desire to be truthful—not to hide anything and not to present oneself as somebody else. Yet when you write there are certain contradictions, what I call laws of form. You cannot tell everything . . . poetry imposes certain restraints. Nevertheless, there is always the feeling that you did not unveil yourself enough. A book is finished and appears and I feel, well, next time I will unveil myself. And when the next book appears, I have the same feeling. And then your life ends, and that's it.[14]

The daimonion seems to be a demon of contradiction between honesty and constraint.

Miłosz desires to distinguish, as Melville put it, between "the wisdom that is woe" and "the woe that is madness." The desire for wisdom in Miłosz outreaches his interest in being artistic. Frost, whom I recognize Miłosz claimed to dislike, once wrote, "I would rather be wise than artistic." One senses that despite his abilities and accomplishments as an artist, Miłosz always felt that the cultural categories, forms, and offices of art were limiting.

In Miłosz's case, the relationship between personal experience and poetic form seems to be related to his psychological experience of the world. It is as though too much emphasis on form and beauty can lead to self-adulation through art. A more spacious form includes the voices of others. It is at this point that I sense Miłosz struggling with his own sense of insanity. While he emphasized the multivocal and polyphonic nature of his art, he also seemed to wonder whether it reflected some kind of schizophrenia. In "To Raja Rao," a confessional poem he wrote in 1969 one year after "*Ars Poetica?,*" he suggests that his own wandering represents also a longing for an impossible promised land. He represents this longing as, perhaps, a disease, a malady as much as a quest for "the real presence":

> Raja, I wish I knew
> The cause of that malady.

For years I could not accept
The place I was in.
I felt I should be somewhere else.

A city, trees, human voices
Lacked the quality of presence.
I would live by the hope of moving on.

Somewhere else there was a city of real presence,
of real trees and voices of friendship and love.

Link, if you wish, my peculiar case
(on the border of schizophrenia)
to the messianic hope
of my civilization.

Ill at ease in the tyranny, ill at ease in the republic,
In the one I longed for freedom, in the other the end of corruption.

Later he added: "If I am sick, there is no proof whatever / that man is a healthy creature."[15]

Among other things, "*Ars Poetica?*" expresses Miłosz's fear of schizophrenia:

What reasonable man would like to be a city of demons,
who behave as if they were at home, speak in many tongues?[16]

Miłosz brings together here Christian notions of sickness of the soul, corrupt forms of speaking in tongues, and contemporary notions schizophrenia. If this kind of speech—wildly polyphonic—is exciting poetry, what reasonable person would like or praise such a thing? He begs the question of whether the artistic worship of the profoundly incomprehensible or irrational truly has value. And what makes them unreasonable is this very specific experience that could at one moment seem like ecstasy, at another prophecy, or at yet another a soul alienated and divided from traumatic experience. This last possibility Miłosz sees as weakness and an indulgence in frailty. Hearing voices and allowing them to speak would be at best a degraded version of the biblical notion of "speaking in tongues." Presumably the ability to speak in tongues was a gift of the Holy Spirit and an act expressive of being taken by the Holy Spirit. Incomprehensibility was evidence of prophecy and divinity. There was also the miracle of gentiles being able to be understood in many languages. We are far from that. Inspiration may be another example of that "passionate intensity" with which the worst have been filled.

Miłosz found his own contradictions and self-interdictions maddening. But his separation from and loss of his homelands must have intensified his sense of wounding and alienation. He was no doubt trying to come to terms with at least a bifurcated self—one living and working in America and yet still deeply attached to Poland and Lithuania. He had equally powerful needs to reconnect and to forget. I think this personal experience of alienation and loss as well as his more general sense of humankind's alienation on the planet attracted him to Wisława Szymborska's poem "Autotomy," which is about a sea cucumber that tries to save itself by dividing its body in two.

In his 1981 Norton Lecture "The Lesson of Biology," Miłosz provides fascinating insight into not only his friend's poem but also his own preoccupations. Miłosz's larger concern was the impact of biology, which he called "the demonic science," on our sense of being human. The Darwinian homology made between ourselves and all other creatures both fascinated and disturbed him. What in such a completely material view of the world would be left of the human soul? Szymborska turns the biological survival strategy of the sea cucumber into a metaphor for the severe divisions made within the human mind to save itself from annihilation:

> It violently divides into doom and salvation,
> Retribution and reward, what has been and what will be.[17]

Szymborska emphasizes "an abyss" (*przepaść*) between these divisions, including those we create or feel from great and tragic loss.

At times it is not clear whether Miłosz wishes to question the absolute reality of biology or has decided to accept it with outrage. Biology represents for him the way the putative rationality of science leads to the irrationality predicament of the human condition: recognizing its materiality but hard pressed to accept it comfortably. Desperation and helplessness rather than rationality are the result. There can be under the circumstances no more of an art of poetry than there can be an art (or science) of salvation. The Horatian notion of *non omnis moriar*—"not all of me dies" or "not everything dies"—seems to collapse in a world in which everything is material:

> Once, a long time ago, another observation of nature . . . provided philosophers and poets with a metaphor for the passage from life to death. It was the observation of the transformation undergone by a pupa when it changes into a butterfly, of a body being left behind by a soul liberating itself. That dualism of the soul and the body accompanied our civilization through several centuries. It does not, however, exist in the poem I quoted. A chasm opens in the flesh of the holothurian, a division into two corporeal "selves" occurs.[18]

Miłosz also sees the parallel in this soul and body dualism to ideals of fame and oblivion in art:

> Beginning with the Renaissance, another kind of dualism was added to the dualism of soul and body . . . the dualism of fame and oblivion, expressed by the maxim *ars longa, vita brevis* and by that great incitement to make one's name live in the memory of posterity: not everything dies, *non omnis moriar*. This might be called additional insurance, running parallel to the Christian one; moreover, such strivings were in harmony with the ambiguous coexistence of the heritage of antiquity and the message of the Gospels.[19]

Szymborska's sea cucumber cannot remain whole, one individual, and survive. Nor can human beings. "We, too, can divide ourselves, it's true / But only into flesh and a broken whisper / Into flesh and poetry," she writes. We are like other creatures but also limited in the kind of divisions we can make. The response to danger and trauma psychologically may be more severe than "a broken whisper." It may be a "howl" or the shrieks of many dissociated selves. And we have learned that for those who have become what Miłosz calls "a city of demons," the tearing of the individual into multiple selves or multiple personalities may well also be a strategy of survival.

Her abyss does not "divide" the holothurian from itself, nor does it represent a gulf between body and soul. In human terms, the "abyss" does not represent a divide between body and soul, past and future, despair and hope. Rather, as she says, "the abyss surrounds us"; it is both inescapable and all-encompassing. What is this abyss? The infinite or nothing? And if "nothing," what kind of "nothing"? Is it the *nichts* of Meister Eckhart or the *ayin* of the Kabbalah? These nothings are actually divine essences. Or, perhaps, is it the abyss of Buddhist sunyata? Sunyata does not signify a divine essence but rather points to the nature of things in their interdependence, coorigination, and lack of selfhood. It is a matter of a relationship as well as the primordial nothingness from which all things arise.

In "*Ars Poetica?*," Miłosz quietly points to an abyss in the notion of the self that seems similar, in some respects, to Buddhist sunyata. It is difficult to remain one person because the human personality is swollen by its constituent elements but is devoid of a central self. In some real and not at all pathological sense, nothing exists in and of itself but only in relation to other things, which are interrelated and thus empty of independent existence. This concept of the self as a kind of nothing works against the notion of poetry as self-created and self-contained space on one side of an abyss. Miłosz gently introduces the metaphor of the self as a house, but one with transient tenants and few barriers. It is "our house," which could be "ours" collectively or "ours" individually. In either case, plurality—polyphony—is unavoidable because the house is never quite inhabited but only haunted:

> The purpose of poetry is to remind us
> How difficult it is to remain just one person,
> For our house is open, there are no keys in the door,
> And invisible guests come in and out at will.[20]

Miłosz returns to poetry and metaphor. But the metaphor serves to remind us of its limitations. He evokes Robert Browning's poem "House," in which the poet criticizes Wordsworth's sonnet "Scorn not the sonnet" and Wordsworth's view that, in the sonnet, Shakespeare "with this key . . . unlocked his heart." Browning thought that Shakespeare would have been a lesser poet had he done so. And his metaphor of the house suggests that it is not readily open to public view. Browning, of course, was a great source of the modernist triumph of the poetic persona. With *The Ring and the Book*, he gave us a multivocal poem, the great *Rashomon* of all poems. For Miłosz, the idea of a poetic persona remained a reality, a psychological necessity, and a great problem.

He was also making a skeptical comment on the nature of scripture and scriptural. In his commentary on Psalms, Origen uses the metaphor of a house with locked rooms to describe the task of scriptural interpretation. One seeks the keys:

> For the Hebrew [a teacher of Origen's] said the whole divinely inspired Scripture may be likened, because of its obscurity, to many locked rooms in one house. By each room is placed a key, but not the one that corresponds to it, so that the keys are scattered beside the rooms, none of them matching the room by which it is placed. It is a difficult task to find the keys and match them to the rooms that they can open.[21]

Origen continues by saying that in principle Paul is arguing the same thing when he writes: "And those things we speak are not discourses instructed by human wisdom, but ones instructed by the Spirit, interpreting spiritual things by means of spiritual things."

Miłosz remains far more tentative about interpretation of the constructs of poetry: there are no keys for the doors. We are ultimately instruments of "spirits" and not necessarily of the divine spirit. In a way, he echoes Horace's deprecation of deus ex machina as a fitting way to end a poetic drama or to interpret one. Like Lev Shestov in *Potestas Clavium*, Miłosz indicates that no one has the key.

According to Miłosz, the poet does lack control because their work is controlled by "a daimonion." He, of course, refers to the daimonion that Socrates describes in the *Apology*, *Phaedo*, and the tenth and final book of the *Republic*. The invoking of the daimonion and indeed the whole tenor of "*Ars Poetica?*" is Socratic. I don't want to complicate matters unnecessarily by saying that it is Platonic. Socrates invokes the daimonion, the little spirit, in the *Apology*. In his defense against charges of corruption by Meletus, Socrates asserts that "a sort of voice comes to me, and when it comes it always dissuades me from what I am proposing to do, and never urges me on. It is this that disbars me from entering public life, and a very good thing too."[22] The parallel between the stances of Socrates and Miłosz is remarkable. They both claim inspiration from the daimonion, but it expresses negation. It refuses public life and all that is not wisdom. That wisdom is the result not of inspiration but of a skeptical process. "If I think that anyone is wise, whether citizen or stranger, and when I think that any person is not wise, I try to help the cause of God by proving that he is not." And indeed Miłosz himself seems to wish to deflate those who claim the cause of God or consider their personal turmoil evidence of wisdom, much less divine knowledge.

I am not trying to argue that Miłosz had a Platonic contempt for poetry as mere imitation. Socrates was himself not entirely consistent when he spoke about the value of poetry. In the *Apology*, he mentions the daimonion as a force that warns him against doing the wrong thing. But in *Phaedo*, Socrates claims to have been visited by what seems to be a daimonion. He has dreams that tell him what to do; in fact, he has been having a recurring dream that he must write poetry. The dream says, "Socrates, practice and cultivate the arts." What could this mean for a philosopher? He believed that it was encouraging him to "do what I was doing already, that is, practicing the arts, because philosophy is the greatest of arts, and I was practicing it."

> I have felt that perhaps it might be this popular form of art that the dream intended me to practice, in which case I ought to practice it and not disobey. I thought it would be safer not to take my departure before I had cleared my conscience and obeyed the dream. . . . When I had finished my hymn, I reflected that the poet, if he is to be worthy of his name, ought to work on imaginative themes, not descriptive ones, and I was not good at inventing stories.[23]

The tension Socrates feels between what is popularly known as poetry and what he sees as the "art" of philosophy may also be a contradiction that haunted Miłosz. In "Dedication," he dismisses poetry that does not save people or nations as a sophomoric exercise. One might also wonder whether Miłosz felt a tension between the descriptive and the imaginative; he deprecated Stevens's idea of the poem as an act of the mind and imagination imposing itself on nothingness. The real was something that existed aside and almost in principle despite the mind or acts of the mind. But Miłosz's faith in the real and his belief that the real had moral content separates him from many of his contemporaries. He believed that moral content could be either good or evil, thus underscoring the uncertainty of his vision. There are spirits that are good and evil, and we have little or no control over their use of us. I would take issue with Miłosz's nostalgia for a time when only wise books were read; ones that help us bear our grief. But he is daring and challenging in his view of what poetry might or should be.

Notes

1. Czeslaw Milosz, "Dedication," in *New and Collected Poems, 1931–2001* (New York: Ecco Press, 2001), 77.
2. David Orr, "The Great(ness) Game," *New York Times Book Review*, February 19, 2009.
3. Czeslaw Milosz, "Reflections on T. S. Eliot," in *To Begin Where I Am: Selected Essays*, by Czeslaw Milosz, edited by Bogdana Carpenter and Madeline G. Levine (New York: Farrar, Straus and Giroux, 2002), 391.
4. Ibid., 391.
5. Czeslaw Milosz, "Robert Frost," in *To Begin Where I Am*, 400.
6. Ibid., 401.
7. Czeslaw Milosz, "Carmel," in *To Begin Where I Am*, 229.
8. Ibid.
9. Czeslaw Milosz, "*Ars Poetica?*," in *New and Collected Poems*, 240.
10. Czeslaw Milosz, "To Robert Lowell," in *New and Collected Poems*, 722.
11. Milosz, "*Ars Poetica?*," 240.
12. Ibid.
13. Ibid.
14. Czeslaw Milosz, "The Art of Poetry, no. 70," *Paris Review*, no. 133 (Winter 1994).
15. Milosz, "To Raja Rao," in *New and Collected Poems*, 254.
16. Milosz, "*Ars Poetica?*," 240.
17. Wisława Szymborska, "Autotomy," in *Map: Collected and Last Poems* (New York: Mariner Books, 2015), 183.
18. Czeslaw Milosz, "The Lesson of Biology," in *The Witness of Poetry* (Cambridge, MA: Harvard University Press, 1983), 45.
19. Ibid.
20. Milosz, "*Ars Poetica?*," 241.
21. Origen, *The Philocalia of Origen*, trans. George Lewis (Edinburgh: T. & T. Clark, 1911), 39.
22. Plato, *Apology*, trans. Hugh Tredennick, in *The Collected Dialogues of Plato*, edited by Edith Hamilton and Huntington Cairns (Princeton, NJ: Princeton University Press), 17.
23. Plato, *Phaedo*, trans. Hugh Tredennick, in *The Collected Dialogues of Plato*, 44.

LANGUAGE

CHAPTER 6

J. H. Prynne's Twist on Charles Olson

JOHN WILKINSON

ALTHOUGH IT WAS Robert Creeley whom Charles Olson named "the Figure of Outward," the phrase was soon and aptly reapplied to Olson's own poetry and poetics by poets and critics at the turn of the 1960s and 1970s.[1] Few American poets seemed as adventurously unconstrained by time and place as this poet of continental drift and Mayan glyphs, of open field prosody, of a new world already populated by advanced societies, a poet of process understood philosophically from Buddhism to the pre-Socratics to Alfred North Whitehead, a poet of high-energy physics and trawling for cod, and of the fine-grain economics of colonialism. For many, Olson's poetry and talks opened fields of possibility; poetry became illimitable. But in recent years few American poets have been so damagingly returned to time and place, hoisted into a caricature of phallic *size*: his literal physical presence, white male dominance, guru-like and interminable "mansplaining," cultural appropriation, and a poetic project arrogating all prehuman and human time and geography. From such a righteous position, *The Maximus Poems* looks like an exemplary folly of its period, and Olson's poetic circle transforms into a homosocial, sexually exploitative, and drug-addled sixties cult greedily taking every kind of permission while bigging up its progressive credentials.

But it is worth asking why Charles Olson's writing has been important to poets as different and compelling as John Wieners, Susan Howe, J. H. Prynne, and Amiri Baraka. Whatever the positioning of a writer in the seminar room, a writer's work lives through its reimagining by poetic successors—for their own reasons and needs. It is rewarding to open *The Maximus Poems* again, for it should be immediately evident that this is less a work that speaks for others than one creating a space for others' spoken and written records, as well as for others' furtherance: it is worth feeling the largesse as well as the folly, and it is worth allowing oneself to feel the beautiful lyric braiding of voices, knowledge, and thought in many of Olson's poems both within and without the *Maximus* project. The polyphony of Olson's poetry is of a rare quality: its sonic and intellectual braiding may idealize an American project, a social bonding in common labor rather than a melting pot—but it is no disgrace for a poet to idealize possibility, sustained through a full sense of the obduracy of the material world and the difficult achievement of human society, attentive to its marks, tracks, and records. This chapter attends to an example of Olson's braided work, through the different lenses of one poem's contemporary reception, its recent critical framing, and a supplementary reading.

The importance and influence of a poetical work as it is received into a different cultural context can declare themselves in unexpected ways. Not only does this apply to the British poet J. H. Prynne's rereading in 1962 of Charles Olson's 1953 poem "The Twist" and his subsequent detailed analysis in 1966; but the redemptive philological project that determined Prynne's reading helped to shape *The Maximus Poems* in its further development as well as making the rupture between the poets in 1967 look all but inevitable.[2] What Prynne read into *The Maximus Poems* as exemplified by his reception of "The Twist" was certain to be disappointed, even if Prynne's disappointment in Olson was as much symptomatic of a disappointment in the cultural and political moment in both Britain and the United States. More locally it followed hard on Prynne's forceful, even violent expressions of frustration at what he came to regard as compromised in the conduct of the worksheet the *English Intelligencer*, promulgated by him in a letter of December 27, 1966, to Andrew Crozier, its editor.[3] Nevertheless, Prynne's review of *Maximus Poems IV, V, VI* in 1969 and his lectures at Simon Fraser University in 1971 in no wise retreat from his admiration of the achievement of the first two volumes of Olson's cosmological project, whose ambitions would be revived by Prynne as late as his own 2011 cosmological poem *Kazoo Dreamboats*; while the intensity of a six-year correspondence (in a profound as well as a literal sense) between Olson and Prynne beginning in 1961, now made available in Ryan Dobran's edition, deeply informs Prynne's early collections *Kitchen Poems* (1968) and *The White Stones* (1969).[4]

"The Twist" has received various critical attention, much of it remarkably prescriptive. Robert von Hallberg set one direction by his disquisition on the nasturtium in *The Maximus Poems*, "derived from *nasus*, 'nose' + *torquere, tortum*, 'to twist,' so pungent is its odor."[5] Von Hallberg does not cite "The Twist" in this connection, and why should he, but this does not deter later critics from assertions like this: "'The Twist,' with its wealth of connotation in the title, opens the theme of the sequence that can be summarized perhaps as the changes in the adornment in which honor is clothed. Specifically, 'twist' means 'nose-twist,' or the nasturtium."[6] However, *The Maximus Poems* is not as a whole to be read as lyric, as Prynne insists to his audience at Simon Fraser: "If we come to this poem of Olson's [i.e., *The Maximus Poems*], we are in the condition of something which is not lyric"; and an etymology does not make a symbol. Although the final sequence of the last volume (vol. 3) of *The Maximus Poems* reiterates "Nasturtium / is still my flower," "The Twist" does not have to be a flower, while the nasturtium and its noxious scent are nowhere to be found in this episode—indeed, the flowery twist in the poem is decidedly no nasturtium. The signal quality of the turning-point flower in "The Twist" is its heliotropism:

> the whole of it
> coming,
> to this pin-point
> to turn
>
> in this day's sun[7]

Nasturtiums are not heliotropic, whereas some varieties of chrysanthemum, a flower equally significant in *The Maximus Poems*—a surprisingly flowery enterprise—do indeed turn to the sun. The definitive heliotropic flower is the eponymous sunflower, recognizable from its earlier appearance in "Maximus, to Gloucester, Letter 14":

> "to tend to move
> as though drawn",
> it also says

Or might it read
"compare
the ripe sun-flower"?[8]

The floral twist is more complex yet, for closely related to the sunflower
and heliotropic also are zinnia, on which "The Twist" puns sonically with the
word "xenia"—and Olson twists a great deal into "xenia." To show how
much, one might return to von Hallberg, who has something curious to say
about "The Twist," bearing on a point of prosody: "In 'The Twist' he [Olson]
distinguishes between Pound's sound and his own:

Or he and I distinguish
between chanting,
and letting the song lie
in the thing itself."[9]

This seems like a mistake—surely "he and I" are united in proposing this
distinction rather than divided. But although Ezra Pound is not explicitly
cited in the poem, von Hallberg's allusion is supported by George F.
Butterick's *A Guide to the Maximus Poems of Charles Olson*, which cites
Olson's notes on a dream involving Pound, boiled down to just these lines.[10]
In context, however, the passage sounds as much like a joke about a baby's
"chanting" and links baby and Pound in a genealogical line through Olson.
The passage continues:

I plant flowers
(xenia) for him
in the wet soil, indoors,
in his house

—in which "he" surely refers back to "a new baby" as much as to Pound, and
"his house" to the house in which his wife stays with their new baby (who
was indeed a boy). In the shifting dreamscape of the proem to "The Twist,"
fertilization, flourishing, and birth are braided so as to implicate Pound's
poetic paternity with Olson's biological paternity; and paternity and
maternity intercirculate in the proem's final lines:

> my neap,
> my spring-tide, my
> waters

"My" here is somewhat ambiguous, for the "my" of the proem's opening lines "Trolley-cars / are my inland waters" refers to the historically and geographically extensive figure of Maximus of Gloucester as much as to the situated Charles Olson, whether in Gloucester or North Carolina. In *The Maximus Poems*, the ocean consistently figures as male and land as female, but "waters" retains the history of the waters that broke with a baby's birth, both as creation myth and domestic event. Such incorporation of the female in the male has been analyzed by Rachel Blau DuPlessis as a trope of hypermasculinity in sixties culture, and specifically as a feature of Olson's poetry developing out of his early investment in Lawrentian phallicism.[11] All of these strands meet in "xenia," whose bisexuality seems exact and not so patriarchally entitled; xenia can be parsed as the effect of pollen on the maternal tissue of an already fertilized plant (or woman or man), so implying the further fertilizing work of the poet. It also refers to the Greek principle of hospitality, and puns on zinnia (as supported by the heliotropic close of the poem). These three meanings are knotted in the dreamed act of planting flowers indoors as distinct from planting seeds or bulbs. The dream might be read both as appropriating Pound's already blooming flowers, and as affirming Olson's still-potent survival in the wet, fecund soil of Pound's grave.[12]

The pleated referentiality of "xenia" might also recall Prynne's point about "monogene" in his review of *The Maximus Poems*: "Thus a single term like *monogene* reaches back into two entwined histories: the geochronology of land-formation and the cytochronology or biochemical evolution," both "xenia" and "monogene" illustrating von Hallberg's contention that "[t]his logographic poem [i.e., *The Maximus Poems*] is structured around a secret set of puns." "The Twist" is filled with tracks, houses, waters, and women, converging on the heliotropic point the poem eventually reaches:

> (August
> the flowers break off
>
> but the anther,

the filament of now, the mass
drives on,

   the whole of it
coming,
to this pin-point
to turn

   in this day's sun,

in this veracity

there, the waters of several of them the roads

here, a blackberry blossom

If *The Maximus Poems* are not to be read as lyric, that instruction cannot preclude noticing the braiding of lyric with epic genre that "The Twist" performs; the human genealogy of epic from Pound to Olson to baby, knots into the lyric bramble before issuing in "a blackberry blossom."[13] Here is the point at which a turn to Prynne's contemporary reading of "The Twist" is invited, since the two poets' exchange about "The Twist" opens on April 30, 1962, with Prynne expressing doubt about the blackberry blossom as a stock lyric gesture, but immediately contriving a reading to dismiss the concern:

> On first reading I was worried over the blackberry blossom: the pressure of circumstances carried me with total conviction to this veracity, but the blossom seemed to carry itself as instance rather than fact, one out of a possible range of alternatives, *any of which would have served*. That is to say, the particular fact (by so devastating a sleight of hand) becomes an emblem of its own unique status, its place in the geographic; not itself real but a pointer to its own necessary reality. And I was wrong, I see, because it is the twist that the intersections of tidal motion define which furnishes the credible ground out of which this bramble can grow. The pungency of turning, the precision at the temporal zenith--here are the map references for this bramble's roots, a quadrant which because

precisely local can belong to any interested person. Exactly there, the whole of it, personal history on the fulcrum of this day's sun.

There is no record of a letter from Olson responding to Prynne's enthusiastic and strikingly overdetermined interpretation—while flowers may be planted indoors in the proem, the poem seems quite innocent of those "roots" Prynne imagines as a subterranean correlative of the "intersections of tidal motion." After all, twisting had been featured earlier in "Maximus, to Gloucester, Letter 15," where far from putting down roots, the twist refers to an interlocutor's complaint against Olson's tendency "to go all around the subject," a different state of affairs while a defensible one.[14] Perhaps the "pungency of turning" alludes to the nasturtium complex identified by von Hallberg, but then equally pungent is the camphoric smell of the tansy, prominent in "Letter 3" ("Tansy for their noses").[15] What is most striking about this passage is the relationship proposed between "any interested person," a specific map reference and, later in the same letter, a substantive. A person ("personal history") is not situated according to his or her first-established roots—rather, roots twist into soil by virtue of a precision of location and of interestedness. "Interest" is not used casually by Prynne but extends its meaning through the first OED definition of the verb: "To invest (a person) with a share in or title to something, esp. a spiritual privilege." It is likely he also registers the importance of the "interesting" in Romantic aesthetics, as discussed recently and reanimated as an aesthetic category by Sianne Ngai.[16] *Credible* ground is produced for "any interested person" through poetic action, and it is "precisely local" at any point on which poetic interest turns and twists, even if, as Edward Dorn asserted, "I am certain, without ever having been there, I would be bored to sickness walking through Gloucester."[17] "Precisely local" is therefore not to be confused with localism; an insistence on "polis / not as localism" is proclaimed early in *The Maximus Poems*.[18] Later in the same 1962 letter, Prynne asserts:

> And what is so fine about The Twist, I recognize (re-cognize), is the
> dense array of substantives which by virtue of their human disposition
> are all proper nouns, absolute resting-places.

Substantives are here accorded a like "human disposition," and to dispose is to corpus(-oris): body, structure, frame, substance, (dim.) corpusculum; corporeus, corporal, fleshly; corpulentus, fleshy, corpulent, < *qᵘer-ep- bind up, make compact, close, thick: cf. creper, crepusculum, carpentum, decrepitus: Sk. kṛp- (form > beauty, cf. forma), M. Pers. karp (body); M. Ir. cri (*qṛpes-); Lit. kurpė (shoe), Pol. kurp (bast). The basic *qᵘer- (x. crassus, crates) in Sk. karōti (makes), karman (work); Lit. kuriu (build). The body is the 'build'. Most prob. to *s-qer-ep- belongs E. scarf (join together < Scand.). E. midrif (< O.E. hrif, belly; O.H.G. (h)ref, body, abdomen) appears to possess a true -i- and so belongs to the cogn. *qer-ei-p- of Lit. kreipiu (twist). [The Lat. may alternatively be derived from synon. *qᵘer-ep- < *qᵘer-: Cym. pryd (appearance), prydu (poetise), O.Ir. cruth (form), M.Ir. creth (poetry). Such a *qᵘer- ('twist') in cortina: cf. E. whorl, whir(l), with *qᵘer-ep- in O.E. hweorfan, O.N. hvirfla (whirl), and prob. in πόρπη, πόρπαξ.]

THE TWIST

Tucker, Concise Etymological Dictionary of Latin, pp. 66–67

BODY	the thing itself	in this veracity
STRUCTURE	the house / was a Jobostorte	
FRAME	Trolley-cars are my / inland waters	
SUBSTANCE	the tide	the air / sea ground the same, tossed / ice wind snow
CORPOREAL FLESHLY FAT	my wife has a new baby	the outer-land
BIND UP MAKE COMPACT	the figures / shoveling	the mass / drives on, / the whole of it / coming, / to this pin-point
CLOSE, THICK	in the wet soil	an apartment house was like a cake
FORM, BEAUTY	as dreams are, when the day / encompasses	the flowers blackberry blossom
MAKE / WORK / BUILD	I plant flowers for him	the ditch that Blyman made / what we are doing
JOIN	those couples did go to I'd have gladly gone to bed with	where it goes out & in
BELLY	the French dress, cut / on the bias	
APPEARANCE	through which I looked	like an oven-door a paper village
TWIST, WHIRL fills itself, at its tides	as they go around the after she left me bend	the river / exactly there at the bridge calyx and corolla by the dog to turn
POETRY	letting the song lie	

put something into its proper place—hence "proper nouns." A substantive must be disposed with a full knowledge of the place proper to it, where its roots can be made vital even if, as in "The Twist," they are nowhere open to view. "The Twist" continues to prepossess Prynne as exemplary of substantives as proper names, and as late in their correspondence as January 31, 1966, Prynne sends Olson what he describes as "a note, as of a new (and rubricated) scholasticism: the stratigraphy of current Language," an analysis of "The Twist." The description is attractively self-mocking, but the enterprise is a serious one despite its occasional tilt into absurdity. The note is here reproduced.[19]

Prynne's early philological poetics, destined for substantial revision but not repudiation, are stated at the very start of his correspondence with Olson: "Things are nouns, and particular substantives of this order are storehouses of potential energy, hoard up the world's available motions" (November 26, 1961). The "stratigraphy" of "The Twist" marks a high point of a poetics and of a poetic practice that Alex Latter dates as significantly modified following Prynne's December 1966 letter to Andrew Crozier printed in the *English Intelligencer*. This poetic practice had been announced in the same work-sheet's printing of "The Numbers," later the opening poem of *Kitchen Poems* (1968 but published in the *English Intelligencer* in 1966), and the first poem in every edition of Prynne's (collected) *Poems*. "The Numbers" ends like a manifesto:

> We *are* alive, the esteem already is
> there in potential. It is
> a firm question, of election,
> the elect angels. Signs or array,
> we should take this, we should
> really do so. There is no other
> > *beginning* on power.
> > Such is to elect terms,
> > to be the ground for names.[20]

All the bulletin poems of *Kitchen Poems* are driven across the page by propulsive line breaks and by italicized single words, few of them substantives but imparting to an unusually discursive poetic text an undiscursive urgency of diction, an almost hectoring insistence—so if *esteem*, the ascription of value, already exists "in potential" and awaits election, that is our responsibility (whoever the angelic "we" might be), a deliberate picking out and rooting as names. Prynne's somewhat Rilkean sense of poetic election may look a little ridiculous at the present distance, like a mixture of sixties optimism and coterie elitism, but its conviction gives a sense of the stakes of his exchange with Olson—that in recognizing another of "the elect angels" beyond the mainly British conclave of the *English Intelligencer*, and in Olson one with a missionary intensity matching his own, Prynne conceived not only a poetic restoration but a recasting of the very conditions for life on earth. The preoccupations of *The Maximus Poems* with the restoration of a place of human dwelling, to use the Heideggerian vocabulary attractive to Prynne at this time, chimed with such an ambition—enacted precisely through a poetic project that under Prynne's influence became strongly philologically driven, driven to elect its terms. Prynne felt Olson's later transformation into a kind of sixties guru as a betrayal of such an essentially selfless vocation, and as an ahistorical capitulation to the power and temptations of the moment—ironically in the light of later aspersions on Prynne's own charismatic influence.[21] In a *Paris Review* interview published in 2016, Prynne is disdainful of the culture Olson fostered at Black Mountain: "Olson and the others practised ascendency over the students and dominated their development, and offered themselves as exemplary models to be followed. [. . .] [T]heir knowledge of scholarship, and their understanding of things outside the ambience of personal interest and behaviour, was extremely casual."[22]

A closer look at Prynne's "stratigraphy" of "The Twist" will be followed by a reading of the poem that complements Prynne's and previous readings. I aim here to contribute to releasing the continuing force and value of Olson's poem.

Prynne's reproduction of the entry for "corpus" in T. G. Tucker's 1931 *Concise Etymological Dictionary of Latin* at the top left of his page generates a structuralist analysis of "The Twist" that at the same time asserts a deep history—and this exactly is the virtue of such a philological reading for Prynne. It is as though Prynne here seeks to drive Olson's flowering poem back into its bud, revealed as philological as it radiates from Tucker's etymological entry for "corpus." The sedimentation of human experience in language is declared the basis of poetry, and by inference "personal" experience becomes subordinate but with the potential to activate the linguistic network if sufficiently intense; hence in Prynne's "stratigraphy" Olson's intensely personal reference to "a new baby" is layered under "my wife has" as a particular form of "CORPOREAL / FLESHLY / FAT"—"FAT" being Prynne's ungallant addition to Tucker's set of cognates. Prynne reads Olson's poem as a map of a linguistic history, a synchronic structure generated from Indo-European roots subtending every English-language speech act but seriously generative (as opposed to accidentally or jocularly) only in the most ardent poetic work. This Romantic philology chimed with Olson's "Logography"—a title naming his Western linguistic turn against

Pound's ideogrammatic method—and influenced Olson toward the etymological preoccupation that can be tracked in *Proprioception*, the group of essay sketches written from about 1959 to 1962 whose chronology from the early "Logography" to "Grammar—a 'book'" shows a recourse to etymological dictionaries emerging contemporaneously with Prynne's earlier letters.[23] In Olson's case this shows the ground already prepared, a track of thinking that awaited and immediately recognized Prynne's information as germane to its project. The noteworthy features of Prynne's stratigraphy of "The Twist"—his excavation of its ground plan to reveal its linguistic strata—include its anachronism, for "The Twist" "was written at Black Mountain in May 1953" before it is plausible to think Olson consciously constructed a poem philologically; as well as its structuralism, whereby the poem is mapped out as a set of differentiations; and also its linguistic idealism, implying that any fully realized poetic text might yield a comparable stratigraphical coherence.[24] To say "fully realized" is to acknowledge that according to this view, judgment of a poem's full realization and seriousness depends upon such philological evidence lying latent and available to be revealed. And the evidence would be *even more* compelling if the subtending structure has not been contrived but emerges out of a "precisely local" twist, out of a "personal history" brought to bear on its "proper names." What was so exciting for Prynne about "The Twist" as evident in his stratigraphy, was that it appeared to demonstrate that true poetic attention drew irresistibly on an etymology of which its writer was almost certainly unaware, twisting back as far as Middle Persian. The discovery of Tucker's entry for "corpus" must have seemed fantastically fortuitous, for that Latin word received into English nowhere appears in "The Twist." Prynne's mapping of the poem then is strict—he resists the temptation to note that "a corpus of poetry" would be tautological in this philological synchrony. Strict, but often ingenious to the point that it stretches belief to breaking point and becomes perhaps knowingly comical. So "CLOSE, THICK" is evidenced by a wedding cake (which is arranged characteristically in aspirational and virginal tiers), and "BELLY" is evidenced by "the French dress, cut / on the bias," going well beyond synecdoche. Strict, in its gridlike structural disposition, but also highly selective, omitting much that other readers have found telling in the poem (for instance von Hallberg's focus on the Pound genealogy). Furthermore, this partial account has nothing to say about the poem's artifice—which may be consistent with the fact that Prynne's own prosody at this time was so dependent on italicized stresses, as though the poetic surface required the reader to engage in philological dowsing at marked points, its prosody being rhetorical rather than lyric, while in Prynne's late quatrain poems endogenous metrical stress would be determinedly eschewed. Logography unites Olson and Prynne, even if in Olson's work logography leads to the marking of a page as a linguistic map of space *and* time, pointing forward to the work of Susan Howe, while in Prynne's verse by contrast it leads to cookie-cutter stanzas—albeit his reconstruction of "The Twist" points in a direction nearer to Howe.

Further inspection of Prynne's stratigraphy shows Olson's poem reconstructed as quite another poem, not only staking out Olson's poem through the etymology of "corpus" but grounding it forcibly in the physical world, centered on the human body. The left-hand column of capitalized words is resolutely corporeal, until "TWIST, WHIRL" serves to organize a constellation of phrases connected with movement. It is such movement that leads to the final entry, "POETRY," specified as "letting the song lie." Given both Olson's and Prynne's strong interest in migration, this "twist" sounds more consistent with the Sapir-Whorf linguistic hypothesis than with formal structuralism: that is, the world-constitutive powers of a language come into focus only through the migration of language speakers and encounters between languages. The twist to the located body, "the thing itself," consists in the recognized unity of the song and the thing achieved through movement. "APPEARANCE," which immediately precedes "TWIST, WHIRL," is the start of such recognition, emerging from the mobilized body in work and in social and sexual congress, then launching outward.

What does Prynne's reading of "The Twist" imply for a reader approaching not just this but any poem? The response might at first seem obvious—that to read a poem must demand a fanatical pertinacity, and familiarity with a range of scholarship unlikely in any reader (to read the Olson-Prynne correspondence is to be staggered anew by Prynne's limitless appetite for scholarship). The abiding influence on Prynne of Olson's social and pedagogical practice is pertinent here—open hours kept through the night for any poet or student caller, and attachment to the lecture, informal discourse, and epistolary exchange as a way of fostering conditions within which Prynne's own writing can be well received, and his scholarly and creative methods propagated through successive generations. The initiate might devote a lifetime to exposition of a Prynne poem, as Prynne has himself devoted a lifetime to exposition of a handful of poems. Attention and interpretation are the watchwords; scholarship that is alive and at the service of art's inexhaustible rewirings. So why should anyone want to read under this rubric, out of Romantic philology through New Criticism and Cambridge-style Practical Criticism? Don't millions listen every day to songs by Joni Mitchell or solos by John Coltrane without such bother? But what does "listen" mean? What does "look" mean in a gallery? The poetry and talking of both Olson and Prynne refuse to quarantine art from thinking, from investigation, from politics, from transcendence even, so keeping art in its place as diversion or entertainment. The poetry of both, even in Prynne's radical departure from Olson's poetics, insists that the thinking art can do is fundamental; it can reconfigure the basis for every other mode of thought. That is not to aver that poetry *must* set such a standard, any more than to imply that a sentimental country-western song delivered in a way that breaks the heart is valueless set against a late Beethoven quartet. But to read a poem like "The Twist" with full attention is to feel aesthetic response at once in the flesh and in the mind and as working there with the felt potential to continue working. The poet drives and is driven by the genetic forces of language, or a society shapes and is shaped by the land and movement across it (or was, before the Anthropocene).

Both Olson and Prynne have been accused of fostering a cenacle, and there is truth in this—but the pertinent question is how open the cenacle has been to those with no admission privileges. In both instances, women have spoken of a sense of alienation, and while there are notable exceptions, both cenacles indeed were predominantly male. Put into the balance, though, that both poets were boundlessly hospitable to unheralded visitors with little formal education, or with mental health and behavioral troubles, while their epistolary reach was astonishing and a major encouragement to the otherwise isolated. Their cenacles were far less exclusive than admission to a research university or to a major creative writing program either then or now. Neither was there any career advantage at the time for students engaging in such open-ended and uncredentialed debate and response.

Prynne's manner of reading would make any poem competent to draw full attention to itself, at one and the same time impossibly difficult and completely accessible. This is what he intends, consistently with his social and pedagogic practice. For Prynne's underlying contention is that a poem apt to compel does so through a subtending linguistic structure that any native reader of its language already knows without knowing it—if a poem *feels* coherent in response to a reader's true attentiveness, however enigmatic and reluctant to yield its secrets it may seem, then it may indeed be trusted to support the reader in linguistically dwelling on earth. A reader does not need to interpret a poem in the sense of accounting for its messages, its argument, its decency, its politics. Of course it is quite another thing to analyze how the poem achieves its effect, just as it is to assay the geological, ecological, economic, and political forces that land the day's catch in Gloucester, Massachusetts. Prynne's approach both creates almost insuperable difficulties and gives any reader a pass on them. That said, such a pass shifts the demand on a reader from the poem and skills in close reading and contextualization, to the capacity for full attentiveness and its quality. Attentiveness figures as an ethical, religious, and political attribute. Preparation for acts of attentive reading might become more important than reading a specific text: are you fit to read? But this should not be taken, as routinely it is, as requiring a certain level of formal education. "Any interested person" in the full sense of "interested" is equipped to approach the poem.

Compare a recent summary interpretation of "The Twist" by an intelligent and informed critic, Peter Middleton, here quoted in full:

In "The Twist" Olson tries to penetrate the unknown as he mingles elements from several dreams from 1953 in which his unconscious mind pictures Gloucester variously as a place where his wife has had a baby in a house at the far end of the trolley line, where he takes a journey with his father during which they watch other people diverge from them, where his wife leaves him to live in a house like a cake, and where that one part of the city he calls "the whole Cut" becomes a village made of paper. It is crucial to the workings of the poem that Olson actually dreamed these dreams; they are not invented nor even primped a little. "The Twist" is a poem about the distorting nostalgias of absence as well as his growing preoccupation with the history of Gloucester (he is writing the poem while living at Black Mountain). What especially interests the poet are his glimpses of the law-like workings of the human universe, the manner in which a series of thoughts, both daylight and dream thoughts, can twist themselves into a complex point: "this pin-point / to turn / in this day's sun, // in this veracity // there, the waters the several of them the roads // here, a blackberry blossom." [. . .] The poem suggests that in daylight dreams become mere toys, and almost that too much consciousness, like urban planning, can mistakenly "tear down" their seemingly out of date construction.[25]

Middleton's summary is orientated to a larger argument and is therefore partial; it must necessarily belie the experience of reading "The Twist," since it encapsulates the meanings of the poem in relation to his larger argument. But even a summary does not have to ignore a poem's formal properties completely. Middleton's account can be held to exemplify the rift between a summary and a poem, since *how* the poem delivers these events, dreams, interests, and suggestions goes unaddressed, so his accurate observation that "a series of thoughts, both daylight and dream thoughts, can twist themselves into a complex point" suggests that "The Twist" is a written record incorporating such *observations* rather than a poem whose procedure enacts such twisting. The effect of reading the poem after Middleton's account is that it seems to concertina into a brief memoir, enriched by the "interests" of the poet as though pastimes, and suffused with sentimentality—"the distorting nostalgias of absence" has a pejorative suggestion that the poem does not support, any more than it supports the suggestion "that in daylight dreams become mere toys." The pertinent passage reads:

> I went home
> as fast as I could,
>
> the whole Cut
> was a paper village my Aunt Vandla
> had given me, who gave me,
> each Christmas,
> such toys
>
> As dreams are, when the day
> encompasses. They tear down

the Third Ave El. Mine stays,
as Boston does, inches up.
I run my trains
on a monorail, I am seized
--not so many nights ago--
by the sight of the river
exactly there at the Bridge

where it goes out & in

The day may encompass, but the toys of childhood and of dream persist within its embrace, for "Mine stays" as does the memory of "the Bridge" and tidal river connecting land and ocean dynamically. That interpenetration of land and ocean is a, perhaps even *the*, governing process of *The Maximus Poems*, and here tidal reach surges to interfuse consciousness and dream—as it will increasingly interfuse economics and myth. The opposition Middleton draws between toylike dreams and urban planning is therefore a fundamental error. But the sentimentality Prynne seeks to purge from the poem, at first in his recoiling from "a blackberry blossom" as a mere fancy and later in his structural analysis, is actually present and kept obtrusively and immitigably so through Middleton's reading. Furthermore, the dominance of a "speaker," in Middleton's account, organizes the poem for all its syntactical and gender complexity into an expression of Olson's nostalgia for a Massachusetts childhood. Prynne's stratigraphy, in its determination not only to purge sentimentality but to deny the quite old-fashioned lyric aspect of the poem, is shown as perverse. What Prynne and Middleton produce through their attention, then, are two radically different poems, but both readings share a compulsion to arrive at a unity, apprehending the poem as a singularity despite duly registering "the manner in which a series of thoughts, both daylight and dream thoughts, can twist themselves into a complex point" (Middleton) and "the twist that the intersections of tidal motion define which furnishes the credible ground out of which this bramble can grow" (Prynne). Prynne's arrival at the "corpus" of "The Twist" is more ingenious than Middleton's, and its implications for future readers may be more productive, although any attentive reader presumably would be immune from distraction by nostalgia, sentimentality, and identification with a first-person lyric voice. For it is *voice* from which both Prynne and Middleton shy away—not the voiced opinions of the poet, but the voice of the poem. Olson's "logography" might seem to justify such avoidance behavior, and much of the archival material in *The Maximus Poems* does depart from the vocal (although a penchant for reported anecdote keeps nonlyric voice active throughout); but even the most spectacular visual twisting of the later *Maximus Poems* can compel lyric performance: "What is the heart, turning / beating itself out leftward" as one remarkable passage begins on the way to an explicitly catechismal rhythmic and semantic take-up, even while comprising the typographical image of a flower.[26]

So how does "The Twist" twist prosodically? In the passage above, the line "had given me, who gave me," is a superversive line for the prosody of "The Twist" according to Simon Jarvis's definition: "A superversive line is that line in a given poem which most eminently exploits the play between syntactic and metrical segmentation, between an ordinary and a special phonology; which peculiarizes verse as verse."[27] On the face of it, there is little odd about this line except a caesura that sounds as though it marks a pause for correction (as it might in a poem by A. R. Ammons, for instance) but doesn't correct anything: rather it determines a kind of rocking, to-and-fro motion. Throughout the passage, the poem, and *The Maximus Poems* the excessive use of commas has such a prosodic effect—not so much of hesitation as of tidal bore balanced with backflow. Such a temporal pendulation is promoted also by a liberal use of parentheses, some unclosed, but more characteristic is the fulcrum of the caesura; so in the opening proem:

And my wife has a new baby
in a house at the end of
such a line, and the morning after,
is ready to come home, the baby too,
exceptionally well & advanced

Again, semantically there is nothing noteworthy here besides the obvious self-referentiality of "at the end of / such a line" and the temporal play between "the end," "after," "ready," and "advanced," but the line break after "end of" makes "such a line" a yearned-for completion rhythmically, and the comma after "after" introduces another counterrhythmic obstruction while "the baby too" reverts to the first line of stanza—it backs up. The beginning of part 1 of the poem offers a similar movement:

> Between Newton and Tatnuck Square the tracks
> go up hill, the cars
> sway, as they go around the bend
> before they take, before they go down to
> the outer-land
> (where it is Sunday,

The opening line clatters with its *t*-sounds like trams on their tracks, whereupon both rhythmic propulsions and *t*'s are suspended to be picked up in "take" and "outer." This stanza might be read as quite closely mimetic of trams and their awkward movement on bends, and so it is, but the prosody of the proem, not only in the earlier lines cited but in such a line as "fills itself, at its tides, as she did" has already attuned the ear to the underlying shuttle of "before they take, before they go down to," made more explicit semantically in the section's final lines "I go up-dilly, elevated, tenement / down" (there is no terminal full stop). It would be tedious to extend such evidence; the temporal and geographical rocking and interpenetration reaches precisely its "pin-point / to turn" in the poem's three closing lines:

> in this veracity

> there, the waters of several of them the roads

> here, a blackberry blossom

Thus prosodically the poem ends on a fulcrum set by the ambivalence of "this veracity / there," the suppression of the medial caesura in the second line plaiting "the waters" with "the roads," and the skewed weight on the initial monosyllables "there" and "here." There is no necessity to search for corkscrew roots under the "blackberry blossom"; what roots and imparts to "a blackberry blossom" its power of heartfelt completion is prosodic, for its absolute presence has been delivered as an equivalence to all that precedes it—it is the "here" and it is *heard*: "here, a blackberry blossom."

Such a prosodic summation has been announced ten lines before as an occurrence at "the anther / the filament of now," harkening back to the "xenia" of the proem—the anther produces the pollen that fertilizes the mother plant, as the present works on the past poetically and implicates each in each. Such interfusion, such tidal back-and-forth, such rocking moves this poem and makes it moving. Prynne's stratigraphy ignores both xenia and anther, and its map categorically cannot register the poem's prosodic performance. Indeed, given that Olson's hugely influential "Projective Verse" essay-manifesto had appeared in 1950 and articulated a process prosody indebted to Whitehead, it is remarkable that Prynne would distribute "The Twist" in such articulations. Writing later, Middleton recognizes that the poem is "interested" in "the manner in which a series of thoughts, both daylight and dream thoughts, can twist themselves into a complex point," but he fails to recognize the consistency of such thinking with the poem's cosmology, its view of history as dynamic and embodied ("history is the function of any one of us"), and its prosody.[28]

Olson's peculiar prosody was developed early. "Projective Verse" (1950) both accurately states its principles and is written, as much of Olson's prose, according to those principles:

I say the syllable, king, and that it is spontaneous, this way: the ear, the ear which has collected, which has listened, the ear, which is so close to the mind that it is the mind's, that it has the mind's speed . . .
it is close, another way: the mind is brother to this sister and is, because it is so close, is the drying force, the incest, the sharpener . . .
it is from the union of the mind and the ear that the syllable is born.[29]

Contemporary with "Projective Verse" is the major poem "In Cold Hell, in Thicket," which opens:

In cold hell, in thicket, how
abstract (as high mind, as not lust, as love is) how
strong (as strut or wing, as polytope, as things are
constellated) how
string, hold cold
can a man stay (can men?) confronted
thus?[30]

The cosmological sweep of *The Maximus Poems* and its generic return to the pre-Socratic *Peri Physeos* (translated by Prynne as "On What There Is" in the subtitle to his *Kazoo Dreamboats*) permits no distinction between poetry and prose, between lyric and document, between logography and prosody.[31] For all Prynne's attention to substantives, Olson's prosody turns about commas and single-syllable words—"here," "there," "is," "how," "thus"—words that act as brakes, as punctuation. While Prynne's *Kitchen Poems* often line-break on grammatical articles and monosyllables, the effect is wholly different—their prosody enforces an emphatic, declamatory forward drive. Prynne's stepped stanzas may often look like Olson's more prosy blocks, but they lack the internal punctuation of lines that impedes the propulsion of Olson's. Nonetheless, in his mapping of "The Twist" around the etymology of "corpus," Prynne responds to the corporeality of Olson's verse, intuitively recognized at least, although attested more theoretically than feelingly. Not only Olson's specific allusions in "Projective Verse" to breath but the prosodic force wresting the onrush of "process" into history as knotted proprioceptively into the body, "the *function* of any one of us," where continuity is marked by the in-and-out of respiration—all this hinges on caesurae forced at particles and commas. Such verse physiology is visually apparent in Olson's highly distinctive long lines broken by commas, a practice unadopted by his contemporaries apart from some influence on Prynne's prosody in *Kitchen Poems*. As the paragraphs from "Projective Verse" show, Olson's prose style can scarcely be distinguished from his long verse lines—indeed, a nominally prose text like *Pleistocene Man* (1965) consists of "Letters" as do many of *The Maximus Poems*. Letter IV of *Pleistocene Man* is headed "Don't read this as a letter," before beginning "It's most like poetry. In fact it *is* poetry" and continuing later in the first paragraph "It has that turn around an impossible corner."[32] Later letters in *Pleistocene Man* may look like verse but are closer to outlines, anticipating by decades the kind of visual outlining programs used on electronic tablets—a technological extension of Olsonian composition by field. Olson's prosody allows *The Maximus Poems* to shift between prose and verse in a cosmological *Peri Physeos* capable of switching like the surviving texts of Parmenides between the rhapsodic, the descriptive, and the analytical—as well as the archival and the anecdotal.[33] Olson's originality lies in bending cosmology to the scaled figures of the earth and sea, Maximus, and Charles Olson in his domesticity, and in braiding them prosodically.

Three ways of reading "The Twist" have now been adumbrated. Although they have first been represented as alternatives, it has become evident that a stratigraphic, a lyrically integrated, and a prosodic reading—each privileging different aspects and passages of "The Twist"—could effectively be twisted into a mode of reading apt to this lyric moment in Olson's cosmological *Peri Physeos*. What do these readings share? They find this complex poem—the term "complex" is unusually precise here—to be governed by a principle of contiguity: philological, conscious/unconscious, geographical, and historical. The manner in which contiguities tend to braid, tend toward unity, tend to interpenetration, and tend to dialectical forwarding is proposed in different ways by the three ways of reading. What are the shortcomings of these readings? Notably all tend to isolate "The Twist" from its place in the larger work, although they have a bearing on how the larger work might be read, through its anchoring in key substantives, through its prosody, and along its autobiographical thread. Crucially, in spite of the intricacy that might be entailed in mapping its philological substrate or in a less cursory analysis of its prosody than is attempted here, both philological and prosodic readings intimate that a reader will feel their workings without a requirement to undertake a like reading or excavation. However, such aesthetic encounter demands unswerving attention of an order that can only be imagined of a dedicated reader of poetry—although oral performance might perhaps compel a less prepared listener. The proximity of Middleton's reading to the New Critical ascription of a "speaker" necessitates a more deliberate strategy on the reader's part; for all that such a style of reading was born out of a democratic motive to make critical reading less dependent on a formal classical education, it demands skills in conscious conceptual exposition, distinct from (but not inimical to) an openness to aesthetic encounter. All three readings testify to the productive richness of "The Twist."

Stepping outside the frame of some powerful feminist and postcolonial critiques of Olson, reading "The Twist" is a reminder that the best of Olson's poems cannot be reduced to examples of his phallicism or of "appropriation," for they work poetically, and true poetic work is by definition never complete—it would cease to be poetic and reduce to dead letters if no longer evolving through readers both accustomed and new. The eventuation of a poem can be blocked, temporarily at least, by forcing its activity into positions, a procrustean distortion quite contrary to the thinking prosody of

"The Twist." Stepping aside from political critique does not propose that the political critiques are illegitimate or mistaken—and indeed, the problem of lyric and the promise of lyric are tied alike to an act of reparation that can be arbitrary and privileged as often as restorative of heart, or appear to different readers as categorically one or the other. What is reactionary in Olson merits a response along with what is farsighted in his environmental politics, for instance; but it is wrong to imagine that progressive positions make for poetry that is effectively progressive, or reactionary positions make for effectively reactionary poetry.[34] The integrative tensions of the twist work against the simplicities of individualism or collectivism, of for or against, of the market or the plan, of in or out, or of then or now. Neither is the convergence of forces marked by a blackberry blossom and Olson's attention to it, a total capture; attention twists with the will to change in both aesthetic experience and political struggle.

A long and deeply felt letter from Prynne to Olson dated March 15, 1966, brings philology, prosody, politics, the body, and the syllable into an explicit twist that illustrates the criticality for Prynne of his exchange with Olson and the exacting standard of loyalty entailed:

> If the language can keep its qualities intact, that recoverable element
> (which in the end is knowledge) will accrue despite all forms of
> apparent supersession. Whom we love, cease to love, or just grow
> strange towards, perhaps through distance: there could be a grammar
> of loyalty which would entail no formal clinging to the specific, but
> which would celebrate our instatement in the human body & the
> community of desire. By quantity of course I mean very locally the
> measures of poetry, and the syllable as a constant element in the
> transformations of speech or myth.

This "grammar of loyalty" draws on a Poundian genealogy that could be expected to unite Olson and Prynne:

> What thou lovest well remains,
>   the rest is dross
> What thou lov'st well shall not be reft from thee
> What thou lov'st well is thy true heritage[35]

But apparently Olson was not attentive. There was no response to this letter from Olson; merely a continual stream of requests for references, books to be sent, and so on. This "community of desire" would not be much longer sustained. Alex Latter reports that by 1968 Prynne was referring dismissively to Olson as "Tithonus of Gloucester [who] never, for all his touch of Pericles, had the wit to go home, shut up, & listen for the other music" (Tithonus was distinguished by unnatural longevity). Indeed, it was just when the fullest impact of Olson and Ginsberg was experienced by British poets that Prynne decided the American poetic project had collapsed.[36] As for studying the subsequent impact of Olson's writing on British poetry, any fuller account might begin from Allen Fisher's long poem *Place* (1971–1980), note Prynne's influence on Fisher, and acknowledge Iain Sinclair's early hybrid poetry-psychic cartographies and advocacy of Olson, Prynne, and Fisher.[37]

Finally, "The Twist" and J. H. Prynne's response to it, not so much in his stratigraphy as more consequentially in his poems, might be held to exemplify the dictum of Robert Walser that "[g]reat art resides in great goings-astray, just as the most poignant grace likes best to dwell in contortions."[38] At times Olson's poetry and Prynne's early poetry have been read as destabilizing master discourses by bringing radically different discourses into jarring proximity. This once unfamiliar strategy looks different now; "The Twist," and so many of *The Maximus Poems*, and the poems of Prynne's *Brass*, feel rather as though they might dream of reparation while striking off violent convergences and disputatious hard edges. Even though the lyric poet in Olson confesses "I run my trains / on a monorail," his monorail holds to the city's grid, the river's curves, and the sun's turning. In the larger project it runs alongside many tracks, with their switches and junctions. There is some impossible position from which they will appear as a unified world of production, exchange, disbursement, goings-astray, thriving, and, as in "The Twist," poignant grace.

Notes

This chapter is deeply indebted to Ryan Dobran, who allowed me access to the uncorrected proof of his edition of the Olson-Prynne correspondence, now published by the University of New Mexico Press. I am more than grateful to him. I am also grateful to members of the Poetry and Poetics Workshop,

University of Chicago, for their comments on a draft of this paper in September 2016, particularly the contributions of Edgar Garcia, Beth Helsinger, and Srikanth Reddy.

1. Olson so names Creeley in the dedication of the first volume of *The Maximus Poems*.

2. Presumably Prynne was reading "The Twist" in the first volume of *The Maximus Poems* (New York: Jargon/Corinth Books, 1960). This chronology discounts any possibility that the poem alluded to the dance and song "The Twist," the first recording of the song being released in 1959 and the best-known version by Chubby Checker in 1960.

3. "I had thought that perhaps something might *move*, if there were perhaps some initial measure of trust, so that the community of risk could hold up the idea of a possible world; we could approximately and in some sense or other mostly be *in* it," and ending, "I would say at this moment that the 'company' you refer to in your last issue, which holds the pen with such discreet fervour, lives its common loyalties like a well-bred whore trying to reform. I rather hope the rats get there first." J. H. Prynne to Andrew Crozier, December 27, 1966, in *Certain Prose of the English Intelligencer*, ed. Neil Pattison, Reitha Pattison, and Luke Roberts (Cambridge, MA: Mountain, 2012), 28–29. See also J. H. Prynne to Charles Olson, October 15, 1967: "I know where I am and where I think you say you are, but where are *we* in that other and more fearful sense? Not in our *houses*, god I so hope, *not in our houses*." In *The Collected Letters of Charles Olson and J. H. Prynne*, ed. Ryan Dobran (Albuquerque: University of New Mexico Press, 2017), 222. Cited henceforward as *Olson-Prynne Letters*.

4. The cosmological works of Olson and Prynne are mediated by Edward Dorn's *Gunslinger* (1968–1975), not least in drawing on pre-Socratic philosophy. See especially *The Cycle* (1971), a lyric interlude in *Gunslinger*, in Edward Dorn, *Collected Poems*, ed. Jennifer Dunbar Dorn with Justin Katko, Reitha Pattison, and Kyle Waugh (Manchester: Carcanet Press, 2012), 475–503. Prynne's review of *Maximus Poems IV, V, VI* was first published in *The Park*, nos. 4–5 (Summer 1969), and reprinted in *Minutes of the Charles Olson Society*, nos. 47–48 (November 2002). It is available online at http://charlesolson.org/Files/Prynnereview.htm. His lectures were first published in *Iron* (October 1971) and reprinted in *Minutes of the Charles Olson Society*, no. 28 (April 1999). They are available online at http://charlesolson.org/Files/Prynnelecture1.htm and Prynnelecture2.

5. Robert von Hallberg, *Charles Olson: The Scholar's Art* (Cambridge, MA: Harvard University Press, 1978), 155.

6. Thomas F. Merrill, *The Poetry of Charles Olson: A Primer* (Newark: University of Delaware Press, 1982), 186.

7. Charles Olson, "The Twist," in *The Maximus Poems*, by Charles Olson, ed. George F. Butterick (Berkeley: University of California Press, 1983), 86–90.

8. Charles Olson, "Maximus, to Gloucester, Letter 14," in *The Maximus Poems* (1983), 64.

9. Von Hallberg, *Charles Olson: The Scholar's Art*, 173.

10. "The dream, from early May 1953, is recorded in notes the poet made at the time: 'Pound's dist. between chant & letting the song lie in the thing itself--& I planting zenias for him in the wet soil (indoors!) of his house.'" George F. Butterick, *A Guide to the Maximus Poems of Charles Olson* (Berkeley: University of California Press 1978), 125. It seems likely that Olson meant "zinnias," confused with the near-homophone "xenia."

11. Rachel Blau DuPlessis, *Purple Passages* (Iowa City: University of Iowa Press, 2012), esp. 108–16.

12. "Flowers" for "poems" was a figure established by the enormously popular anthology of poems *Other Men's Flowers* edited by Field Marshal Lord Wavell, penultimate viceroy of India, and published in 1944. The title draws on Montaigne: "I have gathered a posy of other men's flowers, and nothing but the thread that binds them is mine own."

13. It has been suggested to me that "blackberry blossom" might refer to the Appalachian fiddle tune of that name, but this seems unlikely given Olson's lack of interest in music, verging on antipathy.

14. Charles Olson, "Maximus, to Gloucester, Letter 15," in *The Maximus Poems* (1983), 72.

15. Charles Olson, "Letter 3," in *The Maximus Poems* (1983), 13.

16. Sianne Ngai, *Our Aesthetic Categories: Zany, Cute, Interesting* (Cambridge, MA: Harvard University Press, 2012). See the extensive treatment in chapter 2, "Merely Interesting."

17. Edward Dorn, *Views*, ed. Donald Allen (Bolinas, CA: Four Seasons Foundation, 1980), 34.

18. Olson, "Letter 3," 14.

19. A typographical transcription of Prynne's structural gloss is supplied by Dobran, *Olson-Prynne Letters*, 158, but without the photocopied clipping from Tucker—which obscures the point.

20. J. H. Prynne, *Poems*, 4th ed. (Hexham, Northumb., England: Bloodaxe Books, 2015), 11.

21. It would be apt to note that the death of Olson's first wife, Betty, in a car accident on the night of March 28, 1964, affected Olson profoundly, exacerbating his already heavy drinking. Although Olson refers to Betty enough in the correspondence with Prynne that follows to indicate his continued mourning, Prynne's rather British letter of April 9, 1964, records hearing the news from Jonathan Williams and reads simply: "A terrible thing. I do not presume to 'say' anything, but the ensuing silence is all for yourself. Passengers, ex illo tempore." Dobran, *Olson-Prynne Letters*, 93. There was not much that could be written in direct response to that.

22. Jeff Dolven and Joshua Kotin, "J. H. Prynne, the Art of Poetry no. 101," interview, *Paris Review*, no. 218 (Fall 2016): 177–207, passage cited 183. There is an inevitable revisionism in Prynne's discussion of Olson here, giving little sense of the intensity of their exchange. But the interview is a brief excerpt from a much longer transcript—the interviewers note that "the final transcript came to 152,000 words––495 printed pages" (177). It is to be hoped that eventually the full transcript will be made available in some form.

23. Charles Olson, *Additional Prose: A Bibliography on America, Proprioception, and Other Notes & Essays*, ed. George F. Butterick (Bolinas, CA: Four Seasons Foundation, 1974). Butterick discusses the dating of the sections of "Proprioception" on page 85.

24. Butterick, *A Guide to the Maximus Poems*, 124.

25. Peter Middleton, "Discoverable Unknowns: Olson's Lifelong Preoccupation with the Sciences," in *Contemporary Olson*, ed. David Herd (Manchester: Manchester University Press, 2015), 48–49.

26. Poem beginning "I have been an ability—a machine," in *The Maximus Poems* (1983), 495–99.

27. Simon Jarvis, "Superversive Poetics: Browning's *Fifine at the Fair*," *Modern Language Quarterly* 77, no. 1 (2016): 121–41. The definition is taken from the paper's abstract. Jarvis's term is something of a prosodic equivalent to Michael Riffaterre's "hypogram," which pertains to the semantic core of a text.

28. See Charles Olson, *The Special View of History*, ed. Ann Charters (Berkeley, CA: Oyez, 1970). The section "History: A Definition" begins: "Like it or not, see it or not, history is the *function* of any one of us."

29. Charles Olson, "Projective Verse," in *Human Universe and Other Essays*, by Charles Olson, ed. Donald M. Allen (New York: Grove Press, 1967), 54.

30. Charles Olson, "In Cold Hell, in Thicket," in *The Collected Poems of Charles Olson, Excluding the "Maximus" Poems*, ed. George F. Butterick (Berkeley: University of California Press, 1987), 155.

31. J. H. Prynne, *Kazoo Dreamboats; or, On What There Is* (Cambridge: Critical Documents, 2011).

32. Charles Olson, *Pleistocene Man* (Buffalo: Institute of Further Studies, 1968), 9. But at much the same time Olson fretted in a letter responding to Prynne's poem "Die a Millionaire" (Prynne, *Poems*, 13): "It *is* an essay. And *not* a poem (Isn't it? Any way not at all to abuse, or be the less grateful, myself!" (July 14, 1966). Dobran, *Olson-Prynne Letters*, 196.

33. See Daniel W. Graham, ed. and trans., *The Texts of Early Greek Philosophy: The Complete Fragments and Selected Testimonies of the Major Presocratics*, part 1 (Cambridge: Cambridge University Press, 2010), esp. 211–33.

34. Cf. Theodor Adorno in "Lyric Poetry and Society": "[I]n every lyric poem the historical relation of subject to object, of individual to society within the realm

of subjective spirit thrown back on its own resources—this historical relation must have been precipitated in the poem. This precipitation will be more perfect, the more the poem eschews the relation of self to society as an explicit theme and the more it allows this relation to crystallize involuntarily from within the poem." In *The Adorno Reader*, ed. Brian O'Connor (Oxford: Blackwell, 2000), 217. Such relations "crystallize" around the blackberry blossom.

35. Ezra Pound, Canto LXXXI, in *The Cantos* (New York: New Directions, 1970).

36. Alex Latter, *Late Modernism and "The English Intelligencer": On the Poetics of Community* (London: Bloomsbury Academic, 2015), 104. Latter's account makes it clear that Prynne's disdain was as much political as aesthetic, responding to the reduction of "all the hips and beats and cosmic queers into speechless order." Latter is quoting from the Peter Riley Papers at Cambridge University Library.

37. Allen Fisher, *Place* (Hastings, Sussex, England: Reality Street, 2005). For a brief and insightful history of the London mapping works of Sinclair and Fisher linking their work to Olson and Prynne, see John Kerrigan, "London, Albion," in *The Oxford Handbook of Contemporary British and Irish Poetry*, ed. Peter Robinson (Oxford: Oxford University Press, 2013), esp. 362–69.

38. Robert Walser, "A Painter," in *Looking at Pictures*, by Robert Walser, trans. Susan Bernofsky (New York: Christine Burgin and New Directions, 2015), 32.

CHAPTER 7

The Value of George Oppen's Small Words

KATERINA STERGIOPOULOU

Within the discipline of criticism, nothing is more difficult than praise. To speak of what you love—not admire, not know to be good, not find reasonably interesting, not feel briefly moved by or charmed by—to speak of such work is difficult because the natural correlatives of awe and reverence are not verbal.

—LOUISE GLÜCK, "ON GEORGE OPPEN"[1]

I think always about the thing in which we are. . . . It is not enough to say that we like it or that we do not like it. It is here, we must first talk about it.

—GEORGE OPPEN[2]

I

Despite the "overwhelming impediment" that she outlines in the sentence I have used as my first epigraph, Louise Glück does venture a "tribute" to George Oppen, as "a way of affirming certain values" (29). The value of Oppen's poetry for Glück, then, lies in the values it exhibits and implicitly or explicitly affirms—values both poetic-technical (its directness, its practicality, its "logic") and "moral" (32, 31). Oppen's work seeks, on the one hand, to restore words "to natural health and soundness" and thus "make a language available for common use," and, on the other, to "speak a moral language, a language of salvation and contempt"; and it does so, in Glück's assessment, with "the force of true passion, but none of the smarmy definitiveness, none of the self-righteousness" (31). She judges the poems by the values they themselves propose for poetry (and for life); this may seem either circular or too generous but is, I think, inescapable when evaluating Oppen's work, which is almost exclusively—if not always directly—devoted to asking and thinking the question of the value of poetry: value not only in terms of worth and usefulness, but also, more essentially, its validity (the Latin *valere* is at the root of both our English words).

Glück's assessment of Oppen's poetic value is simultaneously an implicit political claim, suggesting that poetry would be a cure for ailing times. The political or moral dimension may be adduced as a separate one, but it is already imbricated in the way that she talks about Oppen's linguistic/poetic/aesthetic virtues, as seen in her use of "soundness," which metaphorizes "sound" into health. The rhetoric of health is not one that Oppen uses (unlike, say, Pound), and he may have been skeptical of this particular conjoining, and of the implied prescriptiveness of the poet's work (he restores words so others can then use them properly; he offers salvation and contempt).[3] Instead, Oppen's preferred term is "clarity" (the poem is "the structure of meaning which restores the words to clarity"), while he is very cautious about the degree of "morality" that may be present or espoused in his poems (*SPDP* 69). "I DO NOT MEAN TO PRESCRIBE ~~AN OPINION OR~~ AN IDEA, BUT TO RECORD THE EXPERIENCE OF THINKING IT [*sic*]," he notes in his "Daybook," rejecting even the suggestion that his poems might promulgate opinions rather than ideas (*SPDP* 88). Glück in a way acknowledges this when she writes that "at his least good" Oppen is "relentlessly lofty" (30). Indeed, Marjorie Perloff reads Oppen's most famous poem, "Of Being Numerous," against the majority of critics who emphasize its social, political, or moral nature and argues for its fundamental abstraction, claiming that the poem is about itself and its syntax, does not point to a world outside, does not express a populist vision, and does not care about social transformation.[4]

Duncan Dobbelmann has offered a detailed account of Oppen's critical reception over the past fifty or so years, outlining his clearly avant-garde beginnings and descendants but also his recent adoption into a canon of lyric poetry.[5] In a sense, we might say, his poetry came to embody all too well Louis Zukofsky's famous goals of sincerity and objectification; each viewed in separation from the other allows Oppen to be claimed by the competing camps, his poetry to be assigned different values. In some ways, then, it is easy to see Oppen's work as valuable or "important," yet the more evident Oppen's value seems, the harder it becomes to circumscribe it. Complicating matters further is the fact that Oppen is perhaps as famous for what he didn't write as for what he did—Glück, too, singles out his "voluntary silence" (29). Unlike Laura Riding, who eventually repudiated poetry as an instrument for the recording of truth, Oppen published his first book in 1934, at the age of twenty-six, to great acclaim—a foreword by Pound, a review by Williams, Oppen now a member of the new "objectivist" group and, with Zukofsky, small-scale publisher of their work—and then, "[i]n brief, it took twenty-five years to write the next poem" (in Hugh Kenner's words, cited by Oppen himself as "perhaps . . . the correct explanation" [SL 181]). During these years, Oppen worked as a community organizer and a carpenter, fought in the Second World War, and lived in exile in Mexico after being repeatedly harassed by the FBI for his communist associations and leanings. He was not certain about his decision to stop writing, but never wavered about—in fact was proud of—his choice not to write obviously political or communist poetry (SL 22; SPDP 35–37). Oppen's newfound critical appeal has something to do, I think, with the critic's own suspicion/defensiveness about poetry not "doing" anything in the world. Taking the life together with the poetry—as Glück implicitly does when "she continually inflects her judgment of his poetry with evaluations of his character," as Dobbelmann puts it[6] and as many of the quotations I have used above suggest—gives us permission to hold up Oppen as model citizen and model poet: someone who both accords poetry the highest place, wagering that only through poetry can we figure out "[w]hat do we believe / [t]o live with," and who also walked the walk; someone who writes about community and about poverty, but also worked as a community organizer in Brooklyn in the mid-thirties; someone who insists on poetry's separateness from other aspects of life but who cannot be accused of inhabiting an ivory tower; someone who is a veritable maker of houses linguistic and literal; someone who admits, "There's perhaps something peculiarly undemocratic about art, tho the fact bothers me very much" (NCP 52; SL 21).[7] Oppen's poems, then, may appear to present a set of formal and aesthetic values or to "speak a moral language" that reflects the poet's own moral character ("none of the self-righteousness"), both or either of which may be congenial to the reader's own. But since the "right" things that poems are thought to say or do change with their readers, and with time, this kind of assessment is, I think, not enough for their value to rest on beyond this, our, period of Oppen's "canonization."

Glück's most important insight into Oppen's work, though, is that "what would be, in another poet, solemn conclusion becomes in Oppen a development" (30). Oppen's thinking about poetry, its powers and its value, is part of a larger project of fundamental questioning that focuses less on a final and completed "restoration" of language to health or even clarity than on a process of investigation, or "testing." The project echoes that of Martin Heidegger, whom Oppen admired deeply.[8] Though he came to know the German philosopher's work best later on, coincidences in their thinking— that astounded Oppen himself and caused him to worry in the 1960s about whether his own lines, the very "climax of the poem" he was writing, were accidentally plagiarizing Heidegger—date to the late 1920s (SL 136). Heidegger's fundamental insight in Being and Time is that what distinguishes us as human beings (Dasein) is that our being is always an issue for us, even if we forget.[9] Reminding us of that—often in the form of his famous question, "Why are there beings at all instead of nothing?"[10]—is at the center of Heidegger's work. We might modify that slightly and say that Being in general and the being of specific beings and of words are always at issue, always in a state of perpetual clarification in Oppen's poetry. And that deep skepticism, coupled with wonder, that constant deconstruction of meaning, coupled with its construction, that sense of constant development which privileges neither the poet nor the poem qua finished product, lie at the heart of Oppen's work and are its most lasting value—not only for poets or readers of poetry but also for us as literary critics. Against the possible criteria one could use to evaluate poetry—place in literary history, range of concerns, attention to detail of world or word, formal coherence or innovation, contemporaneity, sublimity or timelessness, all of which Oppen could be shown to successfully fulfill (as my list of his virtues above suggests and as could be inferred from my analysis below)—Oppen's poetry urges us to take a step back and talk first about what and how a poem is.

I see Oppen as a hinge figure between modernism and what followed: not willing to give up ambition for/of poetry or belief in the ability of language— and of poetic language par excellence—first to illuminate, then to ground or reshape the social (think of Pound's Confucian motto that "the proper man's words must cohere to things, correspond to them [exactly] and no more fuss about it"), but always attuned to his own self-implication in that process, determined not to be deceived by his own belief, or desire to believe.[11] He is profoundly skeptical of rhetoric—of "'making a poem'" (*SL* 123; *SPDP* 124)—and of poetic emotional outpourings, but at the same time critical of modernism in its "perversion" of what he considers the task of poetry, as poets like Pound or Eliot ventured "bad" lines because of their previously held beliefs. This critique is perfectly encapsulated in his account of Eliot's "Burnt Norton" in a 1959 letter to his sister. Oppen cites the chiseled, intensely visual (imagistic, we might say) octosyllabic poem that opens the second section of "Burnt Norton" and immediately admits: "I know positively that I've not written anything that good" (*SL* 21). He omits the poem's last line—"But reconciled among the stars"—yet returns to it later in the letter, instructing his sister to "[r]ead that passage—it's interesting. Dazzlingly beautiful, and startling how hopeless the 'but' is—" (*SL* 21). It is that "but" and the line it introduces that separate Oppen from Eliot, at least in his mind: Oppen reads that statement of reconciliation as Eliot's "attempt to force these damn things into his poetry in order to do his duty" (*SL* 22). That is, at this moment Eliot is not "writ[ing] [his] perceptions" but "argu[ing] [his] beliefs," trying to convince himself of the salvation Christianity promises by putting it in his poem (*SL* 22). But, the poetic line is the test of truth: "A false statement makes bad verse," says Oppen, and so much so that "[e]ven an Eliot can't smooth it" (*SL* 21). "It's this," he continues, "which makes possible some kind of rational criticism, which saves one from pure whim, pure 'taste'" (*SL* 21). Poetic language itself resists a speaker's desire to say. The comments are less revealing for Eliot—for whom that moment is less of a conclusion than Oppen makes it and perhaps for that reason infelicitously expressed—than they are for Oppen himself, in whose work tensions are precisely perceived and analyzed, but never reconciled. For Oppen, poetic value is inextricably bound to the question and never-ending pursuit of what might be called "truth" in the Heideggerian sense, which emphasizes process rather that result: the truth of Being and beings and of what may allow us to know, to really see them, language. As he notes in his "Daybook," "[s]urely language has not created the real, but has made it visible" (*SPDP* 147).

Language is the medium of the questioning, but by no means a certain or unquestionable system itself. Speaking of his "peculiar faith in small words,"

Oppen acknowledges "feeling that they are in immediate touch with reality, with unthought and directly perceived reality" (*SL* 62), but catches himself before he turns into another Eliot and replaces one kind of theology for another:

> To say "there is a tree" seems the very model of direct, down-to-earth statement. But, except for the number of letters in the words and the age of the words, it is precisely the same kind of statement as it is to say "it is a monocotyledonous plant." Even those simplest or at least commonest words—"tree" or "table" or "chair"—so often appealed to as an escape from philosophic muddying-of-the-waters are classificatory words, are in fact "taxonomy." (*SL* 62)

The seriousness and meticulousness with which Oppen treats every element of his poems' texture is why his poems *succeed* in speaking abstractly, in making powerful philosophical or ethical generalizations that are felt to be true rather than vacuous or forced (like Eliot's reconciliation in Oppen's reading).

From *Discrete Series* (1934) to *Of Being Numerous* (1968), from *The Materials* (1962) to *This in Which* (1965) they form and appear, from the *Myth of the Blaze* (1975) to its *Primitive* (1978) elements, and from *Seascape* to *Needle's Eye* (1972), Oppen's poetry is poised between the singular and the plural and probes these intently and exhaustively, adding to Heidegger's investigation of beings and Being, a deeper examination of "being-with," similar in spirit to that undertaken in philosophy by Emmanuel Levinas or Jean-Luc Nancy. Yet, what makes those ethical or philosophical claims compelling rather than facile is the "smallness" of the poems themselves: the extreme consideration and care with which even the simplest words are chosen and arrayed, and at the same time their restlessness, the ways in which they are pushing against and beyond the boundaries and meanings set for them. Oppen's pursuit of essence and truth is accompanied by an equally strong commitment to particularity, clarity, and immediate revelation (what is there right now); this is perfectly embodied in his fascination with small words like "the" and "a," which counterbalances his exploration of big words like "humanity," or in the syntactic isolation of words in his bare lines (readable, especially in the later work, more as word constellations than as sentences), which is in tension with his insistence on the importance of the whole poem's structure. It is such details of grammar, syntax, diction, and sound—the "concrete materials of the poem"—that Oppen's poems deploy to ground and question, to "substantiate" (*SPDP* 32) attractive propositions, and to forge a compelling link between the personal and universal.

I opened this chapter by quoting both Glück and Oppen on the difficulty, if not the irrelevance, of praise: for Glück, praise is beyond language, while for Oppen, binary evaluation (the vorticists' "blast" or "bless") is inadequate, or at the very best, a second-order process. I also suggested that it is hard to establish criteria to evaluate Oppen's poetry that aren't also in some ways his own. But perhaps this is exactly its primary virtue: because Oppen's poetry is one of evaluation, it can be a model for the work that we do. If so, it would tell us to try to begin at a point where no evaluation has been made, other than the acknowledgment of facticity ("the thing in which we are[,] . . . it is here, we must first talk about it"), and to the extent that a clean slate is impossible, to start at a point of minimal assessment and build up by breaking down, examining and evaluating all the parts that are there as we proceed. The judgment we would reach would hinge on Oppen's peculiar conception of truth (both strict and nonprescriptive), and would be at once about the poet—did she "record the experience of thinking it," whatever "it" is, whatever she thought was worth thinking about and in whatever form she thought it, or is she "'making poetry'" or expounding her beliefs—and about ourselves: a record of our own experience of thinking (with) "it" by having created it anew through our reading, and of our believing it (or not) enough to "live with." Such a critical record would be as firmly and sincerely *made* as the poet's own record of an idea, a form, a world in each poem, but also equally provisionally, with our impulses to canonize or decanonize, sympathize or revile tempered by our minute scrutiny and by the resulting "shar[ing] [of] the century" (as Oppen puts it; see below) with the poet we are reading.

II

The first line of Oppen's untitled first poem in his first book *Discrete Series* anticipates his later work, announcing at once his epistemological and ethical concerns in his characteristic syntax.

The knowledge not of sorrow, you were
   saying, but of boredom
Is—aside from reading speaking
   smoking—
Of what, Maude Blessingbourne it was,
   wished to know when, having risen,
"approached the window as if to see
   what really was going on";
And saw rain falling, in the distance
   more slowly,
The road clear from her past the window-
   glass—
Of the world, weather-swept, with which
   one shares the century. (*NCP* 5)

Oppen's poem of fourteen lines (a sonnet?) begins midconversation; here as elsewhere what seem to be his greatest insights are attributed to another, often an unnamed "you." The ostensible quotation is, moreover, an interpretation of yet another quotation, to be given later in the poem. The poem thus takes place in a specific moment between its speaker and addressee, albeit one that is intercut with a fictional moment from Henry James's short story "The Story in It." It is filled with the mundane—the small activities (reading, speaking, smoking), emotions (boredom, sorrow), surroundings (window, glass, road, rain)—yet its repeated qualifiers and subclauses (a nod to Jamesian syntax perhaps?), its slightly too general words (knowledge, world, century), urge us to read it "as if to see / what really [is] going on."

    An attempt at reconstructing the syntax of what seems to be the poem's main "x is y" statement, using the lines' "Of's" as syntactic markers and discounting the many asides and elisions, yields the following: The knowledge of boredom is the knowledge of what Maude Blessingbourne wished to know, and that is the knowledge "of the world" as specified in the poem's last two lines. The four lines following the quotation describe what Maude "saw"; whether that is the knowledge she sought or not—that is, whether those lines are "what really was going on" or simply what she saw out the window—is, despite the rhetoric of clarity, not clear.

Even if we grant that this is the (syntactic) outline of the poem, questions immediately arise. Is the "of" that anchors the poem subjective or objective? Is this poem about the knowledge that pertains to boredom, that a personified boredom has and perhaps gives us, or about that which we have of it? Second: If the poem means to make a groundbreaking but simple philosophical statement, if it means to say that boredom discloses "what-is," as Heidegger might put it, that knowing boredom means knowing the world more authentically, why does the poem take so long to get there? Why does it go through Henry James? Do the poem's detours inflect the relationships it is building between knowledge, world, nature, time or being, seeing, saying— or define the knowledge it pursues? How do we move from the knowledge of boredom, whatever that is, to that of the world?

Through the poem itself. How to get from a personal vision or experience to a global or universal one is not just the poem's overall question, but what its discrete parts enact. The nesting of speakers/characters facilitates the movement toward an increasing order of generality: we move from "you" to "[Maude Blessingbourne] it" to "one." The quoted speaker's knowledge is subordinated or related to that of a fictional character, Maude Blessingbourne, and then to a more distant/general one in the last lines. The verbs attached to the persons are noteworthy also: we move from "you were [saying]" to "Maude it was" to "one" that *is* not, but "shares," entangled with world and century. As by the end of the poem even Maude has merged into the anonymous "one," so what she sees—whether or not it is "what really was going on"—is presented at an increasing order of generality: "rain," "road," and "the world."

Throughout, the syntax manipulates perspective so that the poem's structure—its meanderings, its retroactive filling in of gaps with "you were saying" or "Maude Blessingbourne it was" or "in the distance / more slowly"—imitates that coming to awareness it speaks of. The phrase "reading speaking / smoking" with its absence of punctuation suggests the unity of the three activities, or perhaps the blurring of the first two into the last, and thus reflects the knowledge or experience of boredom, where activities we consider distinct lose their boundaries, their use-value or purpose having been stripped away. Similarly, the poem's initial gesture toward a philosophical statement about what the knowledge of boredom "Is" necessitates a plunge into the past ("it was"), and, more specifically, into a memory coded as a literary one. Thus the language of philosophy is subordinated to artistic language and the pursuit of identity or essence ("Is," "it was") to ever-escaping activity ("was *going*," "falling," "weather-swept"). Being is subordinated to saying already in the first-to-second line transition (the apparently emphatic line-ending "you were" undercut by the "saying" that turns out to complete the verbal phrase), a detail probably—and I think appropriately—unnoticed in the moment of first reading but which, like boredom itself, gains in significance as the poem progresses.

For a poem whose focus appears to be revelation or clarity of vision, what is seen and its import are particularly unclear. For one, Maude seems to see "what-is" in the sense not only of fullness of space around her, but also of time: the distant past, the present, the future, outlined in each of the second half's "couplets." She sees not simply the rain falling, but its speed. Why would rain fall more slowly in the distance? Perhaps—and this is the most tenuous of my temporal readings, buoyed by the following two—because spatial distance is fused here with temporal distance. The more she looks, the further she looks, the deeper she looks, she experiences the slowing down of time as if she were outside it; the past, we might say, is never felt as the present is, but distorted, slowed down by our examination of it. The poem's last two lines sweep Maude up into the "century"—at the time of her first appearance in Henry James's story as Maud (1903) and even of Oppen's writing (1929) still quite young and hence, I think, holding a sense of futurity (especially if we contrast the "shares" here with the earlier "saw" and "past").

The couplet between what I've called the past and the future is the hardest to parse in the poem: "The road clear from her past the window- / glass." In what sense is the road clear? (And that's of course a question that gets to the heart of the poem and Oppen's poetics of clarity.) In characteristic fashion, these lines put to work small, usually hardly noticed words. If "from her" were missing, the first line would be elliptical but fairly straightforward. If "from" were replaced by "for," the meaning would again be evident: the road is clear for her to see at last; she is now able to see outside, past the window-glass. As the line stands, though, we might read it as expressing distance: the (metaphorical) road from her, from where she stands, to a place past—that is, further than—the window-glass, is finally clear. This prepositional phrase and the lack of punctuation allow additional readings, too, one giving us psychological insight into Maude and the other leaving Maude behind:

Maude could be authentically seeing "what really was going on" in the present moment because she is finally "clear from *her past*," has finally shed her past (her self perhaps, the world of her everyday preoccupations of "reading speaking / smoking"). Or, we/the speaker are now seeing the road past the window-glass as "clear from *her*," free of her, emptied of her specific preoccupations—in this reading, the couplet would provide the transition out of Maude's world to that of the "one" that follows in the next couplet. Most importantly, what our vision focuses on here is, in the end, not "the road clear from her past the window," but the "glass" that interposes between inside and out and is noticed only later (as enacted by the poem through the line break), limiting or at least presenting an obstacle to expansive vision. "From her"—the phrase expressing relation to a person/subjectivity—turns both "past" (time seen also as traversed space) and objects (window-glass) into obstacles to comprehension or clarity, but also allows for the transition to a kind of communal vision. This simple but seemingly out-of-place prepositional phrase thus sums up the poem and underscores its definition of human consciousness as that which complicates and has only limited access to what Oppen will later call the "mineral" world but whose clear acknowledgment is the only way toward a sense of universality or communal belonging.

"Glass" is an important term for Oppen's first book and his work in general because it embodies the potential for vision together with its obstruction or distortion (*NCP* 8, 13, 163–64). There is a sense already in this poem that the glass that stops us in our tracks as soon as we think we have looked outside, past the window, is language itself: the unexpected enjambment and the dash isolate the word qua word, while—together with the "of" that follows—also forcing us to return to the beginning of the poem, where these features have previously appeared. Upon this return, we notice that the poem's other single-word line is "smoking." Smoke, like glass, is also something that prevents seeing but often only slightly; it is equally substantial and insubstantial, there and not there. What Maude (and we) may, in the end, be seeing is her relation to a wider spatial, natural, and temporal world, together with her own (linguistic) enclosure, emphasized, too, by the thicket of alliterative *w*'s in the poem's penultimate line that thus sonically clarify the nature of her "window."

Henry James's "The Story in It"—whose title (taken from the end of the story's last questioning sentence) gives rise, I think, to the way Maude is introduced here ("*it* was")—reflects on the relationship between literature and life and debates the appropriate subject for literature: Is there a story in the tumultuous secret love affair between two of its protagonists or in Maud's own willfully unspoken, unrealized, but no less vivid love? Though James is clearly inclined toward the latter, *his* story is actually about neither but about the question itself, about the potential of story-making. Similarly, in Oppen the whole moment of vision (literal and figurative) in the second half of the poem is introduced not just through a quotation (i.e., through the intermediary of a literary text) but also through a quintessentially literary or imaginative act, through an "as if." In choosing to embed his opening poem in the metapoetic questions raised by James and in making Maud(e)'s story his own (not least through the misspelling of her first name that renders her full name more symmetrical and thus, we might say, aesthetically pleasing)—in having his poem "shar[e] the century" with Henry James— Oppen suggests that the poetic is necessary for accessing the historical, the personal for the general. But what makes this suggestion most compelling is that it is tested out and inscribed in the poem's smallest elements: we can hear in the course of the poem the private "*sorrow*" turning "*slowly*" (the *l* substituting for its fellow liquid consonant) into the collective "*shar*[ing]" of the "*century.*"

III

Just as "[The knowledge not of sorrow]" reads as a philosophical meditation, a pondering on history and on literary writing, and a concrete, detailed account of a particular moment (whether Maude's own or its recollection by the "you" and the poem's implicit speaker), *The Materials'* "From a Photograph" (*NCP* 68) showcases Oppen's unique ability to move from the most particular, the most personal and specific—an actual photograph of his young daughter in his arms (reproduced in *NCP* 288)—to the general, and from the utterly material to the biblical or mythical. It is also another poem about the story in "it," that small word which here provides the crucial hinge between the two stanzas and is emphatically highlighted through the enjambment, stanza break, and surprising lack of capitalization.

Her arms around me—child—
Around my head, hugging with her whole arms,
Whole arms as if I were a loved and native rock,
The apple in her hand—her apple and her father, and my nose pressed
Hugely to the collar of her winter coat. There in the photograph

it is the child who is the branch
We fall from, where would be bramble,
Brush, bramble in the young Winter
With its blowing snow she must have thought
Was ours to give to her.

Appropriately perhaps for a poet just now returning to the materials of his poetry, *The Materials* constantly returns to past events and images: "the Thirties" and the war in "Blood from the Stone," Oppen's childhood home in "Birthplace: New Rochelle," his organizing community in New York in "Return." This poem is no exception. "From a Photograph" also ties in to the volume's obsession with materiality—usually presented as minerality—and the human distance from it, with the contrast between human time or history and what Oppen calls in "Blood from the Stone" "Sidereal time" (*NCP* 53); look, for example, at its second assessment of the child's "whole arms" clutching the father "as if I were a loved and native rock." The poems in this volume are at once more intimate and broader in scope than those of *Discrete Series* (compare, for instance, its opening poem "Eclogue" to "[The knowledge not of sorrow]"), as "From a Photograph" exemplifies, and sometimes the lyric or narrative/historical voice appears to overshadow the complexity of their thinking and construction; yet their claims to personal or universal expression are no less minutely "argued" or substantiated than those of the earlier poems.

This becomes clearer if we compare "From a Photograph" to a similar, though even briefer, poem from *Discrete Series*. In the earlier poem, Oppen places the ephemerality of human life against the persistence both of a Civil War cannon and of a photograph:

Civil war photo:
Grass near the lens;

Man in the field
In silk hat. Daylight.
The cannon of that day
In our parks. (*NCP* 21)

The poem offers two ways of commemoration, both of which are paradoxically able to efface the human: the cannon with its unleashed violence, the photograph with its substitution of image for substance. The poem's verblessness reflects that absence of life, with only the typographical blank and the suggestion of earthly or cosmic time ("Daylight") to effect the movement or transition from one image to the next. In that gap, of course, the poem's speaker or arranger (to borrow a word from Joyce criticism) is tellingly felt as he looks away from the photograph and toward the cannon in that already gone (blank) moment of his present.

"From a Photograph" is similarly split between two moments or at least two moods. In contrast to "[Civil war photo]," though, it begins with "her" and "me." The speaker is not a barely sensed, refracted presence, but (almost) at the center of the literal and metaphorical picture, with his characteristics filled in from line to line: from the initial, unspecified "me" to a "head" to a "father" to a "nose." Still, the photograph is literally timeless: the first stanza has no real verbs, only two participles (the active "hugging" for the child, the passive "pressed" for the father, balancing each other) and a conditional that unites (or could) father and child: his perception of her embrace—"as if I were"—echoed in the similarly conditional "she must have thought" in the poem's penultimate line. The second sentence and stanza are different; the speaker's "there" (rather than "here") in the phrase marking the transition suggests that we are now outside the photograph, just as "Daylight" does in "[Civil war photo]." Then, after the stanza break (a blank echoing perhaps that of the earlier poem), the second stanza's unassuming, lowercase, midsentence opening "it is" sets the syntactic tone: four out of its six verbs are variations of "to be" (two present, one past, one conditional); the only other present active verb is "fall."

The first stanza suggests a familiar portrait of parenthood: the protected small child ("winter coat"), clinging to a lovingly looming parent, craving the stability he provides but also feeling some certainty about her position in the world (rocks are loving, a person as firmly possessed as an apple). By introducing time—if only through grammar—the second stanza reverses that image. While the child seems to be holding on to the parent and while he seems to overshadow her at first ("my nose pressed / Hugely"), "it is the child who is the branch / We fall from." That is, we fall from, are nourished and ripened by our children, dependent upon them for our posterity (again, a theme present throughout *The Materials* with its many seed metaphors). At the same time, another pattern begins to be felt in this private, mundane moment: a more sinister and gendered reading suggests itself, aided by the bucolic imagery, the apple in the *daughter's* hands, and the marked (because of the absence of other verbs) use of "fall."

Yet, as in the beginning of "Of Being Numerous" ("Of this was told / A tale of our wickedness. / It is not our wickedness." [*NCP* 163]), Oppen here weighs the religious narrative against other possibilities and decides against it: the poem reverses itself again and unites father and child in the last two lines, creating the true (rather than photographic or narrative) space in which they "share the century." The statements in the second stanza are prefaced, we recall, by "There in the photograph," a phrase which suggests that the stanza offers a more distanced perspective, but still a perspective onto a "static" image. The photograph allows for a double distillation/capturing of belief: of child in parent in the moment of its being taken, but also of parent in child in the moment of its being viewed (a photograph as a token of one's survival, like a child). But the poem tests and transcends both beliefs. A more nuanced temporal reading of the second stanza makes this clearer: the stanza's first line and a half may finally admit time, but its time is a kind of eternal, definitional present (it is, who is, we fall), from which we then metaphorically fall, moving from relative clause to relative clause (as in "[The knowledge not of sorrow]") and into the uncertainties ("would be," "must have") and final passing ("was") of existence. The poem's title confirms such a reading: we fall "from" the idea of the child as branch and from childhood as we fall "from" a photograph with its implication/promises of survival. Outside the photographic frame (literal and metaphorical), there "would be bramble" or "brush" or "bramble" again; the indecisiveness between the two suggests both a fundamental inability to see outside a human framed perspective, as well as natural fluctuation and variety. The "branch" thus sonically disintegrates in the lines that follow. Unlike the child, the father cannot hold on to his asserted fact ("the child who is the branch"), except perhaps through an imaginary act much like hers, even if less explicitly articulated—the appeal to the personified Winter echoing her view of him as a native rock—an act that receives its final formulation in his imaginative attempt to "share the century," in this case, her thoughts with her. The alliteration, combined with the conditional (another version of "as if") and the relative clauses, mark this space outside the image as a linguistic space and, as in "[The knowledge not of sorrow]," this speculative linguistic space becomes the shared space, the space of the first-person plural.

The poem's end thus upsets both notions of (to some extent material or natural) dependence or inheritance already introduced. The second stanza closes by returning to the child's dependence on the parent, as he tries to imagine her thoughts, and, having now articulated its nature more clearly, refutes it with greater finality. The syntax is difficult to parse, but the suggestion is that the daughter expected the parent to be associated with or symbolize any and all greater natural forces (blowing snow, the oddly capitalized and personified "young Winter"), to provide or control, when in fact neither of them can. It is that inability that fundamentally unites parent and child in the poem's final turn, which gives neither one certainty nor the upper hand but instead embeds both (and us too) in an emphatic pastness or ephemerality: their thoughts finally merge in the last line's "Was," the poem's only use of the past tense. The world is not owned but shared: the child will fall into the predicament of the "we" and of the "was," just as "we" fall out of the photograph in the course of this stanza. Winter's capitalized initial, our childlike humanization of the mineral fact, turns into the real fact of "Was," finally and neatly looming hugely over the stanza's opening lowercase "is," pitting against each other not father and daughter or man and woman but the smallness of being against the vastness of nonbeing, of the present against the past.

The artful manipulation of syntax, tense, and visual texture creates this poem's poignancy. Yet its sense of both hope and loss is perhaps best "substantiated" through the poem's rhythm and sounds. The poem begins by rehearsing a kind of English verse childhood (appropriately with a jumbled rather than straightforward chronology): the clear iambic rhythm of the first line (Her árms aroúnd me—chíld—), the dashes perhaps visually representing the two additional beats we may expect to find in an iambic pentameter, gives way to a heavily alliterative and assonant six-beat line with a caesura (which nonetheless begins iambically, as if filling in the first line's meter a second time: Aroúnd my héad, húgging with hér whóle árms). The third line—with its iambic sway and six stresses—rhythmically combines the two preceding ones, and then the rhythm loosens in the longer last two lines though still roughly maintaining both the iambic beat and the allit-eration. The perspective of the child and of the first stanza is underscored by that persistent alliteration of *h* and *a* established from the very begin-ning, contributing to its "framed" nature. The second stanza begins simi-larly to the first, this time with an iambic tetrameter line, whose last beat is now more conspicuously cut off, indeed fallen, through the enjambment: it ís the chíld who ís the bránch / We fáll from (note also that the verbs carry the stresses here, in keeping with our reading above). Rather than build a full image in a repetitive though ultimately additive movement as in the first stanza, here the fewer words (thirty-five compared to fifty) that are alliterated with comparable frequency (tellingly, the daughter's *a*'s replaced by the father's *b*'s, her *h*'s by his *w*'s, as if we've also fallen further down the alphabet) stumble and clot—the branch, for example, slipping away and barely regrasped in alliteration—in a way that reflects this stan-za's destabilizing and "impoverished" perspective. But the first stanza's *h* comes back at the second's end, with "have" in the penultimate line prepar-ing us for the poem's circular closing on its very first word—"her," now lowercased, much like "it is" under the pressure of "Was." The poem also returns to its first line's rhythmic structure: five words, three beats, clear iambs. (In this, it recalls "[Civil war photo]," whose three-word opening was incrementally expanded to four-, four-plus-blank, then five-word lines before shrinking back down to three.) The absence of the dashes, however, suggests that the "child" is no longer isolated or protected: through the poem, she has entered the world of blowing snow, yet in doing so has also shown the father the necessity of her imaginatively constructive act. Her "as if" is not dismissed as childish fancy, but indeed formally imitated as the poet closes metrically and symmetrically, and thus acknowledges, acquiesces to, and emphasizes his own construction of and dependence on the poem's, poetry's "loved and native rock."

"From a Photograph" manages to be simultaneously and throughout about an actual personal photograph ("what has happened to me"), about the primacy of language and of poetry as against image, and about the examina-tion of—as Oppen puts it in another poem from this volume—"[w]hat . . . we believe / To live with" (*NCP* 52). Though it revolves around a moment of greater specificity and intimacy than "[The knowledge not of boredom]," it, too, like the earlier poem, concludes that essentially it is our inability to see clearly and to be permanently that creates a shared (linguistic) space.

IV

Oppen's next book, *This in Which*, is, as its title suggests, the book of the bramble. If the epigraph to *The Materials*—Jacques Maritain's "We awake in the same moment to ourselves and to things" (*NCP* 38)—reflected that volume's preoccupation with examining the distance between human and material, the self and its mineral world, individual history and human history and between both of those and "sidereal" history, this volume's tracing of the Heideggerian "arduous path of appearance" (as its second epigraph has it) involves a more extended examination of "this in which" things and selves usually or first appear for our grasping: language. This, the book's much longer first epigraph (from Robert Heinlein) suggests, is what may allow us to connect the description of "the creation of the world" to the explanation of "the things that have just happened to *us*" and, in Oppen's own account, allowed for the writing of the more ambitious though "simpler" *Of Being Numerous* (*NCP* 92; italics in original).[12] Because *This in Which* focuses on the question of language—the ways in which it shapes our seeing—it is an appropriate culmination for our inquiry, allowing us to examine more closely Maude's linguistic "windows" and the relationship between the "as if" and the "real."

The volume's best-known poem is "Psalm," and I will dwell on it because it most neatly encapsulates the dialectic that I have been pursuing throughout this chapter. The biblical psalm is typically a lyric poem or song expressing not an individual but a community; it is a hymn of a "collective personality," of the "public cult of the people . . . a collective and single voice of praise" directed to the one God.[13] A psalm, then, may be an "appropriate" medium precisely for inquiring into the possibility of community in relation to an "I" (or the lyric poem as expressing an "I") that is necessarily singular. Given, moreover, that the language of a psalm is supposed to be effective, creational language, and the fact that Oppen's poem is also "self-reflective," about its own parts ("small nouns") and context ("in this in which"), some critics have read the poem as expressing a faith in the creational potential of language.[14] For Burton Hatlen, the poem conveys the meeting of mind with the things of the world, a "holy song of praise and celebration."[15] "Psalm," however, is not straightforwardly what its title might indicate because, as Glück suggested, Oppen takes as a starting point—the exclamatory "that they are there!"—what others might have considered a conclusion.

But first I want to examine briefly another poem—equally important for the book's definitions of language—that shares some of its images with "Psalm" (and with much of Oppen's later poetry) and will help illuminate it. "The Occurrences" begins with a statement that could easily be a motto attributed to the putative back-to-basics poet of *The Materials*: "The simplest / Words say the grass blade" (*NCP* 144), aligning simplicity of nature to simplicity/materiality of word/language. But the back-to-basics poet is not George Oppen.[16] Here is the first stanza of the poem in full:

The simplest
Words say the grass blade
Hides the blaze
Of a sun
To throw a shadow
In which the bugs crawl
At the roots of the grass;

In fact, what the simplest words (are said to) say consists not in bright revelation but in shadowing, obscuring—Oppen echoes here the smoke and glass of "[The knowledge not of sorrow]," and will return to these images in later poems (*NCP* 274, 281). As the word-blade (the writer's engraving instrument) rises, *that* is what we see instead of the sun (a sun) that has nurtured and prompted it, the light or heat, truth or passion, that has given rise to the desire for expression or recording—we see the blade and not the blaze of its occasion. Yet in hiding "a sun," in necessarily moving away from it by speaking about it, the "simplest words" are also protective of a different kind of life: one of little buglike beings (or letters?) crawling at, building the very roots of language/speech. Indeed, the poem's third and last stanza makes explicit the necessity of this downward plunge of our attention:

> watch
> At the roots
> Of the grass the creating
> *Now*   that tremendous
> plunge

Instead of leading us upward to the sun toward which the grass theoretically strives, the simplest words focus our attention downward, "At the roots of the grass," at the creating process rather than its result (the grass blade itself) or impulse (the sun)—the active aspect of every now, the linguistic, letteral creating that precedes any discovery of a sun. The imperative "watch," however, is addressed to a specific figure who makes his appearance in the poem's seemingly incongruous middle stanza:

> Father, father
> Of fatherhood
> Who haunts me, shivering
> Man most naked
> Of us all, O father

Who is this figure and why does he belong in this poem? For one, he too is metaphorically plunged/fallen: from the highest (father of fatherhood itself) to "Man most naked / Of us all." This is perhaps an illustration of the movement described in the poem's other stanzas as the speaker—explicitly present only here—turns away from a haunting distant, perhaps divine, notion of fatherhood (that is to say, never approached/grasped though potentially intuited, much like the blaze of a sun above) toward an earthly one that simultaneously also turns the speaker's or poet's haunted loneliness ("me") to a communal experience ("us all"). That is, what the poem enacts is the shift from "a sun" that is indefinite (indefinable?) and privately haunting to "the roots" from which "we all" begin, from an aspired-to purity/transparency/clarity of expression to the messier process through which we try to get there. Oppen liked to refer to the etymology of "occurrence"—a word he frequently used, including again as the title to a different, later poem (*NCP* 212)—as "running against" (*ob* + *currere*). We might think of the simplest words as the occurrences of the title, standing in for the constant and active running of language against both nothingness and the privacy of individual experience. It is that reorientation that has to take place also on the human, subjective/interpersonal level of the second stanza (supplementing the first stanza's "objective," philosophically or poetically declarative tone) for the creating *"Now"* to be seen in the poem's last stanza. This poem is a more self-conscious, linguistically shaded version of the movement we have already seen taking place in "[The knowledge not of sorrow]" and "From a Photograph."

The next encounter of creature, grass root, and simple or small word is in "Psalm," a poem about that creative process and its limitations.

PSALM

Veritas sequitur . . .

In the small beauty of the forest
The wild deer bedding down—
That they are there!

          Their eyes
Effortless, the soft lips
Nuzzle and the alien small teeth
Tear at the grass

          The roots of it
Dangle from their mouths
Scattering earth in the strange woods.
They who are there.

          Their paths
Nibbled thru the fields, the leaves that shade them
Hang in the distances
Of sun

          The small nouns
Crying faith

> In this in which the wild deer
> Startle, and stare out. (*NCP* 99)

"Psalm" appears to be the record of a revelation, disclosing something as though for the first time: "That they are there!" The deer unexpectedly emerge from concealment in all of their Heideggerian facticity ("that")[17] and seem to reveal to the poet and to us the "truth." The image and emotion of "Psalm" seem akin to what Oppen will call in "Of Being Numerous" "the pure joy / Of the mineral fact // Tho it is impenetrable // As the world, if it is matter, / Is impenetrable" (*NCP* 164); Hatlen translates it into the later poem's "sad marvels" of existence.[18] Rachel Blau DuPlessis has argued that Oppen, especially after *Of Being Numerous*, searches for the basic element providing value and finds it the natural world; she suggests that the fact that things of the natural world are undoubtedly there may be Oppen's "major consolation."[19] Using "Psalm" as an example from the earlier poems, she claims that one can ground oneself in the "this in which" that is the world and that, moreover, "Oppen sees no barrier between perception and expression. Seeing deer allows him to say deer."[20] But that is only where the poem begins. It seems to me that Oppen's "Psalm" is not simply a celebration of "nature" or of "language," a moment of respite from his usual interrogatory mode, but a questioning of both these terms, as each threatens to overcome the other. Otherwise, there would be little to differentiate this poem—in Oppen's mind—from Eliot's forced reconciliation of man to the stars in "Burnt Norton."

The language of "Psalm" complicates Oppen's putative poetics of revelation of world/earth even before the poem explicitly does so by referring to "nouns" in the last stanza; at that point, we are forced to reread the whole poem and realize that the "descriptions" we took as truth, the verbs that seemed so "accurate," are our classifications or even projections, our (or Oppen's) "simplest words." But already in the first four stanzas Oppen signals this ending through the positioning of the deer's observer. Though the deer are looked at, they themselves appear to be seeing; in addition to observant "eyes," the poem gives them "beds" and an implicit concern about "shade," and it sees them carving their own "paths." In this way, it gradually turns them into a "who" (rather than a "that") that "is there," and moreover, "stares out." The deer are thus couched in a distinctly human, if not existential, vocabulary, which betrays the presence of the human observer watching and recording them, desperate to find in their worldly at-homeness a model for being. We are still seeing through the glass or the photograph more than peering into "the thing itself"; more importantly, in doing so throughout, "Psalm" undercuts not just the revelatory value of its beginning (with respect to the world), but also that of its end (with respect to language).

This can be read in two ways. On the one hand, the "I" or speaker is there only through this "they" of the deer; the "I" of the poem gives its space, its "there" to the deer and lets in "their" time, their mode of being, as that of the wholly other, the "alien." We are indeed "awaken[ing] in the same moment to ourselves and to things" as the "I" and the deer are both constituted in and by this encounter (*NCP* 38). Or—and this is by no means an exclusive or—we cannot awaken to things because our language blocks us; once we speak, we anthropomorphize. Hence also the subtly sinister tenor of the poem's diction: "wild," "alien teeth," "tear," "dangle," "cry," "startle." All these words suggest intrusion, with its corollary threat of exploitation. "Things" do not speak themselves; as Walter Benjamin wrote in an early essay, "Because she is mute, nature mourns," or, more specifically, "the sadness of nature"—sad because named "not from the one blessed paradisiac language of names, but from the hundred languages of man"—"makes her mute."[21] The deer, then, might be displayed as "matter" unknowable, impenetrable except through our categories and words that necessarily oppose their being and that they in turn resist. The transferred image from "The Occurrences" supports this point: the nuzzling deer eat the poet's grass and dangle its roots, destroying/ consuming the poet's ability to capture them in language as the fullness of "grass" is chewed down into an "it" in the awkward circumlocution that begins the third stanza. This undecidability about the nature of the appearance of things, the access language provides, and the "message" we are supposed to get from their interaction in the poem is reflected in Oppen's choice of epigraph: Aquinas's famous dictum "veritas sequitur esse rerum" here appears chopped off, as if to suggest that the poem is what fills it out. But, as in "[The knowledge not of sorrow]," rather than being (of things), we have saying, and whether truth has followed or will follow it remains unclear.

The fragmented state of the epigraph alerts us to another way in which "Psalm" dramatizes the effort (rather than the success) of speech, the "creating / Now" of "The Occurrences": the poem speaks visually, or silently, through its very pronounced white spaces and line arrangement. Every stanza wins its beginning from the nothing, wresting its words from silence. The phrases that form the indented first line of each stanza all begin with deictic/declarative/definite "th" words: "their eyes," "the roots of it," "their paths," "the small nouns." These phrases form the poem's skeleton and spell out a slightly different story, proposing an alternative narrative route that proceeds, as in "[The knowledge not of sorrow]," from the specific to the general: eyes seeing, trying to get to the roots of it (the origins and causes, the knowledge of what they see, of the matter, of the world), get to the roots—which turn out also to be routes, paths—and, those roots/routes, then, are possibly contained in the "small nouns," which literally designate all three of the preceding phrases and perhaps annul or subsume them in much the same way that the whiteness of the page prevails when the poem ends. Another visual aspect: the persistent doubling of elements, the not immediately audible double letters in the poem's words ("small," "deer," "scattered," "nuzzled," "effortless," etc.). These two aspects of the poem evoke its paradoxical, suspended state, between the nothing, the absence of ground and "world," and the excess of world, its greatness.

This tension between scarcity and plenitude is reflected in the poem's chosen animal. The word "deer" is double, singular and plural, in the singular also embodying the plural. "Deer," moreover, is an Old English word, coming from the still-used German *Tier*, animal; the word was used in the archaic phrase "small deer" to denote any small animal. The deer, then, stand in a paradigmatic, synecdochic relation to the rest of their "peers" in the animal kingdom, just as this poem does to the rest of the volume (since it includes the book's title and its original epigraph, later replaced by Heinlein and Heidegger). In this way as well, they (deer and poem) are one and many, and in this might lie the "success" of this small noun.

Does then truth follow from this appearance—however conceived—of things, as the epigraph gestures toward promising? Do the nouns say something, function as something other than a means to bring the "world" to the possession of humans? That they might is the cry of faith of the "small nouns," Oppen tells L. S. Dembo:

> That the nouns do refer to something; that it's there, that it's true, the whole implication of these nouns; that appearances represent reality,

whether or not they misrepresent it: that this in which the thing takes place, this thing is here, and that these things do take place.[22]

As in the poem, so in this "explanation," though, Oppen is quick to displace "reality" (Aquinas's "esse rerum") into "this in which," and in so doing, to substitute a deictic phrase for a noun. "World," too—though I have been using it—does not appear in the poem. In its stead, we have the slant homonym of "woods" and then the "this in which." The "small nouns," which abound in this poem, are crying faith in something that is explicitly and intentionally *not* a noun, thus simultaneously expressing and rejecting the desire for an ideal language of perfectly representational nouns.

In the poem, the "this in which" is what the deer stare out of. It is introduced through an ambiguous "in," which can be read both literally, as a spatial preposition, and metaphorically. Insofar as the deer are in it, it is the world and perhaps even their world in contradistinction to our world. Yet the small nouns also cry faith "in" it, which would suggest that the "this in which" designates the space of the poem—unless, that is, we read against the syntax prescribed by the stanza break and, attaching the preposition to "faith," think of the nouns as crying *faith in*, trying to *believe in* the "this in which" which would be the world (but could still be the poem). The "this in which" is formulated thus in anticipation of our trying to parse it; it is not "world" or "poem" in order to prevent a simple reading of it as "ground," as the comfort of what-is-there. This deictic replacement of "world" (always a manmade one) or "earth" or "the mineral" (and as such retreating and so unnamable) has no meaning except in utterance, except in the context of an I-You pair; as linguist Émile Benveniste writes, deixis is "contemporary with the instance of discourse that carries the indicator of person."[23] Deictics are "'empty' forms" put forth by language, "which each speaker, in the exercise of discourse, appropriates to himself and which he relates to his 'person,' at the same time defining himself as *I* and a partner as *you*."[24] Being fundamentally relational, then, "this in which" does not have a ground or a cause but encodes, we might say, this poem's absent "you," the addressee necessary for the poem to mean anything at all. The "this in which," this relation is "before" the small nouns, allows the small nouns to be, though it can barely be differentiated from them in the end; it retreats as they appear, claiming belief "in" it.

Indeed, the poem doesn't end on this linguistic note and returns instead to the "wild deer" that "startle, and stare out," shifting its emphasis from "in" to "out." What startles the deer? Or, rather—since the active voice of "startle" is infrequently used to describe an intransitive state of "startling" as "being startled"—whom do they startle? Does the "and" that connects "startle" and "stare" necessitate, because of parallel construction, the reading of "stare out" as transitive, the deer staring somebody out, out-staring even, seeing better, but also intimidating or disconcerting (and does that mean their otherness and strangeness have remained)? Is the invisible I/speaker that has been looking at the deer throughout this poem also invisibly here as the unmentioned object or locus of their staring on which the poem concludes? Or does the comma before "and" allow "stare" to be intransitive in the sense of looking intensely out to something? We might also read "stare out" as an intransitive phrase—and this would turn the deer back into objects—in the sense of something "staring out at us," being "unpleasantly prominent or striking." This short phrase that ends the poem encapsulates, as "from her" did in "[The knowledge not of sorrow]," the power dynamics explored throughout. Moreover, the grammatical multivalence of the phrase ("startle" and "stare out" both transitive and intransitive, the deer both subjects and objects) also beautifully and minutely calls back to the Latin epigraph, for "sequitur" (*sequor*) is a deponent verb, a passive grammatical form used to express an active meaning. Rather than get to the "esse rerum" at the end of the poem, we formally and sonically (hear the *s*, *t*, *r*'s and the *e* and *u* sounds in all three verbs) return right to the beginning, as in "From a Photograph."

If the deer, then, do stare out at us readers, at the poet, and stare us out, what is their demand or accusation? Do they stare out because they cannot be encompassed by the page? Do they startle us still because we finally understand that they fundamentally do not belong to the page or to our language? As the speaker at the very end of the poem reaches outside himself, finally explicitly acknowledging the role of language—as a fluid, socially or communally negotiated process—in enabling his vision, so the deer perhaps attempt to make their final escape. This may be, at least, what the nouns are crying faith in after all: that the deer will manage to stare "out," to interrupt the poem while being "in" it. As Oppen puts it, "one is left with the deer, staring out of the thing, at the thing, not knowing what will come next";[25] "not knowing" is "truth that follows," a truth that always follows any potential articulation of "the truth." Neither world nor poem are made, finished things even when so vividly presented or exquisitely crafted, but, this poem suggests, hope to be this in which or from which something else might erupt, break (as did the Aquinas quotation in the epigraph), and break out.

V

Peter Nicholls says of Oppen's poems that they are "caught between the large, catastrophic forces of 'history' . . . and the minute temporality of the 'commonplace' and 'everyday.'"[26] As Oppen tells L. S. Dembo apropos of two of his longest and most famous poems:

> "Route" is very closely connected to "Of Being Numerous," the learning that one is, after all, just oneself and in the end is rooted in the singular, whatever one's absolutely necessary connections with human history are. . . . That's right, but I'm also writing about the human condition. All I actually know is what happened to me and I'm telling it. . . . I've written about what happened and the place it happened, and that, I suppose, is the only philosophy I could possibly understand.[27]

Writing "out of one's own experience, out of one's own emotion, out of what one knows," as Oppen puts it elsewhere,[28] means of course "starting from" the singular and accounts for the poems' sense of lyrical intimacy. At the same time, it also suggests the movement of this writing, from oneself, out(side) of oneself, toward something that is not oneself, toward the "other" or "humanity," whose possibility Oppen incessantly investigates and attempts to map out first and foremost by testing his language, the connections that (in theory) shared language can forge or foreclose. His poems, as we have seen, are on the one hand as tightly woven as can be, their thought "substantiated," expressed in their smallest elements in such a way that makes even the most abstract phrase seem felt and earned, illuminating, and "true." And on the other hand, they are restless, developing (to use Glück's word) beyond their artfully crafted confines and their apparent content, showing that the simplest may not be simple and that the small or obvious may in fact be hardest to see or understand; this quality of "staring out" becomes ever more apparent in Oppen's work of the 1970s.

I have focused here on some of Oppen's earlier and shorter poems rather than on his great longer sequences because they provide a model and framework for appreciating the workings of those longer poems—they "begin to show the pattern of what [he has] to add" as a poet (*SL* 21). The value of Oppen's poetry lies in his way of merging and mediating between the particular and the universal, the specific and the abstract, the temporal/existential ("what happened to me") and the essential ("philosophy"), the personal and the anonymous, the timely and the always relevant, *without* resolving the tension, without one side overshadowing the other or being only the means through which the other is expressed. Thus, we might say, as Oppen did of his friend Charles Reznikoff, that he too "wrote / in the great world // small for this is a way // to enter / the light" of "kitchen // tables" and "mountains" alike (*NCP* 306). May we as critics do the same.

Notes

1. Louise Glück, "On George Oppen," in *Proofs and Theories: Essays on Poetry* (Hopewell, NJ: Ecco Press, 1994), 29; subsequent citations are in-text.
2. George Oppen, *Selected Prose, Daybooks, and Papers*, ed. Stephen Cope (Berkeley: University of California Press, 2007), 137; henceforth abbreviated as *SPDP* and cited in-text. The following abbreviations are also used throughout: *NCP* for George Oppen, *New Collected Poems*, ed. Michael Davidson (New York: New Directions, 2002); and *SL* for George Oppen, *Selected Letters*, ed. Rachel Blau DuPlessis (Durham, NC: Duke University Press, 1990).
3. See L. S. Dembo, "George Oppen," interview, *Contemporary Literature* 10, no. 2 (Spring 1969): 165–66, 172–74. For Pound, see Ezra Pound, *Literary Essays of Ezra Pound*, ed. T. S. Eliot (New York: New Directions, 1968), 22, 24, 42–48.
4. Marjorie Perloff, "The Shipwreck of the Singular: George Oppen's 'Of Being Numerous,'" *Ironwood* 13, no. 2 (Fall 1985): 193–204; recently revised at http://marjorieperloff.blog/essays/oppen-numerous/.
5. Duncan Dobbelmann, "'A Ferocious Mumbling, in Public': How George Oppen Came to Be Canonized," *Paideuma* 40 (2013): 191–209. Richard Swigg's *George Oppen: The Words in Action* (Lewisburg, PA: Bucknell University Press, 2016) begins with a similar assessment.
6. Dobbelmann, "A Ferocious Mumbling," 202.
7. For Oppen's own reflections on his life, see Dembo, "George Oppen," 159–61,

175–76; see also Mary Oppen, *Meaning a Life: An Autobiography* (Santa Barbara, CA: Black Sparrow Press, 1978), esp. 151–63, 185–202.

8. See Dembo, "George Oppen," 169; *SL* 134–37, 156–57; *SPDP* 137, 146–47; and Peter Nicholls, "Oppen's Heidegger," in *Thinking Poetics: Essays on George Oppen*, ed. Steve Shoemaker (Tuscaloosa: University of Alabama Press, 2009), 91–119.

9. Martin Heidegger, *Being and Time*, trans. John Macquarrie and Edward Robinson (New York: Harper and Row, 1962), 32.

10. Heidegger, *Introduction to Metaphysics*, trans. Gregory Fried and Richard Polt (New Haven, CT: Yale University Press, 2000), 1.

11. Ezra Pound, *Poems and Translations*, ed. Richard Sieburth (New York: Library of America, 2003), 712.

12. See also George Oppen, "An Adequate Vision: A George Oppen Daybook," ed. Michael Davidson, *Ironwood* 26 (1985): 17.

13. John Martone, "The Psalmic Poetics of George Oppen," *Poesis* 6, no. 1 (1984): 47.

14. E.g., John Martone, ibid.

15. Burton Hatlen, "Between Modernism and Postmodernism: Truth and Indeterminacy in the Poetry of George Oppen," in *The Idea and the Thing in Modernist American Poetry*, ed. Cristina Giorcelli (Palermo, Italy: Editrice Ila Palma, 2001), 59.

16. Compare with the certainties of Pound's Canto 83 ("When the mind swings by a grass-blade . . ."), a passage that Oppen may well be rewriting here; Ezra Pound, *The Cantos* (1970; New York: New Directions, 1996), 553.

17. Heidegger, *Being and Time*, 173.

18. Burton Hatlen, "Opening Up the Text: George Oppen's 'Of Being Numerous,'" *Ironwood* 13 (1985): 271.

19. Rachel Blau DuPlessis, "George Oppen: 'What Do We Believe to Live With?,'" *Ironwood* 5 (1975): 73.

20. DuPlessis, "George Oppen," 75.

21. Walter Benjamin, "On Language as Such and on the Language of Man," in *Reflections: Essays, Aphorisms, Autobiographical Writings*, by Walter Benjamin, ed. Peter Demetz, trans. Edmund Jephcott (New York: Schocken Books, 1989), 329–30.

22. Dembo, "George Oppen," 163.

23. Émile Benveniste, *Problems in General Linguistics*, trans. Mary Elizabeth Meek (Coral Gables, FL: University of Miami Press, 1971), 219.

24. Ibid., 227.

25. Dembo, "George Oppen," 163.

26. Peter Nicholls, "Of Being Ethical: Reflections on George Oppen," in *The Objectivist Nexus: Essays in Cultural Poetics*, ed. Rachel Blau DuPlessis and Peter Quartermain (Tuscaloosa: University of Alabama Press, 1999), 250.

27. Dembo, "George Oppen," 172.

28. Reinhold Schiffer, "Interview with George Oppen," *Sagetrieb* 3, no. 2 (Winter 1984): 10.

CHAPTER 8

On Harryette Mullen

SCARLETT HIGGINS

HARRYETTE MULLEN IS a boundary breaker who has brought together the techniques of experimental writing and the concerns of feminists. And yet this is not the primary reason that I would advocate for her inclusion in any account of the significant US poets of the second half of the twentieth century. Instead, the reason for my advocacy is that her poetry is fun to read. Much poetry may be pleasurable to read in its sensual treatment of language, or satisfying in its provocation or affirmation of readerly insights; although these things may be true of Mullen's writing, this is not what I mean. Rather, her poetry is fun in a way that reminds me of the fun of reading nursery rhymes, or other types of songs and chants often aimed at children; a similar fun may be found in hip-hop lyrics. These patterned forms use language to engage the body and brain as they both beg to be voiced rather than apprehended on the page.

Another aspect of the fun of Mullen's poetry is its frequent recourse to humor. This is not the humor of Frank O'Hara, not that of Billy Collins, nor of Charles Bernstein. Mullen's humor is sometimes a silly, almost childlike humor related to language play (as above); other times it is an ironic humor that finds in the swerves and twists of language usage a layered—and not always entirely pleasant—social history. I appreciate the fun and funny aspect of Mullen's poetry as both a reader of poetry and as a teacher of it. As a teacher, I have found these qualities of Mullen's work to be a better counter to common student reluctances toward reading poetry—"it's boring" or "I don't understand it/can't relate to it"—than any other writers I have yet encountered.

Yet it is difficult to evaluate Mullen's poetry because she writes book-length texts more than discrete poems.[1] Moreover, her variations of style make it impossible to speak of a coherent "voice." What is constant is curiosity: she goes for that which seems not to fit. Her poetry maps out a subject matter overlooked by other poets: the objects and habits commonly associated with female appearance. While conventions for engaging women's experiences are well settled, the strangeness with which she approaches female appearance in particular makes her poems remarkable. *Trimmings* (1991) is an acute analysis by someone estranged from any recognizable cultural context: an outsider peering in. *Muse & Drudge* (1995) expresses several consciousnesses; her speakers come at clothing and cosmetics with love and hate, too. Her affective model could be Pope's *The Rape of the Lock*.

Mullen the experimentalist actually draws on ancient traditions of poetry. She writes playfully, with puzzle devices and game rules. They render some poems obscure, though it is an obscurity unlike that of modernist poetry. Some texts are riddles that can be solved—"What walks on four legs in the morning, two in the afternoon, and three in the evening?"—and others, unanswerable ones—"Why is a raven like a writing desk?" Her language experiments are driven most by melopoetic wordplay. Her poetry absorbs much that is pleasurable and playful in habits of speech in English even while not consistently imitating speech on the page. Her language is deep and wide in reference and association. Single terms have multiple references even while serving as roots of a branching series of associations leading readers to some apparently remote lexical field. Some poems abandon sense almost entirely in favor of rhyming and chiming sounds. Others avoid their most central, structuring term: readers must decipher both the poem's subject and the poet's intention. No question, she goes very far with melopoeia and wordplay. This is why one speaks of her as experimental.

There is tension in her work between experiment and experience. Experiments are open-ended. What are often called experiences are units of recognizable sense. Mullen learned from Black Arts Movement writers and from feminists that identity has predictable effects, apparent in everyday experience, such as applying for a job or getting pulled over for a speeding ticket, as well as in large-scale, statistics-driven analytics, such as poverty and incarceration rates. But from Language poetry, she learned that these identity-effects are generated by language. Her poetry is didactic concerning identity, yet open-ended concerning language. My appreciation derives from this crossing of language experimentation and political engagement. Two ways of thinking, usually distinct, are constantly collaborating on her pages.

There is no narrative of progress in her work, only remarkable shifts, more or less drastic, among nodes of formal and thematic concern, including stereotypical female appearance and experimental melopoetic wordplay, language games, and personal anecdotes. In her brief essay "Imagining the Unimagined Reader," she speaks of her work's variety of form, style, and theme: "One reason I have avoided a singular style or voice for my poetry is the possibility of including a diverse audience of readers attracted to different poems and different aspects of the work. I try to leave room for unknown readers I can only imagine."[2] These "unknown readers" have become a group. Even as she has made drastic shifts in style and theme, she has rarely left behind anything significant, or any of her following.

"Resistance Is Fertile," from *Sleeping with the Dictionary* (2001), tropes on the signature tag line ("Resistance is futile") of the Borg, the *Star Trek* universe's overarching villainous race of colonizing super-aliens from the 1990s and early 2000s. The Borg believe that incorporation into their collective is the highest form of being; "other" races are not just colonized but assimilated fully so that survivors lose all former distinctiveness and become Borg. The accrued scientific and technological learning and genetic advantages of this group become part of the Borg collective; cultural markers of difference are not retained. Humanity struggles against these aliens for individuality and freedom; this fight plays out in ideological terms nearly identical to those of the original 1960s-era *Star Trek* series in regard to the Cold War, though with updated technology. Other significant sources for this poem include Georges Perec's novel *La Disparition*, or *A Void* in its English translation—conspicuously referenced by the word "avowal" in the line "Libertarian runs on avowal movement platform," as A. (Anton) Vowl is the name of *A Void*'s protagonist—and Gertrude Stein's poem from *Tender Buttons*, "A Brown": "A brown which is not liquid not more so is relaxed and yet there is a change, a news is pressing." Both *A Void* and *Tender Buttons*, like this strain of Mullen's poetry, work through a process of disavowal in language, a type of periphrasis whereby the most significant term of a text is withheld.

The disavowed term in "Resistance Is Fertile" becomes clear partway through Mullen's prose poem, which uses not only *Star Trek* terminology but, in a chained fashion (such that nearly every sentence repeats or reuses an element from the previous sentence and introduces a new element), reimagines phrases, images, and tropes from fields as diverse as politics, advertising, medicine and health care, cooking, data analysis, technology, and the mythology surrounding the fictional vigilante (the) Batman. These fields have something in common: each, in everyday language use, involves the digestion, incorporation, processing, or exclusion of waste material. For example, "We call you irresponsible, say you're indigestible, and it's undeniably true it's tough to swallow you. Your data resisted analysis, but if you are not consumed, your flawed construction only proves that we are perfection cubed." (Most Borg spaceships are cubes.) The poem's exclusion of its central term becomes more pointed as it reaches its conclusion: "Pundits pooh-pooh as law and order candidate Bruce Wayne leaves his potty to go on a turd-potty ticket: Libertarian runs on avowal movement platform. Our constipation requires frequent amendments to free up the tree of liberty." This poem is fun to read, and feels silly in its childlike humor. The lines rely for both humor and sense on strategic mispronunciation or mishearing. Potty sounds like party, turd like third, a bowel like avowal, and constipation like constitution. The humor of these references follows Stein's play on "anus" in "a news is pressing." The "potty talk," the playfulness, and the language failures here are reminiscent of how children use language—and how children of all ages are surprised and delighted to discover that "serious" poems can do this.

Despite its childlike jokes, the poem builds to a serious conclusion, brought to the surface by the lines that relate Bruce Wayne/Batman's vigilantism to politics. The question becomes: if resistance is in fact fertile (not futile), what does this fertility produce? The resistance to assimilation, whether by the Borg, the digestive process, computer data analysis, or political force, becomes a cleansing, corrective necessity. It allows the built-up detritus characteristic of any large system to be flushed, which, in the long run, creates stronger, healthier systems that can withstand difficulties: "[R]esistance challenges the ant farm to adapt. . . . You are the virus that keeps it in tune." Excrement—whether the literal waste product or as a figure for something else that's deemed unnecessary or unwanted—is defined by its exclusion, and yet is an essential part of any healthy, well-functioning system, whether organic or virtual.

Trimmings contains the first group of Mullen's work to be explicitly inspired by the writings of Stein. Mullen has said that she found "a complexity of meaning . . . in the utter simplicity of [Stein's] syntax," and that she wanted to write both with and back to Stein.[3] Equally, she credits the influence of the Language writers, particularly Ron Silliman's *The New Sentence*, on this second phase of her poetics.[4] These lines from *Trimmings* are crisp and pleasurable to speak or hear:

> Clip, screw, or pierce. Take your pick. Friend or doctor,
> needle or gun. A dab of alcohol pats that little hurt hole.
> Hardly a dimple is soon forgotten brief sting. Stud, precious
> metal. Pure, possessive ring. Antibody testifying with im-
> munity to gold, rare thing. So malleable and lovable, wear-
> ing such wounds, such ornaments.

Much like Stein's portraits of the interior objects of women's domestic spaces, this poem on ear piercing estranges something "normal" via language. Mullen uses a minimalist list to enumerate terms for ear piercing with little contextual elaboration, and particularly without naming the act itself. The first phrase, "Clip, screw, or pierce" describes earrings, typically attached via either a spring mechanism that clamps down, a movable metal piece that makes the opening larger or smaller, or a slender post with detachable backing. Detached from nouns, these prosaic terms—used to describe earrings in advertisements, jewelry packaging, or casual conversation—read explicitly as violent and/or sexual, clarifying one type of violently sexualized language that is often used in casual conversation. All typically used as adjectives, they read here as verbs, part of what gives these lines their intensity. The two brief lists that follow, "Friend or doctor, / needle or gun," again describe the two most common ways of having one's ears pierced. It can be done at home, by a friend, or in a doctor's office; either a needle or a piercing gun can make the hole. Out of context, the terms sound medicalized or violent, though this procedure is ideally neither.

The ending lines of this prose poem—"So malleable and lovable, wear- / ing such wounds, such ornaments"—make up a sentence missing a subject. Its implied subject, a woman with pierced ears, whether an "I," a "you," or a "she," is both "malleable" and "lovable," the implication being that she is lovable because malleable, and because she is willing to be wounded and ornamented, wounded in order to be ornamented. This poem leaves open the subject of address, so that it could be any of the three. Ear piercing becomes a minor wounding that any woman might share, a "little hurt hole. / Hardly a dimple . . . soon forgotten brief sting." But this poetic technique, decontextualizing the language of ear piercing into minimalist lists, allows it to stand in for the panoply of ritualistic woundings to which women may submit in pursuit of beauty and/or love. The unnamed speaker-subject of this poem (and of all those in *Trimmings* and *S*PeRM**K*T* [1992]) speaks as a detached observer, which gives the poems surprising power.

Mullen's effort to reinvigorate Stein's investigatory practices enabled this detached observation. However, this intense but elegant investigation into the possibilities of both written and spoken English is evident through-out Mullen's oeuvre, as is her attention to the objects and rituals of stereo-typical femininity. One of the most discussed sections of *Trimmings* is that in which she explicitly "writes back" to Stein's poem, "A Petticoat," from *Tender Buttons*:

A light white disgraceful sugar looks pink, wears an air, pale compared to shadow standing by. To plump recliner, naked truth lies. Behind her shadow wears her color, arms full of flowers. A rosy charm is pink. And she is ink. The mistress wears no petticoat or leaves. The other in shadow, a large, pink dress.

This is a rereading (or misreading) of both "A Petticoat" and Édouard Manet's painting *Olympia* (1865), scandalous in its time for its presentation of the traditional odalisque posed gazing directly and unhesitatingly at the viewer. Manet's form of portraiture in *Olympia* hides within his painting several revisions of the long tradition of the odalisque, many of which suggest that this is a portrait of a prostitute. Most shocking to contemporary viewers was the model's direct gaze straight ahead: she appears to look right where a viewer would be.

When interpreted in conjunction with each other, it becomes clear that Mullen has adapted aspects of Stein's "A Petticoat"—which contains many of the same terms as Mullen's poem: "A light white, a disgrace, an ink spot, a rosy charm"—and *Olympia* to find her own basic strategies. She combines Stein's first two terms into one ("A *light white disgrace*ful sugar looks pink") and resignifies on the remaining two as she directs Stein's diction toward Manet's painting. While Stein lays out various ways that a woman's petticoat can signify meaning about the (white) woman, Mullen uses *Olympia*'s structure of two visually opposed women (one white, nude, reclined, looking ahead; the other black, brightly clothed, standing, looking down) to break these terms apart and amplify their meanings, a move that Cynthia Hogue has described as redrawing the border between the painting's two female figures as "fluid, disordered by its permeability to an exchange of ordering signs."[5] In doing so, Mullen juxtaposes the terms of both Manet's painting (and its reception) and Stein's own interpretation of what Mullen terms the "pink and white" femininity indicative for centuries of both female innocence and female sexuality. She does this in Steinian fashion, with language stripped of specific nouns or identifying references. Mullen's own version of Steinian wordplay here works through heavy assonance, consonance, internal (and some end) rhymes, and the repetition of specific words, here the color "pink" (or variants like "rosy"). The opening line, "A light white disgraceful sugar looks pink, wears an air, pale / compared to shadow standing by," shows all of these features clearly, as well as Mullen's conspicuous avoidance of the word "black" in favor of "shadow" (twice) and "ink" (once) and, after the third word in the poem, "white." White is the dominant color of Manet's painting: the woman's body is almost shockingly white—given how much of it is on display, with no scarf or other colored fabric draped over her to break up the large field of white—and she lies upon a bed with white sheets and a white pillow. Whiteness stereotypically represents innocence, specifically female innocence, an innocence that, as Mullen notes in the poem's first line, is deeply questioned in this figuration: *Olympia*'s white is "disgraceful sugar" that "looks pink."

The central formal strategy of this poem is the clustering of these three color terms, two of which are nearly absent, while the third is overly present. The two absent terms are loaded ones: they refer to a dichotomy of two extreme options; they are also the two terms upon which the racialized discourse in the United States has depended until quite recently. The opening line of this poem implies that the whiteness of the central figure of *Olympia* is a put-on, one that only survives due to the corresponding blackness of the other woman figured in the painting. Without this central opposition, this whiteness would appear for what it is, "disgraceful sugar" that looks "pink." The black woman behind the central figure is pictured in opposition to her. She is standing, looking down rather than straight ahead, conspicuously clothed in pink. Mullen writes: "Behind her shadow wears her color, arms full of / flowers. A rosy charm is pink. And she is ink." Pink, the overly present term, is what binds these two women together. The "light white disgraceful sugar" *is* pink, while the woman who is presumably her servant wears the color that her mistress fails to wear, as if she does the duty (of being pink) that her mistress has so brazenly shrugged off. She holds flowers and wears a pink dress, but while the naked "white" woman, the "rosy charm," *is* pink, she "is ink." Several of Mullen's critics have read this last line as a response to Stein's own claiming of "ink" as a woman writer; in this reading, Mullen claims that the black woman also has a stronger claim to the tools of writing. "Ink" is also, of course, the word "pink" with the "p" removed, wherein "pink" represents both the actual skin tone of many "white" people and, in slang, female genitalia.

This poem's extended wordplay on the stereotypical terms of white femininity and its relation to clothing or other forms of bodily decoration is continued throughout *Trimmings*. Mullen's beautiful facility with language and particularly her polysemic wordplay is on display as she exposes the construction of this "white and pink" femininity to the detriment of all women (who are trapped into relationship with it, whether they like it or not), but particularly women of color, who are excluded from this stereotypical version of femininity. Mullen accomplishes this through a repetition—frequently with a difference—of common phrases used to describe women and femininity, but stripped of the typically surrounding, contextualizing words that would normalize these phrases. In "Girl, pinked, beribboned," Mullen, in two and a half lines, packs the poem with antiquated terminology surrounding female innocence and the ritualized skepticism surrounding this innocence. This girl is not "pink" but "pinked" (her pink is not natural, but an accessory) and "beribboned," recalling *Olympia*'s throat ribbon, a conventional adornment of prostitutes at the time. She is an "[a]lternate virgin at first blush," wearing a "starched petticoat besmirched. Stiff with blood." She, like any formerly "new" item that has been used, is "[a] little worse for wear."

This poem pairs well with the next, "The bride wore white." It is naturally about wedding dresses ("Posed in modest bodice à la mode"), but really it is about the quasi-humiliating rituals surrounding the question of the bride's virginity. White and pink are the wedding cake ("Cake with sugar rosebuds and white frosting") of which "[e]veryone gets a piece," also a possible reference to the bride's sexuality. The jokes about her are "[o]ff-color . . . borrowed and blue," references both to the "oldness" of the well-worn jokes about her virginity and to their implications (blue), as well as to the traditions surrounding items that the bride must wear (something old, something new, something borrowed, something blue). The bride ends the poem "frozen" in white lace, her smile the "tip of the iceberg." In this lexical layering, the woman is clothed in humiliation as she walks down the aisle, the butt of ancient but persistent male humor regarding her sexual purity and fidelity as represented by the color "white."

The investigative, language-oriented experimentalism of *Trimmings* and *S*PeRM**K*T* marks a strong shift away from what Mullen has described as her first book's "derivation and celebration of [her] mother's (spoken) voice."[6] In *Muse & Drudge*, she brought together aspects of this earlier vernacular- and character-based lyricism from *Tree Tall Woman* (1981), inspired by the Black Arts Movement, and the formal experimentation of *Trimmings* and *S*PeRM**K*T*. This book-length poem consists of a series of loosely linked quatrains of code switching, arranged four to a page, that visually refer to ballad and blues forms. Critics have rightly argued that these poems are heavily influenced by the blues in both form and content.[7] Written in a vernacular style with melopoetic references to music and popular culture, the poems do not have one unifying consciousness but rather move quickly from lyric subject to lyric subject. This formal strategy—whose most obvious predecessor is Langston Hughes's *Montage of a Dream Deferred*—constructs a chorus of voices, mostly black and female, who do not share one perspective. The poem's musical language and layered wordplay represent a version of spoken American English, reproduced on the page as if it were a palimpsest. The poem is modular, without a narrative arc that is sustained between or among pages (though some pages can be thematically grouped), and so the individual pages can be read in any order that the reader chooses.

Muse & Drudge opens with an invocation of a female blues singer/ musician whom Mullen names Sapphire (after the racially stereotyped shrewish black female character produced by the *Amos 'n' Andy* radio, and later television, show). Sapphire here is also in part Sappho, primal female poet. The book opens with the lines, "Sapphire's lyre styles / plucked eyebrows / bow lips and legs / whose lives are lonely too" (the last five words cite the close of Billy Strayhorn's "Lush Life"). Mullen's musically inflected word and sound play draws on traditional resources of music and poetry as she also brings new life to the debased language of advertising, truisms, and stereotypes. I will take as exemplary for my discussion two pages of quatrains that invoke several of the recursive sets of image/word complexes of *Muse & Drudge*, the pages with quatrains beginning "keep your powder dry" and "honey jars of hair."

The book's title, *Muse & Drudge*, invokes stereotypical images of black women in the media—as overtly sexualized, divaesque models, actresses, and singers (the muse), or as low-down, despised "welfare mothers," criminals, and manual laborers (the drudge). It refers to a quotation from Zora Neale Hurston, that the black woman was the "mule of the world." In the set of lines beginning "keep your powder dry," Mullen combines these two sets of images into a hybrid "muse of the world" who "picks / out stark melodies / her raspy fabric / tickling the ebonies." This (not mule but) muse of the world has become a mus-ician, who can "sing their songs / with words your way / put it over to the people / know what you doing." The female blues singer here plays her own music, picking out "stark melodies / her raspy fabric / tickling the ebonies"; the "ebonies" are both the black piano keys (half tones) and the black people of her imagined audience. She can sing "their songs / with words [her] way," which sounds very much like what Mullen does in her poetry.

The quatrains beginning "honey jars of hair" elaborate this "muse/mule" trope: "mule for hire or worse / beast of burden down when I lay," a rearranged quotation from the spiritual "Glory Glory (Lay My Burden Down)," which returns in the fourth line of this quatrain, "lawdy lawdy hallelujah when I lay." This spiritual contains the common message of many such songs, that the pains of this world are best remedied through salvation in the next; the speaker's burden is her own body to be laid down at the end of her life. The first two quatrains on this page play with the "muse of the world" image, and the lines "honey jars of hair / skin and nail conjuration / a racy makeup art-ist collects herself / in time for a major retrospective" combine images of the female body as the grounds for artistic practice, in the senses of both creative magic ("conjuration") and self-fashioning. The art of applying cosmetics is ephemeral. Even professional "makeup artists" need photographs of actors or models to exhibit their art; Mullen's artist here must collect "herself" for this "major retrospective," a line ironic in its contradictions (a living body cannot be a retrospective).

The last quatrain on the page fairly bursts with wordplay: alliteration, assonance, and consonance as well as a palindrome ("avid diva"):

tragic yellow mattress
belatedly beladied blues
shines staggerly avid diva
ruses of the lunatic muse

The "tragic yellow mattress" is one of the shopworn phrases Mullen resurrects through decontextualization: "mattress" rather than "mulatto," a descriptor for a woman prized as a sexual object. The blues are "belatedly beladied" in that women's contributions to the artistry of blues music were until recently not well understood except for a few famous singers. The words "shines" and "staggerly" both refer to aspects of African American (male) folklore, but in the syntax of these phrases, both also refer to the "avid diva."[8] These singers were "avid divas" but also the fronts of a muse who may be crazy or fonder of the moon than the sun, as are most performers who tend to work at night. This "lunatic muse" returns to the "muse of the world," from the "honey pots of hair" section, who takes control of the blues to sing with "words [her] way," a clearly "avid diva" of the "stark melody."

The quatrains beginning "keep your powder dry" likewise begin with a list of truisms regarding the need to prepare for an assault:

keep your powder dry
your knees together
your dress down
your drawers shut

Mullen here relates the invocation of planning for warfare ("trust in god but keep your powder dry") with stereotypical advice to a young girl on how to deal with male sexual advances, her body the grounds of contestation that she is responsible for protecting. In these lines, articles of clothing (as well as parts of the body) reverse their function to become protective armor rather than decoration designed to attract, while the girl is now equated with a soldier who cannot rely on a higher power for safety. The quatrains in this section of the poem each explore the possibilities of written and spoken English (or, the representation on the page of the spoken language), showing how the language's fluidity of meaning creates—as much as it records—a great deal of what we commonly think of as identity within its shifts and turns.

In this final section, I will discuss a paradox in Mullen's work. One element she expresses in "Imagining the Unimagined Reader" is her desire for poetic immortality: "I write, optimistically, for an imagined audience of known and unknown readers. Many of my imagined readers have yet to encounter my work. Most of them are not even born yet."[9] She imagines her work, written in idioms and on subjects of her moment, to be read twenty or more years into the future, a hope that surely most writers share with her. Mullen has attained a level of success that only a handful of experimental poets ever achieve. However, she has been candid about the effects of her decision to turn away from her early voice-based, workshop-style poems— those clearly situated within the gendered, racial, class-based, and regional context of *Tree Tall Woman*. This move shifted her audience, largely, as she has noted, from black to white, but also limited it. Maya Angelou was invited by President Bill Clinton to read her poem "On the Pulse of Morning" at his inauguration in 1993 (right at the moment Mullen had shifted away from a style that would have positioned her to be a successor to poets like Angelou and Nikki Giovanni), and Elizabeth Alexander (b. 1962), not Mullen (b. 1953), was asked to read at President Barack Obama's inauguration in 2009.

Competing with her desire to reach an "unimagined" reader is a persistent attraction to riddles and puzzles. Her cryptographic writing creates secret codes within the poems. Some of these codes exist as messages to very particular readers (such as "Ask Aiden," or "Kirstenography" in *Sleeping with the Dictionary*, which are directed at family members). Others are not directed to anyone in particular. These contesting concerns—for a very general audience and for very particular ones, too—create a freedom of meaning within the poems. Readers take this work on their own terms, creating their own meanings. In many "puzzle" or "riddle" poems, it is evident that there *is* a "hidden" meaning to be found. The quatrain beginning "marry at a hotel, annul 'em" in *Muse & Drudge* is one such elusive "puzzle" poem:

> marry at a hotel, annul 'em
> nary hep male rose sullen
> let alley roam, yell melon
> dull normal fellow hammers omelette

Any careful reader of this quatrain will notice a surprising number of repeated sounds, both in the sense of Mullen's common recourse to assonance, consonance, and internal rhymes, but more so in that there are frequently repeated letter combinations in these lines, more than would be expected from any "ordinary" series of phrases. These lines, which read like children's nursery rhymes, are all created primarily out of the letters of the author's name, "Harryette Rommel Mullen." The following quatrain,

> divine sunrises
> Osiris's irises
> his splendid mistress
> is his sis Isis

is more densely packed with repeated and patterned phonemes, in my view, than any other in *Muse & Drudge*, creating a passage that is musically deep even while it may appear bereft of meaning. Mullen describes these lines as "something close to pure word-and-sound play," but she also indicates that the poem "alludes to the project of Afrocentrism."[10] She discloses too that "marry at a hotel, annul 'em" is anagrammatically related to her name and describes the quatrain as "admittedly nonsensical."[11] Beyond these lines' obvious musicality and the pure pleasure that that entails, they relate to two other claims Mullen has made about her poetry: that some of her lines "aspire to certain moments in jazz when scat becomes a kind of inspired speaking in tongues, or glossolalia, moments when utterance is pure music"; and that other readers may find sense in her work she did not originally see.[12] The combination of surface-level musicality with buried, obscured, or playfully hidden meaning opens this work up both to these "unknown" readers as well as to the "sense of play and pleasure" that is too often missing for many reluctant readers of poetry.[13]

Mullen's playfulness and pleasure become increasingly evident in her fourth book, *Sleeping with the Dictionary* (2001), written under the influence of Oulipo.[14] In this abecedarian book, sense frequently is subordinate to sound and lexical play. Again, Mullen's cryptography suppresses the most significant word in some poems. Just as she conspicuously avoids the terms "black" and "white" in her prose poem written back to Stein and Manet, in "Denigration," as in "Resistance Is Fertile," she avoids using the poem's obvious central term. She substitutes for this central exclusion a series of alternatives, some etymologically related and others not, but all of which contain the letters "neg-" or "nig-." Rather than the juvenile playfulness of "Resistance Is Fertile," this poem is characterized by painful irony, as the excluded term represents centuries of racism. This poem nonetheless plays with the connotative, accrued sense and social histories of the alternative terms. It is structured as a series of questions uttered by a naïve speaker, who asks, "How muddy is the Mississippi compared to the third-longest river of the darkest continent?" and "Does my niggling concern with trivial matters negate my ability to negotiate in good faith?" The first of these reads like a grade-school exam and the second like a defensive concern for trustworthiness. Yet both contain strange contortions: the first substitutes the phrase "darkest continent" for "Africa" and avoids the answer to its question, the Niger; the second's repetition of words with "nig-" and "neg-" suggests that the speaker is embarrassed by the thought of the suppressed term.

The most remarkable example of Mullen's language play is the series of lines that refer to the controversy surrounding the word "niggardly." Although this word's denotation—"stingy" or "miserly"—has nothing to do with the nearly homophonous racial epithet, its use was the occasion for the firing and then eventual rehiring of Washington, DC, mayoral aid David Howard in 1999, whose use of this term to characterize a budget discussion was misunderstood by a colleague as racist. Mullen refers to the controversy in her lines, "Though slaves, who were wealth, survived on niggardly provisions, should inheritors of wealth fault the poor enigma for lacking a dictionary? Does the mayor demand a recount of every bullet or does city hall simply neglect the black alderman's district?" "Denigration"'s central term is unutterable in "polite" company. Mullen has made it central to the poem in both subject and structure. Although people who care about language might insist that "niggardly" is an utterable word, it has now also become unalterably associated with the racial epithet in question, largely due to these controversies about its use. (There were at least four other such incidents in the 1990s and 2000s.) "Niggardly" inexorably drags with it all the connotations of the racial epithet. The evident interconnectedness of linguistic and social history leads one to sense other connections evident among the terms Mullen includes in this poem. The *American Heritage Dictionary*, Mullen's source, asserts that many of the terms she uses in this poem are related to each other linguistically in that they derive from the root "ne-," meaning "not," and thus refer, ultimately, to a negation.[15]

Any evaluation of Mullen must reckon with wordplay: people either love or hate puns. Samuel Johnson, author of *Dictionary of the English Language* (1755), the most significant English dictionary prior to the *Oxford English Dictionary*, was apparently one of the haters. His definition for "quibble" (a contemporary synonym for "wordplay") includes this quotation from Joseph Addison: "This may be of great use to immortalize puns and quibbles, and to let posterity see their forefathers were blockheads." Johnson also purportedly wrote that "[t]o trifle with the vocabulary which is the vehicle of social intercourse is to tamper with the currency of human intelligence. He who would violate the sanctities of his Mother Tongue would invade the recesses of the paternal till without remorse."[16] Mullen's wordplay finds humor or meaning in an explicit flaunting of the language rules that a dictionary is meant to determine. She makes obvious how words mean variously in various contexts—or in any context—or sound like other words that mean differently. Even my possibly apocryphal Johnson quotation derives power from wordplay regarding incestuous linguistic theft.

Johnson's "Preface to Shakespeare" (1765) established the now rarely cited universality criterion for poetry. His claim, for instance, that Shakespeare's greatness is largely due to his ability to provide audiences with a true portrait of humanity has little to do with Shakespeare's historical moment. "Whatever advantages he might once derive from personal allusions, local customs, or temporary opinions," Johnson argues, "have for many years been lost." Johnson holds that language and meaning survive over time, that future readers will understand Shakespeare's English and see, too, its value. And they do. Mullen's lexical play relies on local, timely references. One might argue, then, that it will be hard for her to outlive her moment. But there is more to the calculation.

Mullen's musicality goes well past her moment; she recalls a time when the musical qualities of poetry were an aid to memory. Meter and rhyme helped an oral culture to remember and find pleasure. Her puzzles, riddles, and cryptography, too, though they generate sense, encourage readers to create meaning of their own. A future reader might not understand the *Star Trek* references in "Resistance Is Fertile," but this would not leave the poem meaningless. More recently, "resistance" was taken up as a call to action by those opposed to the political strategies of the US government after the 2016 presidential election. Thus the term took on a renewed sense that harkens to the French resistance against German invasion. Puns and lexical play lose their initial sense in time, but they may equally open to a new or renewed sense in time. Mullen combines playful patterns of sounds and sense; her poems allow readers both to examine a particular historical moment and to create a meaning relevant to their own.

Notes

1. Of her five books of poetry published since her first book, *Tree Tall Woman*, which was written in 1981 and is formally anomalous, four of these are book-length texts. Only *Sleeping with the Dictionary* (2001) is a collection of discrete poems.
2. Harryette Mullen, "Imagining the Unimagined Reader: Writing to the Unborn and Including the Excluded," in *The Cracks between What We Are and What We Are Supposed to Be: Essays and Interviews* (Tuscaloosa: University of Alabama Press, 2012), 8.
3. Harryette Mullen and Barbara Henning, "Snail Mail: From Coast to Coast; Correspondence on *Trimmings* and *Muse & Drudge*," in *Looking Up Harryette Mullen: Interviews on "Sleeping with the Dictionary" and Other Works*, ed. Barbara Henning (Brooklyn: Belladonna, 2011), 13.
4. See her discussion of Silliman's "paratactic sentence" and the poetic possibilities of compression, "An Interview with Harryette Mullen by Cynthia Hogue," in Mullen, *The Cracks between What We Are and What We Are Supposed to Be*, 242.
5. Cynthia Hogue, "Harryette Mullen's Revisionary Border Work," in *We Who Love to Be Astonished: Experimental Women's Writing and Performance Poetics*, ed. Laura Hinton and Cynthia Hogue (Tuscaloosa: University of Alabama Press, 2002), 89.

6. Harryette Mullen, "Telegraphs from a Distracted Sibyl," in Mullen, *The Cracks between What We Are and What We Are Supposed to Be*, 19.

7. For example, Evie Shockley states that Mullen's goal is to "sample and quote blues voices . . . as representations of black women's expressions and subjectivity." Evie Shockley, *Renegade Poetics: Black Aesthetics and Formal Innovation in African American Poetry* (Iowa City: University of Iowa Press, 2011), 106.

8. The story of criminal Lee Shelton, known as "Stagolee," "Stagger Lee," or "Stack-O-Lee," became a part of the blues tradition shortly after his murder of Billy Lyons in 1895; John Lomax recorded songs retelling the story as early as 1910. The traditional toast "Shine and the *Titanic*" tells the story of a black stoker whose attempts to warn the *Titanic*'s captain of the ship's impending disaster are ignored. He eventually saves himself by leaping into the ocean and swimming to shore.

9. Mullen, "Imagining the Unimagined Reader," 3.

10. Mullen and Henning, "Snail Mail," 8.

11. Ibid.

12. Harryette Mullen, "Kinky Quatrains: The Making of *Muse & Drudge*," in Mullen, *The Cracks between What We Are and What We Are Supposed to Be*, 17. Mullen wants to "allow . . . space for divergent interpretations by a heterogeneous audience, or by myself at different moments of my encounter with the poem as one of its possible readers" (Mullen and Henning, "Snail Mail," 8).

13. "An Interview with Harryette Mullen by Daniel Kane," in Mullen, *The Cracks between What We Are and What We Are Supposed to Be*, 212.

14. Oulipo, or Ouvroir de Littérature Potentielle (Workshop of Potential Literature), is a group of writers working with the belief that literature written under a system of structural constraints would produce works of immense possibility, particularly when these constraints were taken on in an attitude of play. Although writers (particularly poets) have worked with traditional constraints of form (such as the sonnet or sestina) for centuries, Oulipian writers more often use constraints designed around mathematical formulas, such as the N+7 constraint, in which the author starts by looking up each word in an existing poem in the dictionary, moving forward seven words, and then replacing the original word with this new one. The group was founded in 1960 by French mathematician François de Lionnais and writer Raymond Queneau. Georges Perec's novel *La Disparition* is perhaps the most famous Oulipian text.

15. Harryette Mullen and Barbara Henning, "From A to Z: Conversations on *Sleeping with the Dictionary*," in Henning, *Looking Up Harryette Mullen*, 60.

16. Although this quotation is widely attributed to Johnson, the source for it seems to be Oliver Wendell Holmes's book *The Autocrat of the Breakfast-Table* (1858), in which he states that the quotation is from "the great moralist."

FORM

CHAPTER 9

#CageFreePoetry

CHARLES BERNSTEIN

Now, who shall arbitrate?
Ten men love what I hate,
Shun what I follow, slight what I receive;
Ten, who in ears and eyes
Match me; we all surmise,
They this thing, and I that: whom shall my soul believe?

—ROBERT BROWNING, "RABBI BEN EZRA" (1864)[1]

THERE IS NO perfect in poetry, but there can be more perfection. Every success has a countermeasure of failure: the better you do one thing, the more you fail to do something else. That is why monotheism in poetry is a crime against aesthetics. Which does not mean anything goes: anything is possible, but only a very few things get through that eye of a needle that separates charm from harm. And often what appears as harm has got the charm.

Harder for a rich man to write a good poem than to buy a good painting. The hardest part: *why bother?*

When you are on the losing side of literary judgment as long as I have been, you count your losses as gains, in the poetry economy. For every poem I love, a baker's dozen hate it, and sometimes I feel (delusions of agency) that my endorsement of a poem is sufficient cause for others to shun it. Those ten, or ten times ten, will say *Robert Lowell* to my *Larry Eigner*. Who do I think I am, Sancho Panza? Am I just a voice crying in the wilderness or am I a just voice pleading aggrievement? Indeed, my gang's outlier taste is often viewed as canonical by those who feel their mainstream taste is slighted by a cognoscenti that shuns them. Is anyone in poetry free of aggrievement? The ones who get the prizes say, "Why has no one heard of me?" The ones that don't sing in unison, *the system is rigged*, as if they are at a Bernie Sanders rally (or maybe shills for Donald Trump). I have composed many arrangements for this chorus. Being Jewish helps with the cacophonies. There hasn't been a *real* Jewish poet since Solomon and his Songs, but at least we can agree that he was pretty God-damn good.

My soul believes only its own ears, Ibn Ezra. I can't be wrong about that. If I love a poem, can I love it tastelessly? Or is it that I love its tastelessness? Reb Bint Eliza would say that the discussion of taste is more important than the preference for one taste over another.[2] "I don't want to know what you prefer but rather what's your criteria?" the rebbe would always say.

Once two poets came to King Solomon each insisting that the poet they most revered was the greater poet. Solomon said that each of them should burn the books of the poets and read only the Torah. What a jerk! (Don't confuse the author of the Song of Songs with the earlier king; King S. would surely resent that he is best known for poetry he couldn't and wouldn't have written.)

Even so, maybe King Solomon would have echoed his poet avatar and said that it is not the poem but its kiss that matters: let the poem kiss you with the kisses of its mouth, for love is better than wine. There are many poets who say the kiss of a lover is far greater than any poem. —But kisses grow cold and hard while a poem will never betray you.

"Rebbe, are you arguing that the Bible says that sex is better than art?"

"No. The kiss in the Song of Songs symbolizes aesthetic experience, which is akin to Shekinah, the presence of God. And while each of us might say our lover is the best of all lovers, we accept the plurality of loves as it would be monstrous to think there are only a few great loves and the rest are minor. Love is plentiful and always next to us. The difficulty is in acknowledging its presence rather than shunning it."

I am in mortal danger, but not from an erotic
Lovesickness of a desperate suitor;

My desire is to be with the mighty Monarch who has
No weakness; He is the fountain of my craving;
My anguish is hidden in the recess
Of my heart; my face does not show it,
>   Lest they say of me: "His base passion killed him
>   Why does he put on airs?" (Ibn Ezra)[3]

In 1974, I was doing a drug education talk for teenagers at Camarillo State Mental Hospital near Los Angeles. The place Charlie Parker made famous with "Relaxin' at Camarillo." At the time, I was the health educator at Freedom Community Clinic in Santa Barbara. My friend Stu Rubinstein and I were talking about LSD and marijuana when one of the teenagers mentioned sniffing glue. I must have blanched because the kid came back hard: "I get just as high on my glue as you do on your LSD." I interpreted this as his saying, "You contemptible bourgeois snobs, you think your Courvoisier is so much better than my Thunderbird, but isn't what you want same as me?" Democratic vistas; but after all, glue causes brain damage, so whatever its potency, it's a "bad" way to get high. But then, lots of popular entertainment also causes brain damage, even if we call it mind damage. Is potency the issue or is it the kind of potency or is it the pedigree of the potency? You could certainly make a case that "low-grade" poetry is less intense than what you get from "high" art. —And if you can't make that case then I will. I'll take my Creeley over your Bukowski any day of the week, buddy. For the lover of Bukowski, Creeley will seem too elusive, while for the lover of Creeley, Bukowski will seem not elusive enough.

So is what's most significant the poem itself or the experience a reader gets from the poem? I could write a Creeley-like poem that might have the same power for someone who never read him. Sometimes imitations will have more impact because they cut to the chase quicker. "Candy / Is dandy / But liquor / Is quicker." Who said that? Was it Dorothy Parker, Tim Leary, or Ogden Nash?[4] We aesthetes will always insist that when you go back to the original, you'll see the difference. The copy is a gateway drug for the power of the real thing. But it could as easily be said that the great poem initiates the reader into taking aesthetic pleasures beyond the poem: listening with a livelier consciousness and seeing with a crocked eye.

The poem is not the end of aesthetic experience but its beginning.

Feeling superior to the self-righteous makes you that. If I say that my taste is better than yours, I have just proven my tastelessness. My taste is better than no one, but it is mine. Even so, I don't own it, it owns me.

Nowadays the professors of culture speak more of "distinction" than "value" since distinction can be quantified in a way value can't. Western poetry from the Romantic period on has accorded the greatest value to poets who had, in their own lifetime, the least distinction. It is a measure of distinction to have a poem in the *New Yorker*, but I have never heard anyone argue for the aesthetic merit of the poems in the *New Yorker*.[5] The magazine sets the bar so low for poetry that when it does on occasion publish a poem that breaks the mold, it generates attention that overshadows its more typical commitment to the mundane. The distinction of having a poem in the *New Yorker* is similar to the prestige of a prize: everyone wants it but few get it. But there can also be another level of distinction involved: showing you can write an aesthetically good poem in such a way that it can "pass" muster, like having your cake and eating it too, or being a cool nerd. The ultimate prestige is for the great poet who manages, against all odds, to get recognized as great. The great but obscure poet is still a loser. Even if the system is rigged, the point is to beat the odds. That's far more prestigious than writing a poem could ever be.

If one of your criteria for the value of poems is that they unsettle, it doesn't mean that every poem that aims to unsettle is equally good or that a poem that is deeply conservative might not be better than one that is all about undermining received opinions. But still I'd prefer to read poems that are at least trying to unsettle than ones that treat poetry as a dead art.

Taste is a matter of experience. You can educate your taste as you can open your experiences to new vistas. Knowledge and awareness are not opposed to judgment; they are its foundation. As a poem is an opening to experience, so taste is not the end of aesthetics but the onset, as of a fever. Judgment is never final; it is a place to begin a journey in art, a point of departure on a trip without fixed destination.

Taste is rooted in perceived preference. To deny or invalidate your preferences is not modesty but travesty. Tastes are *essentially* provisional even if you remain locked in the prison house of your predilections.

Aesthetic judgment is more precisely articulated by comparison with poems that are alike than by comparing poems of wildly different forms or periods.

Taste is not a matter of wrong or right. Moral principles of wrong and right impede the grasp of taste: that is the still-scandalous principle of aestheticism.

For many readers of poetry, identification with the poet, solidarity with the moral or political sentiment of the poem, or prior knowledge of the prestige of the poet is more important than the formal, stylistic, or aesthetic qualities of a poem. Psychologists will talk about branding or affectional projection and sociologists about predetermined ideological dispositions. How can taste be any more than an extension of tribalism, class, or commodification? Capitalists may celebrate the triumph of the market while anticapitalists will stress the importance of counterhegemonic alternatives. The idea that taste could ever be more than a puppet of economic and ideological forces seems as precarious as a piece of china in *The Spoils of Poynton*.

Changes of taste require changes of consciousness: the aesthetic clash between refinement and coarseness is a symptom of discordant senses of the world. I prefer Larry Eigner to Robert Lowell and find Eigner the more refined, but it's a different kind of refinement from the patrician Lowell, as different as Cambridge from Swampscott or as gentile to Jew. To prefer Eigner requires a readjustment of aesthetic criteria. It is not a matter of what Eigner stands for but what he does ("thro' acts uncouth, / Toward making," as Browning puts it in "Rabbi Ben Ezra").

The proof of Eigner's poems is in the experience they allow. Depending on where you are coming from, Eigner may well be an acquired taste. But for the kind of aestheticism I want, all tastes are acquired. You feel it on the tongue before you prize it in the mind. It stings before it stuns. And yes there is something of a conversion narrative here, a transvaluation that can only come after habitual or received judgments are called into question, suspended for a moment in an imaginary place of possibility. The dialectical process of aversive judgment, pushing against the given of authority or moral law toward the possible, is grounded in taste just as experience is the ground of ethical judgment.

It is a shibboleth (תְּלִבֶּשׁ) for those who turned against the New Criticism that the meaning of a poem is essentially bound to its historical context and the identity of the author (except we would avoid the word *essentially*). Much ink has been spent on redressing how this doctrine has turned critics and professors from close reading to distant learning. Here's my three and three-quarters sense: it is the dialectical relationship of the form of the poem to its social context that makes aesthetic meaning possible. A failure to address the ethnic and local particulars of Robert Frost fails to grapple with his poems even if that is the basis of his hegemony. Similarly, reading the work of a "minority" writer only in terms of her or his subaltern experience robs the poem of its aesthetic particularity. The history of racist exclusion of black poets from the canon is most powerfully addressed by a discussion of the forms and styles of specific poems and their contribution to the art of poetry. Valuing poems thematically, exclusively as expressions of the subaltern, risks reinscribing racist ideas of authenticity. The answer to the problem of the color line in American poetry is not primitivist paternalism but a prolonged and detailed consideration of the history of poetry, language, and song by African Americans, with special attention to the formal inventions that have been an unacknowledged foundation of radical North American poetry.

Reception of poems is dogged by asymmetrical patterns of evaluation. The "same" poem by a male or female (white or black) poet will be evaluated differently—both by the proponents of an identity-free canon and those whose priority is the inclusion of underrepresented voices in the canon. Eccentricity by a male poet might be valued as formally innovative while formal innovation by a woman poet is written off as eccentric or affective.

I am under no illusion: my prioritizing of the aesthetic and formal aspects of a poem is fundamentally out of step with the preference of many readers for personal stories and moving anecdotes. My criteria for what makes a poem good are irreconcilable with those who favor narrative continuity and emotional expression achieved through the overcoming of language play and ambiguity.

Evaluation is always interested. The construction of disinterestedness is itself a form of interest. If, as the cliché has it, Western "high" culture favors those perceived as white Christian heterosexual men, this form of identity preference does not favor all white people or all men or all heterosexuals but rather those whose work is marked by, and conforms to, an idealized identity.

Is Elsa von Freytag-Loringhoven a better poet than Frost? It depends on the criteria.[6] Surely she is the better Dada poet.

"No Images," from 1926, is the only poem I know by Waring Cuney

(1906–1976). Its value is not diminished for me by its being singular, even if that means that this often-anthologized poem is both obscure and famous.

> She does not know
> her beauty,
> she thinks her brown body
> has no glory.
>
> If she could dance
> naked
> under palm trees
> and see her image in the river,
> she would know.
>
> But there are no palm trees
> on the street,
> and dish water gives back
> no images.[7]

Each stanza is a broken sentence with the middle stanza's five lines being one line longer than the first and third stanza. The "echo" theme of seeing one's reflection in the water takes a startling turn in "No Images," connecting it to the radical modernist aesthetic of resisting mimesis. "No Images" transforms the modernist aversion to representation into a dialectical engagement with racialized images. The second stanza projects an unalienated site that evokes Africa but avoids the primitivist romanticizing of the "jungle," common at the time. The stanza's opening word *if* insists on the role of the imaginary not as a prior reality but as a counterpoint within the present. The elegant syncopation of the Williams-like lines of this stanza is free of any trace of traditional poetic diction. "Naked" stands alone on its own line, unbaring the image, bringing us up not only against the *naked* word but also against the "brown body" that is at the center of both the poem's gaze and its aversion of gaze. This nakedness is contrasted with the inability to "know," echoed from the first line of the poem. In "No Images," this inability is self-knowledge and recognition of value ("glory"). It is only in the penultimate line of the poem that the site of alienation is located: dirty (and so opaque) "dish water." The dish water could be the subject's own, but there is the suggestion that she labors as a domestic worker, whereby her life is taken away from her rather than being "given back." Through Cuney's negative dialectics, the loss of image literally *reflects* the loss of the beauty of her body.

Compare this poem to "Man and Wife" by Robert Lowell. What would happen if I gave the kind of flatfooted, clueless, exoticizing reading of this canonical poem that so many champions of Lowell give to poems that are not to their taste:

Written in the New England section of the US and first published three decades after "No Images" in 1958, Robert Lowell's poem begins—

Tamed by *Miltown*, we lie on Mother's bed;
the rising sun in war paint dyes us red;[8]

In contrast to "No Images," the diction is stiff and suggests that the poem is possibly written by a second-language speaker (as suggested by the missing personal pronoun before "Mother" and the overpunctuation). The poem is strikingly anachronistic—almost sixty years after *Un coup de dés*, it fails to reflect the poetic revolution of Stein, Pound, Eliot, or Hughes: consider the naïve rhyme of "bed" and "red" and the primitivist idea associating a red sun with war. But this first impression can be overcome if we take into consideration the cultural background of the author and read the poem from an ethnographic point of view. The cultural limitations of the poem—its "uptightness" and recognition of the difficulty of sustaining heterosexual relationships ("Now twelve years later, you turn your back")—become its strength. "Man and Wife" seems to be bruising up against a "high" education and breeding that hamper a freer emotional life ("too boiled and shy / and poker-faced to make a pass") and acceptance of more open form ("tamed," "you / hold your pillow to your hollows like a child"). That is, once we see that the poet comes out of a repressed, alcoholism-prone ("boiled," as in aesthetically cooked), Anglo-Protestant-American background, once we take in its class origins ("all air and nerve"), we can see its immediate appeal to other Anglo-Protestant-Americans, who may suffer from the same problems, such as emotional and intellectual sedation, drug addiction, or overdosing (*Miltown* is not a reference to a factory town but to a prescription sedative, a popular form of legal doping in the late 1950s). Yet while "Man and

Wife" would be primarily of interest to heterosexual Anglo-Protestant-Americans of the upper crust, the poem gives other readers insight into this unique form of life.

—But enough of such costume foolery! Both poems are great, in their fashion, and both turn their forms on themselves. Lowell's poem is less interesting for what it "confesses" than for how its candor works like acid on the form.

I prefer art that opens up possibilities rather than art that perfects a possibility. That may mean liking "lesser" poems to "greater" ones. Of course, nowadays, *minor* is *major* and the concept of "minor literature" is the new critic's siren song. The signal work on this distinction, for the thirtieth consecutive year, is *Kafka: Toward a Minor Literature* by Gilles Deleuze and Félix Guattari, though if Kafka is minor, what does that make all the other twentieth-century fiction writers far more minor than he is? Oh but: they mean minor as a modality not as a marker of diminished achievement. It is a commonplace that "outsiders" later become insiders. The most conventional poets are dying to be called "avant-garde" even though they detest actual avant-garde practices, in the process trashing their weirder fellow poets for taking up the oxygen that God designated for the conforming. It all gets so confusing. I want to make a case for genuinely "minor" figures—poets who didn't write as much, have the impact, or achieve the level of innovation as their "major" counterparts. At the same time, I want to sing the praises of reading a range of innovative and iconoclastic modernist and contemporary poets, not just the "best"—not so we can rescue a neglected poet for the canon (though I am all for that), but because poetry is best read through multiplicity rather than singularity. I do not, however, extend this same capacious interest to the ensemble of conforming poets. In that case, I do prefer only the best! But that is because my interest lies in nonconforming poetry from the past century and more.

A Bach fugue is a closed experience, even if infinite in its variations and transcendental in its feel. Familiarity allows even the startling changes of tempo in Glenn Gould's Bach performances to feel fresh while confirming a received idea of perfection. The experience of Brian Ferneyhough's music is different: it remains provisional and unexpectable, averting a listener's ability to fully come to terms with it. Ferneyhough's music is open in the sense that its value is undetermined (is it great?), but also undeterminable (it averts perfection).

Canonical art does not offer a challenge to the arts of invention but rather to the arts of convention, to artwork that offers a pale imitation of values no longer fully obtainable.

Francis Janosco, a high school teacher in Darien, Connecticut, recently asked me and a few others to nominate poems written since 2000 so that his senior class could exercise their judgments by picking what they perceived to be the best.[9] I was thinking of Robert Duncan's remark in 1963 ("Pages from a Notebook"): "I make poetry as other men make war or make love or make states or revolutions: to exercise my faculties at large." I asked the teacher to tell his students that I don't believe in "best" in the abstract since what I may most value in a poem is likely to be despised by other readers. Poetry is more like politics in that sense, but the stakes are aesthetic. In making this list, I assumed that the students were relatively new to poetry, and I selected works that are very different in approach, so their preferences would reflect as much the kind of poem they are interested in as the "best." I picked the following poems to raise issues that I hoped would spark discussion.

Lyn Hejinian, *The Unfollowing*, Hejinian's new book, in which each line is supposed to be a non sequitur. The poems are each fourteen lines, but Hejinian says they are not sonnets. Would other combinations of the lines make for equally good poems? Why do non sequiturs put into this form become connected to one another? Could this be a structural allegory for human organization in families, groups, cities, nations?

David Antin, "Hiccups"—Antin gives improvised "talk poems" and then transcribes the talks. You can read the written version and also listen to the audio on which Antin based the text. What's the difference in experiencing the recording versus reading the poem? Is it one poem or two? Why call this a poem?

Maggie O'Sullivan, *All Origins Are Lonely*. O'Sullivan is the only poet here from Great Britain. She sometimes publishes her work with her own collages.

Tracie Morris, from "Slave Sho to Video aka Black but Beautiful" (audio file). There is no "text" version of this poem, only the recording of the performance.

Felix Bernstein, "If Loving You Is Wrong." This one is by my son. How does nepotism affect the selection of the "best"? The poem lists the number of Google search hits for each of the dozens of contemporary poets listed. Is this a legitimate form for a poem? Do "hits" represent popularity, distinction, or value? The poem ends with a reference to David Antin's quip, "if robert lowell is a poet i dont want to be a poet   if robert frost was a poet   i dont want to be a poet if socrates was a poet   i'll consider it."[10]

Ron Silliman, "from Caledonia." Silliman has been publishing since 1970. This is his most recent online magazine appearance.

Tonya Foster, "In/Somniloquies," from *A Swarm of Bees in High Court*, along with a commentary I wrote on the work. Do you read the poem differently after reading the commentary?

Robert Grenier, two "scrawl" (hand-drawn, visual) poems with rough translations. Many people would not consider these drawn works poems at all. How does handwriting affect the meaning?

Christian Bök, *Eunoia* ("o"). Each chapter is composed with just one vowel (lipogram).

Elizabeth Willis, "The Witch." Are you one?

Charles Bernstein, "War Stories." This is not my best poem, but a good one for discussion. Does that make it a better candidate for this classroom use?

Ibn Ezra as channeled by Browning:

Rather I prize the doubt
Low kinds exist without,
Finished and finite clods, untroubled by a spark.

In a recent letter to our mutual friend Li Zhimin, Susan Stewart wrote, "I expect art to create new knowledge and new feelings."[11] No doubt she was echoing Wallace Stevens's "new knowledge of reality."[12]

A here we've never been. Where we've always been. Where we are now.

Feng Yi, a visiting scholar at Penn this year, puts it this way: "This is the moment for me to test whether I can be an immigrant to the uncertain, the unknown and the foreign, whether I am acceptable and open enough, whether I can adapt to the new or not."[13]

Once Reb Bint Eliza was asked, "What poems will abet making the next world?" None, she answered. After a few minutes three people walked by, talking wildly and bursting into uncontrollable laughter. —"What those people are exchanging is making the world to come."

I can't get no perfection. But I can get new possibilities, new directions, new horizons.

Then, welcome each rebuff
That turns earth's smoothness rough,
Each sting that bids nor sit nor stand but go!
Be our joys three-parts pain!
Learn, nor account the pang; dare, never grudge the throe!
("Rabbi Ben Ezra")

(Provincetown, Summer 2016)

Notes

1. Robert Browning, *Poems of Robert Browning*, ed. Charlotte Porter and Helen A. Clarke (New York: Thomas Y. Crowell, 1896), 207–12. Browning based "Rabbi Ben Ezra" on poet and philosopher Abraham Ibn Ezra (ca. 1089–1167). "Ibn" is the Arabic form for *ben* (son of).
2. Rabbi Eliza first appears in "Sign Under Test," a poem of mine collected in *Girly Man* (Chicago: University of Chicago Press, 2006). *Bint* is the Arabic form for *bat* (daughter of).
3. Abraham Ibn Ezra, *Twilight of a Golden Age: Selected Poems of Abraham Ibn Ezra*, ed. and trans. Leon J. Weinberger (Tuscaloosa: University of Alabama Press, 1997), 31.
4. Ogden Nash, "Reflection on Ice-Breaking," in *Hard Lines* (New York: Simon and Schuster, 1931), 83.
5. See my related commentary in "The Pataquerical Imagination: Midrashic Antinomianism and the Promise of Bent Studies," section CII, in *Pitch of Poetry* (Chicago: University of Chicago Press, 2016).
6. I read the Baroness's "Teke Heart" at the Museum of Modern Art for a Dada show: jacket2.org/commentary/teke-baroness-elsa.
7. William Waring Cuney, *Storefront Church*, Heritage Series 23 (London: Paul Breman, 1973), 7. Cuney's only other poetry collection is *Puzzles*, ed. Paul Bremen (Utrecht: DeRoos, 1960), limited to 175 numbered copies. Cuney wrote "No Images" when he was eighteen; it won the 1926 *Opportunity* literary contest. Lorenzo Thomas calls Cuney "a minor poet who produced a major poem." Thomas discusses several of Cuney's poems as well as the blues lyrics he wrote with Josh White. See Thomas's "Whose Images? Waring Cuney and the Harlem Renaissance Idea of the Poet's Work," in *The Heritage Series of Black Poetry, 1962–1975: A Research Compendium*, ed. Lauri Ramey in consultation with Paul Breman (Farnham, Surrey, England: Ashgate, 2008). I first heard "No Images" sung, a cappella, by Nina Simone: see jacket2.org/commentary/cuney.

8. Robert Lowell, "Man and Wife," Poets.org, www.poets.org/poetsorg/poem/man-and-wife.

9. Links for the poems can be found at writing.upenn.edu/bernstein/syllabi/Janosco-best-poems.html.

10. David Antin, *Radical Coherency: Selected Essays on Art and Literature, 1966 to 2005* (Chicago: University of Chicago Press, 2011), 273.

11. Susan Stewart, e-mail correspondence, August 1, 2016. See Stewart's *The Poet's Freedom: A Notebook on Making* (Chicago: University of Chicago Press, 2011).

12. Wallace Stevens, "Not Ideas about the Thing but the Thing Itself," in *Collected Poetry and Prose* (New York: Library of America, 1997), 451.

13. Feng Yi, e-mail correspondence, April 26, 2016.

CHAPTER 10

"Funny Ha-Ha or Funny Peculiar?"

Recalculating Charles Bernstein's Poetry

MARJORIE PERLOFF

The problem with teaching poetry is perhaps the reverse of that in other fields: students come to it thinking it's personal and relevant, but I try to get them to see it as formal, structural, historical, collaborative, and ideological. *What a downer!*[1]

BEMUSED AND JOKEY as this observation sounds, it points to the particular anomaly of Charles Bernstein's poetics. From the beginning, when the twenty-six-year-old author of "Stray Straws and Straw Men" declared that poetry should "emphasize its medium as being constructed, rule governed, everywhere circumscribed by grammar & syntax, chosen vocabulary: designed, manipulated, picked, programmed, organized, & so an artifice, artifact,"[2] Bernstein has thought of himself as a formalist, a maker of rigorous structures, an enemy of "the natural look." And yet a frequent charge against him—a charge Bernstein has never quite been able to shake—is that, however interesting and valuable his critical, theoretical, and pedagogical formulations, the poems themselves often seem incoherent and undisciplined. Indeed, mainstream poetry reviewers, from Calvin Bedient and Dan Chiasson to Charles Simic and Helen Vendler, have either ignored Bernstein's poetry or taken the occasional potshot at it.[3]

Part of the problem is that Bernstein, who was, with Bruce Andrews, the founding editor of *L=A=N=G=U=A=G=E*, the journal that initiated the movement by that name, has come to be regarded as the representative Language poet, and hence his work is all too often held synonymous with "Language poetry" in general. Here is the Canadian poet-critic Jason Guriel in a 2010 essay for *Parnassus: Poetry in Review*:

> How does a Language poet know when her poem is finished, or at least ready for the typesetter? (It strikes me that a non-linear and non-representational poetry of fragments that resist closure could go on forever.) Does a Language poem end where it does because its author got winded and, well, a poem has to end *somewhere*? What does her revision process look like? Why is it "Surfeit, sure fight," and not "Sure fight, surfeit"? Why couldn't the lines in "Solidarity Is the Name We Give to What We Cannot Hold" and "Let's Just Say" be shuffled into a different order and still enable the reader to come up with the same point about the wobbliness of words? And if the lines *can* be shuffled into a different order, why should the reader read the poems at all? . . . How many Language poems does it take to unscrew the signified from the signifier?[4]

Note Guriel's use of the female pronoun as if to claim that the strictures on Bernstein's poetry apply to *Language poetry tout court*. It's as if Ezra Pound were to be blamed for the shortcomings of the minor Vorticists published in *Blast!* or André Breton equated with some of the lesser French poets in the various surrealist anthologies. But the charge of formlessness has been made so frequently, at least in the anglophone world,[5] that I propose here to take it seriously. Discussions of Bernstein's poetry—and the bibliography is now enormous[6]—have focused on theory, using this or that poetic passage primarily to buttress particular arguments about poetics. Critics elucidate the principles of Language poetry, applaud (or question) Bernstein's critique of lyric, comment on his relentless attack on Official Verse Culture, and so on. What is missing is the actual reading of the poems themselves as well as of the individual volumes.[7]

In what follows, therefore, I want to make an experiment. I shall read one of Bernstein's longer poems—for the long poem is his primary genre—as well as a few of his recent short lyrics, *not* as examples of Language poetry but as poems to be read, first and foremost, on their own, even as Eliot's "Prufrock" and *The Waste Land* are discussed and admired by those who may never have read "Tradition and the Individual Talent" or "Hamlet and His Problems." Such an experiment is especially important today when the tendency is to discuss what I call "poetics minus the poetry,"[8] to rely too heavily on statements of intention at the expense of practice. Thus we regularly hear all about Charles Bernstein's "views": his commentary is available for all to read on social media, and his poetry readings, lectures, and interviews are easily accessible at PennSound. But what about the *poems* themselves?

In his brief preface to *Content's Dream*—a preface that is itself framed as prose poem ("Night falls, is used to; when all the cues seem larks and constancy's a brocade fan")—Bernstein poses the question, "Funny odd or funny peculiar?"[9] The reference here is to one of the commonly posed questions of my own childhood: "Funny ha ha or funny peculiar?," which is to say, was that meant to make you laugh (ha ha)? Or was it meant to make you feel a little uncomfortable? Funny peculiar? Bernstein gets rid of the *ha ha*: in his ironic universe, nothing is merely funny or of no consequence; it's all *funny peculiar*, otherwise known as *odd*. *Dark City* (the title of one of Bernstein's best volumes) is decisively funny peculiar: its oddities point to what Bernstein will call, in a recent book, *The Pitch of Poetry* (2016), the *pataque(e)rical*.

Getting the Wine into the Bowl

"A non-linear and non-representational poetry of fragments that resist closure could go on forever": Jason Guriel's stricture is hardly new. Consciously or not, such criticisms echo W. B. Yeats's famous critique, made in the introduction to his idiosyncratic selection for *The Oxford Book of Modern Verse* (1936), of his younger friend Ezra Pound's Cantos:

> Like other readers I discover at present merely *exquisite or grotesque fragments*. . . . Can impressions that are in part visual, in part metrical, be related like the notes of a symphony? . . .
>
> When I consider his work as a whole I find more style than form; at moments more style, more deliberate nobility and the means to convey it than in any contemporary poet known to me, but it is constantly

interrupted, broken, twisted into nothing by its direct opposite, nervous obsession, nightmare, stammering confusion. . . .

Style and its opposite can alternate, but *form must be full, sphere-like, single.* Even where there is no interruption he is often content, if certain verses and lines have style, to leave unbridged transitions, unexplained ejaculations, that make his meaning unintelligible. . . . Even where the style is sustained throughout one gets an impression, especially when he is writing *vers libre* that he has not got all the wine into the bowl.[10]

Eighty years later, this objection to *The Cantos* is still being voiced. Reviewing David Moody's biography of Pound for the *London Review of Books*, the poet Robert Crawford (who had himself recently published a major biography of T. S. Eliot) says of *The Pisan Cantos*, "Shot through with lyricism and flights of polylingual associative brilliance, *The Pisan Cantos* also contain much rambling and rant. The rant can be energetic; the problem is the rambling. . . . Pound constellates a vast collection of allusive snippets around the sometimes scarcely perceptible thread of his life-story."[11] And in a provocative piece called "*The Cantos* as Pedagogy," Michael Kindellan and Joshua Kotin argue that Pound's "tendency to insinuate connections between unconnected or barely connected things" testifies to "the ideogrammatic method's reliance on baseless assertion."[12]

The distrust of "unconnected" fragments dies hard. Despite decades of sophisticated commentary on the very careful craft of *The Cantos* on the part of critics from Hugh Kenner, Guy Davenport, and Christine Brooke-Rose to Richard Sieburth and Yunte Huang,[13] Pound's poetic mode continues to arouse suspicion. At issue is the understanding that, as the Brazilian poet-theorist Haroldo de Campos put it so succinctly in his important book *Ideograma*, "relations are more real and more important than the things they relate."[14] As de Campos, here following Roman Jakobson's seminal treatment of the "poetic function," notes:

Whereas for the referential use of language it makes no difference whether the word *astre* (star) can be found within the adjective *désastreux* ("disastrous") or the noun *désastre* ("disaster"), or whether there are affinities between *espectro* ("specter") and *spectator* ("spectator"). . . . [F]or the poet this kind of "discovery" is of prime relevance. In poetry, warns Jakobson, any phonological coincidence is felt to mean semantic kinship.[15]

"What the Chinese examples enhanced for [art historian Ernest] Fenollosa," de Campos continues, "was the homological and homologizing virtue of the poetic function." In the words of an earlier concrete poet, Öyvind Fahlström, "like-sounding words belong together; plays on words depend on them. . . . Thus if I hear of 'firing,' I am not sure whether someone has been shot, burnt or dismissed. Figs are related to figment, pigs to pigmentation."[16] Indeed, such aural, visual—and often etymological—connections are what make poetry poetry. "Little Boy Blue, come blow your horn . . .": in ordinary discourse, there's no relationship between color and blowing a horn, but in poetry the fact that the past tense of "blow" is "blew"—a homonym for "blue"—no doubt led the anonymous maker of the nursery rhyme select that color rather than red or green.

In nineteenth-century poetry—Baudelaire's "Le Voyage," which furnishes de Campos with his first example above, is a case in point—the seemingly sequential story line—from childhood imagination and desire to the disillusionment and remorse of old age—would seem to be fairly straightforward, but, as critics have long noted, it is the tension between the overt meaning of a given line or phrase and its subtext that is so striking. "Mers" (seas), for example, rhymes a number of times with "amers" (bitter), as if to warn us that the vast and tempting oceans are treacherous. Similarly, "paysages" rhymes with "nuages" and "capitale" with "fatale," and throughout there are elegant antitheses that turn out to be false leads and absurd hopes: in the final couplet, for example, "Plonger au fond du gouffre, Enfer ou Ciel, qu'importe? / Au fond de l'Inconnu pour trouver du *nouveau*!," the very repetition of *o* and *u* and of the *ou* diphthong in *gouffre* (gulf, abyss) and *trouver* (find) suggests that the anticipated *nouveau* (new) will be all too familiar.

With such sound figuration in mind, let's look at the opening poem in *Dark City* (1995), "The Lives of the Toll Takers."[17] The form of this and Bernstein's other long poems is often assumed to be a latter-day version of Charles Olson's famous "Projective Verse," the process poetics or "composition by field," governed by the famous principle, first spelled out by Robert Creeley, that "form is never more than an extension of content" and that in the "energy-construct" resulting, "one perception must immediately and directly lead to a further perception." For Olson and his fellow "New American" poets, projectivism or "open form" meant that each poem establishes its own form in an exploratory, unpredictable act of writing, prompted and shaped by the "pressures" of the poet's own voice—more specifically, the poet's breath.[18]

Open form, claiming its ancestry from Pound and William Carlos Williams, was the dominant mode of the 1960s and 1970s poetic avant-garde, from Black Mountain to the Beats, to the San Francisco and New York poets. But it is important to note that Bernstein's interpretation of Pound is very different from, say, Allen Ginsberg's. The ideogrammic method, as de Campos explains, emphasizes not the shaping breath or the move from one perception immediately leading to another but the homology, based on sonic, visual, or semantic echoes, of individual items—what Hugh Kenner referred to as Pound's "subject rhymes."[19] Then, too, the mode of Bernstein's poems, in contradistinction to, say, George Oppen's or Denise Levertov's, is that of satire. "The Lives of the Toll Takers" is a Popean *Dunciad* of sorts, its burlesque comedy replete with cerebral punning, elaborate wordplay, and parodic rhyme, in the vein of Byron's *Don Juan*:

> But—Oh! ye lords of ladies intellectual,
> Inform us truly, have they not hen-peck'd you all?

For Byron's *ottava rima* or Pope's heroic couplets, Bernstein's poem, which runs to 435 lines (although line count is deceptive because some lines have only a single word or syllable, while others are part of a prose paragraph, and there is much blank space between given passages), substitutes the mobility of typographic play: the poet's unit becomes not the stanza but the verbal fragment in tension with the overall page design. At the same time, at the phrasal level, Bernstein's sound structures often recall the high pitch of Hart Crane, as in "Slow / Applause flows into liquid cynosures," or "The dice of drowned men's bones he saw bequeath / An embassy."[20] Neither narrative nor the meditation of a grounded speaker in a particular landscape, nor the Olsonian "energy-discharge," the structure of "The Lives of the Toll Takers" is best characterized as montage: its connections are metonymic and paratactic rather than syntactic, its structure less temporal than spatial, although the sequence does drive to a tentative conclusion with its final word "besides," which leaves everything wide open for the reader, allowing as it does for the widest range of possibilities to come. And *besides* . . .

Working the Streets

Consider, for starters, the resonance of the poem's title. Not The Lives of the Saints or The Lives of the Poets or The Lives of the Rich and Famous, but "The Lives of the Toll Takers." We are all familiar with those anonymous men and women in glass booths or open-air stations, collecting toll money on our freeways and bridges and handing us change. The job of toll taker, mechanical and endlessly repetitive as it is, is not even an essential one, since today toll takers are largely being replaced by machines. Even in 1995, when Bernstein was composing the poem, toll takers were becoming obsolete.

Then again, toll takers do have lives: surely they have unique experiences like anyone else, pleasures and sorrows all their own.[21] And figuratively they are everywhere among us: people performing routine jobs just to make a living, or, in the opposite sense, those whose jobs exact a toll on themselves and others. "Working that job," we might say of Bernstein's character "The Klupsy Girl," "certainly took a toll on her." Moreover, the rhythm of toll taking is the rhythm of recurrence—and hence, by definition, boringly repetitive. Even then, however, there are unforeseen changes of rhythm, as when in Francis Ford Coppola's *The Godfather*, Sonny Corleone stops at the toll booth on the causeway to Queens only to find that the attendant has been replaced by his murderer. Such "speed bumps" become a challenge for the poet.

Here are the poem's first twenty lines:

There appears to be a receiver off the hook. Not that

you care.

Beside the gloves resided a hat and two

pinky rings, for which no

finger was ever found. Largesse

 with no release became, after

not too long, atrophied, incendiary,

 stupefying. Difference or

différance: it's

 the distinction between hauling junk and

 removing rubbish, while

 I, needless not to say, take

out the garbage

(pragmatism)

Phone again, phone again jiggety jig.

 I figured

 they do good eggs here.

 Funny $: making a killing on

junk bonds and living to peddle the tale

(victimless rime)   (*All the Whiskey*, 150–51)

At first reading (or hearing), "Lives" may seem casual and improvisatory—a
kind of stand-up comedy routine. But this "funny peculiar" passage is
actually highly structured. It begins with a bit of everyday conversation:

before the advent of cell phones, it was common to pick up the phone to make a call, only to find that one of the extensions in one's home or office was off the hook. It makes perfect sense to remark on this to a relative or friend, and when the latter does not respond, to complain, "Not that you care." You don't need to make a call! The exchange, in any case, provides the key leitmotif for the entire poem. In the world of the "toll takers," communication is blocked: nothing comes through the channel but noise. Thus the conversation between "I" and "you" breaks off and shifts to a kind of pseudo-Victorian narrative: "Beside the gloves resided a hat and two / pinky rings, for which no / finger was ever found." Pinky rings: In Victorian England, members of the royal family initiated the custom of wearing a wedding ring on one's fifth (pinky) finger, but in modern America, one usually associates pinky rings with images of gangsters: the Godfather Vito Corleone wears one. In "The Lives of the Toll Takers," however, the rings have no fingers to encircle: another sign of extreme dislocation. The disconnect—again in very formal and slightly archaic English—is an emblem of "Largesse / with no release," a largesse "atrophied, incendiary, / stupefying." Perhaps the reference is to the exchange of these rings, to wedding vows that don't work out or promises that have been broken and lead to unspecified trouble. In any case, something, in this old-fashioned tale, is very amiss but we don't know what.

No solution is forthcoming from our contemporary Great Thinkers. Jacques Derrida's insistence that there is a clear-cut distinction between *difference*, as we ordinarily use the word, and the *différance* of language, where no word has a fixed meaning but, on the contrary, *defers* meaning endlessly, is parodied in Bernstein's "distinction between hauling junk and / removing rubbish, while / I, needless not to say, take / out the garbage." Let's, even if it's offensive ("needless not to say"), not succumb to the highfalutin distinctions of French theory: American "pragmatism" (as in William James) is surely preferable.

And so on to the everyday lives of our toll takers. "To market to market to buy a fat pig, / Home again home again, jiggety jig." The nursery rhyme is adapted so as to put emphasis on the phone again—a "phone" that quite logically replaces "home" in our market economy where the "right" call makes the trade, never mind going to "market" in person and buying anything as tangible as a "fat pig." "I figured / they do good eggs here": a fellow trader, no doubt, is explaining why he or she chose a particular local restaurant for breakfast. Note that even a choice this mundane is one that has been "figured." The "funny money" ($) now cited is literally counterfeit, but in our culture all money is in a sense counterfeit—an empty signifier with nothing to back it up. "Making a killing on / junk bonds and living" not just to tell the tale, as the idiom has it, but to peddle it, this being a tale of junk bonds exchanged in what is a "victimless rime" (rhymes with "crime"). The crime ("rime") is ironically victimless in that the victims of Wall Street "killings" are anonymous and too numerous to specify. Our nursery rhymes, it seems, are not so innocent.

To recapitulate: the first twenty lines of "The Lives of the Toll Takers" use a variant of Pound's ideogrammic method to juxtapose fragments of conversation, Victorian narrative, pseudo-philosophical phrase making, parodic nursery rhyme, and familiar clichés and adages, repeatedly altered just enough to be recognized even as they are carefully skewed, so as to create a portrait of a domestic world so in thrall to business interests that the language of peddling and making killings no longer seems exceptional: it is simply the discourse of everyday life.

Who is speaking? Sentences like the first—"There appears to be a receiver off the hook"—may be attributed to a friend or relative, as in a drama or film, but the words may also be the poet's own, as in "I, needless not to say, take / out the garbage," and "I figured . . ." "The Lives of the Toll Takers" is by no means "personal" in any direct way, but that is not to say there isn't a very particular voice speaking here—a voice I can recognize and separate from the voices of other Language poets, New York poets, and so on. Bernstein's "I" functions as an angle of vision, a subject position, responding to a related set of propositions. And the vision, however depersonalized, is that of a bard: his lines are marked by elaborate alliteration, assonance, consonance, and internal rhyme, as in "*Beside* the gloves *resided* a hat and two / *pinky rings*, for which no *finger* was ever *found. Largesse* / with no re*lease.*" Enchanted, so to speak, by the associations his own words call up, the poet bombards us with clichés, slogans, aphorisms, proverbs, puns, familiar catchy tunes, pop songs, and nursery rhymes—individual motifs repeating themselves, always in bowdlerized form, as in "Phone again, phone again jiggety jig," "laughing all the way to the Swiss bank," and "the prison house of language," the latter a reference to Fredric Jameson's famous critical study, denouncing the formalist focus on the word as such, rather than on the word as symptomatic of larger cultural and political issues. It's as if Bernstein's antennae, unable to hear a familiar phrase without picking it up and turning it inside out, are almost feverishly attuned to the vagaries and contradictions of living in the marketplace of late twentieth-century America. Everything is always already mediated and waiting to be decomposed or reframed. But it is also the case that the references point to New York City—the New York of the tabloids and *Variety*, of TV comedy and nightclub humor, of subways and street crossings. And these references are in turn interwoven with more literary material: Bernstein's radius of discourse is that of the secular Jewish New Yorker turned, improbably, to himself, artist and intellectual.

The opening page of Bernstein's poem, in any case, sets the stage for what is to come in the lives of the toll takers and specifies what toll their environment takes on them and thus on the reader. In this connection, it is useful to note what sorts of references are not to be found in a Bernstein poem like this one. Unlike, say, John Ashbery's or Robert Creeley's, Bernstein's is a curiously asexual world: energy and power, far from having overtones of love and desire, are channeled into business, finance, and media activity. The poet is surrounded by people buying and selling; his competition is never with rival lovers; it's with other poets and with those (perhaps relatives) who want him to be successful in the accepted sense of the word. Voluble and entertaining, playing the prankster with his friends, this poet is nevertheless curiously isolated, standing on the sidelines, where he can take in the foibles and follies of his contemporaries. Thus Bernstein's is a *Dunciad* of overheard conversation and cartoonish gesture. His is a very social world as viewed through the lens of an antisocial observer.

Now consider how the threads of the opening page are developed in the course of this thirty-page poem. The recitation of absurd rhymes and jingles, always just a word or two *off*, recurs throughout, for example:

There was an old lady who lived in a
Zoo [for "shoe"],
she had so many admirers

  she didn't know what to rue [for "do"]—

or the continuous wordplay on the aphorism, "A picture is worth a thousand words," here becoming—cynically, "A picture [fixture] is worth more than a thousand words," and later, "(A picture is worth \$44.95 but no price can be put into words)," and so on. All the variants on the original adage circle around the concept of "worth." In the original adage, by now a cliché, a visual representation is much more graphic than a verbal account of the same thing: think of the photographs of Hiroshima or the Vietnam War that literally changed the course of history. But Bernstein literalizes the notion: in fact, a successful picture (painting) *is* worth more than "a thousand words," even as the price (\$44.95) can never be a measure of a given artwork's real worth. And the further irony is that Bernstein himself is using words, not pictures, to map his universe.

Or again, consider the variations on the song made popular by Frank Sinatra, "Button up your overcoat / When the wind is free / Take good care of yourself / You belong to me!":

<blockquote>

                                    Button

your lip, cl
asp your tie, you

re on the B team

</blockquote>

"Button Up Your Overcoat" is a cheery love song, *"Button / your lip"* a kind of threat, urging the addressee to shut up, to remember how to put his tie clip on correctly, the conclusion suggesting that the advice just given hasn't been taken since *"you / re"* on no better than *"the B team."* And indeed the toll taker's fate is set: in a scratchy echo of "A rose by another name . . ." we read "A job / by any other name / would smell as / sour."

No wonder: for the "lives of the toll takers" function, as the last page of the poem tells us, not in *"an operating system"* but in *"an / op / erating environm / ent."* The phrase splutters out: "in computer software," according to Wikipedia, an *operating environment*, also known as an integrated applications environment, is one in which users run application software. "It consists of a user interface provided by an applications manager and usually an application programming interface (API) to the applications manager." Such an environment is of course rigidly controlled, but the "control" is not the artist's, as Bernstein proposes in "Stray Straws and Straw Men," but that of an impersonal system that governs exactly what the user can and cannot do, as rigidly as the movement through the toll both controls the driver's options. But the wrenching of the phrase, with the comma getting its own line—

> *It's*
>
> ,
>
>   *s'an*
>
>   *op*
>   *erating environm*
> *ent—*

implies that this operating environment simply doesn't function. Not with a receiver off the hook . . .

The blocked communication channel is, as I've already noted, one of the key motifs throughout the poem. And, to trace another ongoing thread, communication failure is everywhere related to *money*. This is, after all, a poem about paying tolls, and its scene is one of buying and selling, hot tips and broken promises, junk bonds and stock options. Bernstein's is not so much the genteel world of Wall Street as it is the rough-and-tumble world of the uptown neighborhoods and suburbs, of deal making and business breakfasts, "laughing all the way," not just to the bank, as the idiom has it, but appropriately to the Swiss bank, where international customers deposit and launder their assets, perhaps "in gold bars." "Exemptions," "off-peak" trading, "A depository of suppositories," "current fees" that "barely cover expenses," and a host of other business references pile up and culminate in such plaintive and absurd questions as—in a twist of Bob Dylan's "If dogs run free, then why not we?"—"Catalogs are free, why not we?"

Self-help manuals and bits of good advice on everything from buying gold to composing successful poetry permeate the poem. The debasement of poetry into poe-biz is a theme throughout. One of the funniest of the self-help bits, this time on the poetry front, is the following True Confession:

> I had decided to go back
> to school after fifteen years in
> community poetry because I felt

> I did not know enough to navigate
> through the rocky waters that
> lie ahead for all of us in this field.
> How had Homer done it, what might Milton
> teach? Business training turned
> out to be just what I most needed.
> Most importantly, I learned that
> for a business to be successful, it
> needs to be different, to stand out
> from the competition. In poetry,
> this differentiation is best
> achieved through the kind of form
> we present.

Grotesque as these lines, written in the early 1990s, sound, today they have become almost normative: one finds such suggestions everywhere in promotions of "creativity" and "entrepreneurship" in the "humanities." The key word is *form*, reduced, in our own *operating environment*, to *format*—to mere technique chosen from a Microsoft Word menu or manual. And when form is reduced to format, *language* is inevitably unhinged:

> never only
> dedef
> ining, always rec
> onstricting (libidinal
> flow just another
> word for loose
> st
> ools).

Language, abused, copied, misconstrued, recycled, takes a heavy toll. Words and morphemes fly apart, the line breaks and cuts acting to distort words and phrases almost beyond recognition. Dialogue repeatedly presents us with such misconstrual: the "triple play / on all designated *ghost* morphemes" leads to the qualification "(you mean morphemes)" and the immediate huffy response, "[don't tell me what I mean! /]" signed by someone with the initial

"J." Throughout the poem, not *X* but *Y* is a frequent construction: "Simplicity is not / the / same as simplistic"; "Not angles / just / tangles"; "No 'mere' readers only / writers who read, actors who inter- / act"; "not this or this either, seeing five sides to every issue." Since the channel is full of noise, the words start to fly apart, morphemes are opened up and contain unexpected paragrams, and when, on the penultimate page, "significant" questions start to come up, culminating in "Daddy, what did you / do to stop the war?," the computer crashes:

[p-

=Jovwhu2g97hgbcf67q6fbqujx67sf21g97b.c.9327b97b987b87j7
7TD7KTQ98GDUKBHG G9TQ9798 ICXQY2F108YTSCXAGS62JC.

Text is now finally reduced to garbage. But then again, the numbers on the screen are mostly sequences containing 6, 7, 8, and 9. Perhaps this *is*, after all, a language that can be decoded? It's a natural impulse, in any case, to *try* to decode it. On the other hand, in toll taker land, as we read on the poem's penultimate page, "It's not / what you / know but / who knows / about it / & who's likely to squeal." Here, too, is a pragmatic solution, if a very cynical one. And "besides . . ." The poem's last word resonates with possibility. Perhaps, it implies, there *is* a way out. Or at least a further explanation. And besides: let the reader complete the sequence and pay the toll.

Shoring the Fragments against One's Ruins

In relating the seemingly "unrelatable," Bernstein's is an art of excess, baroque in its piling up of manifold exemplars of the follies and mendacities of our Waste Land, an unreal—or, more properly, hyperreal city that splinters into fragments before our eyes as "the profit and the loss" of Eliot's "Death by Water" is carried to its absurdly logical conclusion. Indeed, as we make our way through single-word lines and prose paragraphs, through Tin Pan Alley songs and computer coding instructions, we watch the breakdown of the "'operating environment' (op / erating environm / ent)" until there is nothing left except a series of numbers spewing out from all the computers and calculators in sight. The poem's rhythm of recurrence always takes the most subtle differentials into account: one letter or phoneme can make all the difference, as in the overheard remark, "Funny, you don't look / gluish."

Bernstein's art of excess is not easy to maintain. If there is a downside to this poem's exuberant and elaborate verbal play, it is, I think, that certain allusions will date, for example the references on the second page to "a 1965 'short stabs' poem / by Ted 'bowl over' Berrigan" and the aside, "Barbara Kruger is enshrined in the window / of the Whitney's 1987 Biennial" on the following page. It's not that Berrigan and Kruger aren't significant art figures of the late twentieth century, but it isn't clear—at least not to me—why they are singled out for inclusion in the riff on the commercialization of poetry and painting: the specificity of reference seems at odds with the hyperreality of the scene. Again, some of Bernstein's effects are too easy: for instance, "Andy / Warhol is the / P. T. Barnum / of the / (late) / twentieth century," followed by the too-clever pun, "there's a /succor dead every twenty seconds."

But then think of how many lines of *The Waste Land* manuscript Pound crossed out. It is almost inevitable, as Edgar Allan Poe insisted, that a long poem will have lapses. On the whole, "The Lives of the Toll Takers" maintains its difficult juggling act. And once the reader gets the hang of the poem's spatial form—the cutting and positioning of words and phrases on the page, forcing us to see what the Russian futurists called "the letter as such," as in

    word for loose

    st
    ools)—

where the hiss of "st" and chiasmus of "loose / stools" says it all, the poem's careful construction becomes obvious.

To understand this and related Bernstein poems, in any case, we need to bypass current clichés about schools and movements. Language poetry is regularly read against its seeming precursors: the New York school, objectivism, Black Mountain. But if we take Harold Bloom's *The Anxiety of Influence* seriously, we begin to see that, however much Bernstein may protest that he has been influenced by Louis Zukofsky and Robert Creeley, by

Gertrude Stein and George Oppen, his real affinities are for those two great modernists whose politics and ideological stances he so often found objectionable—the Eliot of *The Waste Land* and Ezra Pound.

In a controversial essay called "Pounding Fascism," originally presented as a Modern Language Association talk in 1985, Bernstein insisted that one must recognize—and decry—Pound's fascism even as his best work inadvertently undermines his own theories:

> Pound's great achievement was to create a work using ideological
> swatches from many social and historical sectors of his own society and
> an immense variety of other cultures. This complex, polyvocal textuality
> was the result of his search—his unrequited desire for—deeper truths
> than could be revealed by more monadically organized poems, operating
> with a single voice and a single perspective. But Pound's ideas about what
> mediated these different materials are often at odds with how these types
> of textual practices actually work in *The Cantos*.[22]

This is an important point. Here is a representative passage from Canto 80 in the Pisan sequence:

> It is said also that Homer was a medic
> who followed the greek armies to Troas
> so in Holland Park they rolled out to beat up Mr. Leber
> (restaurantier) to Monsieur Dulac's disgust
> and a navy rolls up to me in Church St. (Kensington End) with:
> > Yurra Jurrman!
> To which I replied: I am *not*.
> "Well yurr szum kind ov a furriner."
> > Ne povans desraciner[23]

The "mishearing" of English and German in the London of World War I brings together a dizzying set of references, looking ahead in its multivocalism to the "misseaming" of Bernstein's own "Dysraphism" or "Amblyopia." But the Pound of *The Pisan Cantos* could move easily from his burlesque rendition of German accents and off-color war stories to the high seriousness of "dove sta memoria": the elegiac note that opens *The Pisan Cantos* with the famous line "The enormous tragedy of the dream in the peasant's bent shoulders" (Canto 74) and concludes the sequence with the words:

> If the hoar frost grip thy tent
> Thou wilt give thanks when night is spent. (Canto 84)

In a similar vein, Bernstein's baroque excess is often qualified by a dark lyric note. In recent years, for example, he has turned to the love song and ballad for imaginative transformation. The impetus seems to have been the tragic death of his adored daughter Emma (age twenty-three) in 2008; the question, from a critical perspective, was how a poet so given to irony, parody, burlesque, and satire, a poet who had always avoided autobiographical, much less confessional, poetry, would address such a rupture. Here is "Today Is the Last Day of Your Life 'til Now":

> I was the luckiest father in the world
> Until I turned unluckiest
> They shoot horses, don't they?
> In the mountains the air is so
> Thin you can scarcely say your
> name. I dreamt I was a drum.
> In the dream, I dreamt I was a
> School boy afraid of school. I dreamt
> I was drowning. Far away, the
> crush of snow refracted the still muted
> light. As if punishment was not
> punishment enough.[24]

This comes from *Recalculating* (2013), in which Bernstein includes many translations and adaptations that have obliquely given this would-be anti-expressivist poet permission to treat of his own lost love, from "Auto-psychographia" (after Fernando Pessoa) to "Be Drunken" (Baudelaire) and "Le Pont Mirabeau" (Guillaume Apollinaire). In these translations, the poets in question provide the mask that the reticent Bernstein evidently feels he needs, but what about the "straightforward" "Today Is the Last Day of Your Life 'Til Now," with its play on "Today is the first day of the rest of your life"?

Aren't those opening lines, "I was the luckiest father in the world / until I turned the unluckiest," almost painfully raw in their reference to the loss of the person this poet most adored?

As in his satire, Bernstein solves the problem by avoiding all personal reference. We know nothing about Emma—not even her name and certainly not the circumstances of her death or memories of her life. Nor do we know anything about this father's own life—no excuses, no explanations. The aim is to project *how it feels*, avoiding all mitigating circumstances or occasions for self-pity. This is a poem about grief, pure and simple. "They shoot horses, don't they?" Even horses are routinely taken out of their agony, he notes, so why not he? The line's allusion to the 1969 film about a group of losers and derelicts is apropos: the poet has reached bottom. "I dreamt I was a drum" is less a narrative of dream content than a visceral description: to feel like a dream is to feel one's head and heart pounding unbearably, even as to dream that one is "a school boy afraid of school" is an impossible situation. The poet's dreams are unbearable but also wish fulfillments: no doubt, he would like to drown but already the "still muted / light" is coming up, "refracted" by a "crush of snow." It seems that there is no choice but to go on, "As if punishment was not / punishment enough."

I don't know a contemporary elegy more moving than this one unless it is the title poem of *All the Whiskey in Heaven*, which I have heard Bernstein read many times. Again, on first hearing, I found the language of excess almost too painful: the "No, never, I'll never stop loving you" seemed too much the stuff of a Frank Sinatra pop song, and the transparency of the whole ballad seemed, well, not quite seemly:

> Not for all the whiskey in heaven
> Not for all the flies in Vermont
> Not for all the tears in the basement
> Not for a million trips to Mars
>
> Not if you paid me in diamonds
> Not if you paid me in pearls
> Not if you gave me your pinky ring
> Not if you gave me your curls

Not for all the fire in hell
Not for all the blue in the sky
Not for an empire of my own
Not even for peace of mind

No, never, I'll never stop loving you
Not till my heart beats its last
And even then in my words and my songs
I will love you all over again.[25]

This is a pseudo-ballad, the lines largely failing to measure up to the *abcb* ballad rhyme, except in the clichéd "pearls" / "curls" rhyme of stanza 2, and the rhythm faltering awkwardly, as in line 4 where the flowing anapestic rhythm of the first three lines is curtailed. Such short-circuiting befits the irreverent title: heaven hardly seems the place where one will get all the whiskey one wants; too much whiskey, after all, is hurtful, and its intake is usually associated with the road to hell rather than to heaven. The nectar of the gods would be nice, or perhaps champagne: heaven might be the place to keep these flowing, but whiskey? No. And the catalog that follows now turns bizarre: I will never stop loving you, not for all the flies in Vermont! Aren't these the opposite of what we want of immortality? "Tears in the basement"? Hardly. And even astronauts are not eager to make "a million trips to Mars."

The second stanza begins by coming back to the more acceptable pop theme: "Not if you paid me in diamonds / Not if you paid me in pearls." But "pinky ring"? Who even wants one? And the gift of curls would mean they were not on the lost girl's head. As the ballad continues, it becomes more and more disjointed: the fire in hell is equated with the blue in the sky. All the talk of heaven and hell and empires is pure posturing: this elegist won't give up his pain "even for peace of mind." And so, in the final stanza, the hackneyed "I'll love you till my heart beats its last" is rejected, the poet exclaiming that he cannot conceive even of a *death* that will end his pain. Indeed, the one thing that is eternal is neither heaven nor hell: it is *pain*.

Interestingly enough, the excess of the satiric poems becomes, for Charles Bernstein, the very stuff of the love elegy. Hyperbole, contradiction, the juxtaposition of unlike items, the "bad taste" of unpleasant suppositions, the explosion of conventional form: these create a poetic complex as rich as it is strange and distinctive. The longer poems, often sequences of short units like those in "All the Whiskey," are ambitious in their reach and range even as Pound's *Cantos* have the serial form of accumulation, splicing together smaller lyrics for greater resonance. It is, to return to Jakobson's definition of the poetic function, the *way of relating*, not the *what* that *is related*, that counts. And to study those modes of relating in Bernstein—those senses, as Fahlström noted, in which "firing" can refer to shooting, burning, or the dismissal of an employee—is to appreciate one of the signature poetic oeuvres of late modernism.

Notes

1. Charles Bernstein, "Recalculating," in *Recalculating* (Chicago: University of Chicago Press, 2013), 174.

2. Charles Bernstein, "Stray Straws and Straw Men" (1976), in *Content's Dream: Essays 1975–1984* (Los Angeles: Sun & Moon Press, 1986), 40–49, passage cited 40–41.

3. See, for example, Helen Vendler's review of Jorie Graham's *Sea Change*, "A Powerful, Strong Torrent," *New York Review of Books* 55, no. 10 (June 12, 2008), http://www.nybooks.com/articles/2008/06/12/a-powerful-strong-torrent/; cf. Dan Chiasson, "Entangled: The Poetry of Rae Armantrout," *New Yorker*, May 17, 2010, http://www.newyorker.com/magazine/2010/05/17/entangled/. Citing Bernstein's "Dysraphism," Chiasson writes, "the tired puns, the mugging post-everything politics, the harangues, the joyless *jouissance*. Boy did it catch on. . . . Bernstein, an eminent professor at Penn, was recently signed up by Farrar, Straus & Giroux, Robert Lowell's publisher."

4. Jason Guriel, "Words Fail Him: The Poetry of Charles Bernstein," review of *All the Whiskey in Heaven: Selected Poems*, *Parnassus: Poetry in Review* 33, nos. 1–2 (2013): 370–89, http://parnassusreview.com/archives/1791/. The reference to "Surfeit, Sure Fight" is to "Dysraphism," line 86.

5. The situation—as I shall comment below—is very different abroad: Bernstein has won major prizes in Austria, Germany, and Hungary; he has been widely translated in China, Japan, Korea, Brazil, Chile, and Mexico; and he frequently gives readings in France, Italy, and Scandinavia.

6. See Charles Bernstein's author page at the Electronic Poetry Center at the State University of New York at Buffalo for a very full and up-to-date bibliography of primary and secondary sources.

7. I have, over the years, commented on a number of key Bernstein poems, though not usually in their entirety. See the following, in chronological order: on "Dysraphism," in "The Word as Such: L=A=N=G=U=A=G=E Poetry in the Eighties," in

The Dance of the Intellect: Studies in the Poetry of the Pound Tradition (Cambridge: Cambridge University Press, 1985), 228–32, and again in "Can(n)on to the Right of Us, Can(n)on to the Left of Us," in *Poetic License: Essays on Modernist and Postmodernist Lyric* (Evanston, IL: Northwestern University Press, 1990), 11–14; on "Safe Methods of Business" vis-à-vis John Ashbery's "Business Personals," in *Radical Artifice: Writing Poetry in the Age of Media* (Chicago: University of Chicago Press, 1991), 185–97; on "The Lives of the Toll Takers," in *21st-Century Modernism: The "New" Poetics* (Oxford: Basil Blackwell, 2002), 173–79, and "Representing Speech in Conceptual Poetry," *Dibur Literary Journal*, no. 1 (Fall 2015), http://arcade.stanford.edu/dibur_issue/spoken-word-written-word-rethinking-representation-speech-literature-0/. My discussion of Bernstein's Walter Benjamin libretto "Shadowtime" is found in Chapter 4, "Writing through Walter Benjamin," in *Unoriginal Genius: Poetry by Other Means in the New Century* (Chicago: University of Chicago Press, 2010), 76–98.

8. A case in point is Barrett Watten's *Questions of Poetics: Language Writing and Consequences* (Iowa City: University of Iowa Press, 2016), which barely considers an author's poems, except as exemplifying this or that theoretical or political move.

9. Bernstein, preface to *Content's Dream*, 10.

10. W. B. Yeats, introduction to *The Oxford Book of Modern Verse, 1892–1935*, ed. W. B. Yeats (Oxford: Oxford University Press, 1936), xxiv–xxvi.

11. Robert Crawford, "He Was the Man," review of *Ezra Pound, Poet: A Portrait of the Man and His Work*, vol. 3: *The Tragic Years, 1939–72*, by A. David Moody, *London Review of Books* 38, no. 13 (June 30, 2016), 32–33.

12. Michael Kindellan and Joshua Kotin, "*The Cantos* and Pedagogy," *Modernist Cultures* 12, no. 3 (2017): 345–63.

13. See my chapter "'No Edges, No Convexities': Ezra Pound and the Circle of Fragments," in *The Poetics of Indeterminacy: Rimbaud to Cage* (1981; Evanston, IL: Northwestern University Press, 1999), 155–99.

14. Haroldo de Campos, "Poetic Function and the Ideogram / The Sinological Argument," in *Novas: Selected Writings of Haroldo de Campos*, ed. Antonio Sergio Bessa and Odile Cisneros (Evanston, IL: Northwestern University Press, 2007), 287–311.

15. With respect to the words *astre*, *désastreux*, and *désastre*, de Campos refers to Charles Baudelaire, "Le Voyage," part IV, stanza 1:

> Nous avons vu des astres
> Et des flots; nous avons vu des sables aussi;
> Et, malgré bien des chocs et d'imprévus désastres,
> Nous nous sommes souvent ennuyés, comme ici.

16. Öyvind Fahlström, "Hipy papy bthuthdththuthda bthuthdy: Manifesto for

Concrete Poetry," in *Öyvind Fahlström on the Air: Manipulating the World*, ed. Teddy Hultberg (Stockholm: Sveriges Radios Förlag/Fylkingen), 109–20, esp. 115.

17. Charles Bernstein, "The Lives of the Toll Takers," in *Dark City* (Los Angeles: Sun & Moon Press, 1994), 9–28. Reprinted in Charles Bernstein, *All the Whiskey in Heaven: Selected Poems* (New York: Farrar, Straus and Giroux, 2010), 150–79. I cite the text from *All the Whiskey* here, due to greater accessibility. For an earlier discussion of the opening lines of "Lives," see Perloff, *21st-Century Modernism*, 172–79.

18. Charles Olson, "Projective Verse," in *Human Universe and Other Essays*, by Charles Olson, ed. Donald Allen (New York: Grove Press, 1967), 51–61. "Projective Verse" has been widely reprinted; it appears in virtually every anthology of American poetics of the period, beginning with Donald Allen's *The New American Poetry, 1945–1960* (New York: Grove Press, 1960). See Eleanor Berry and Alan Golding's entry for "Projective Verse" in *The Princeton Encyclopedia of Poetry and Poetics*, 4th ed., ed. Roland Greene and Stephen Cushman (Princeton, NJ: Princeton University Press, 2012), 1109–10.

19. Hugh Kenner, *The Pound Era* (Berkeley: University of California Press, 1991), 92–93.

20. See, on this point, Perloff, *Radical Artifice*, 185–87.

21. In the *San Francisco Chronicle* (May 31, 1999), there is an article by Carolyne Zinko on this very question:

> There's the slap, the snatch, and the ball of change.
> These are the moments that make up a day in the life of a Bay Area toll taker. Five hundred times an hour, eight hours a day, as the cars approach endlessly, like lemmings to the sea.
> Toll collectors must make change with as few bills as possible, and balance the cash drawer at the end of each shift.
> They must count cars and axles that come through their lane. They must give directions. They must be happy. And above all, no matter how cranky the motorists are, they must never snap back.

And Zinko tells the story of one particular toll taker, Peter Klein, sixty, who has held the job for twenty-six years and says he has come to enjoy observing and classifying the various toll payers who pass through his booth (Perloff, *21st-Century Modernism*, 173–74).

22. Charles Bernstein, "Pounding Fascism (Appropriating Ideologies: Mystification, Aestheticization, and Authority in Pound's Poetic Practice," in *A Poetics* (Cambridge, MA: Harvard University Press, 1992), 121–27, passage cited 123.

23. Ezra Pound, *The Cantos* (1970; New York: New Directions, 1993), 523.

24. Bernstein, *Recalculating*, 158.

25. Bernstein, *All the Whiskey in Heaven*, 297.

CHAPTER 11

The Recipe for Charles Wright

JOHN FARRELL

All the while we thought we were writing for the angels,
And find, after all these years,
Our lines were written in black ink on the midnight sky.

—CHARLES WRIGHT, "LITTLEFOOT 18"

IF THERE WERE a recipe for writing a fine poem, no one would use it, and not just because the recipe would have already been filled so many times that readers would be tired of it. The very idea of a poem that can be reliably assembled out of preexisting elements, without a display of imagination or skill, is contrary to poetry's nature. The audience for poetry is restless for new and varied satisfactions, demonstrations of skill that exploit new possibilities in the medium. Even the oldest wine must come in new bottles. Moderately educated readers who could enjoy a poem, even one written along the lines of the best-chosen exemplars, without comparing it with the run of human powers and the state of the art—which is to say, with their past experience of reading—would have no need for a new poem at all. They might as well be content with the ones they know.

Value in poetry depends essentially on the poet's demonstration of skill in the choice or invention or arrangement either of words or thoughts or happenings, some or all of these. Not everything need be new, of course, but even in the most traditional and stereotyped performance, there must be something in the amalgam that transforms the combination of well-known elements into an unforeseen and valuable experience. The merest hint that the performance is explicable—that it was copied from another source, for example—is enough to deflate its interest. It is no fault for Ashbery to sound like Ashbery, or Bishop to sound like Bishop, but for another poet the effect would be fatal even if the mimicry were perfect. It is the act of composition we are responding to, not just the words. As Edward Young put it, "He that imitates the divine *Iliad* does not imitate Homer."[1] To imitate Homer, you need to make your own poem. And for Ashbery to imitate himself *too* often also becomes a fault, a lapse into mechanism.

The recipe-proof nature of poetry vetoes every reductive theory of value. If class or status or political interest could account for the success of a poem, all a poet would have to do to achieve success would be to express ideas that appeal to a certain class, foster a certain cause, or provide a certain degree of status to readers. But things aren't that simple. Even the people for whom works are intended or whose point of view they express do not necessarily enjoy them on that account. And if certain psychological themes were enough to animate a work of art, furnishing them would be easy. Had Poe been right that the death of a beautiful woman is a surefire poetic subject, there are plenty of ways to conjure up beautiful women and kill them off. But such tricks soon wear thin. Freud thought that *Oedipus the King*, *Hamlet*, and *The Brothers Karamazov* were the three greatest works of literature because they dramatize the universal wish to kill the father. If he had been right, then all works would be about this theme, and they would all be equally moving. So much for psychoanalysis.

I do not mean to say that the factors cited by psychologists or social theorists have no explanatory value, but they do not have the value claimed for them. They provide half-truths at most. All Quattrocento madonnas present roughly the same attitudes, the same ideas, ideology, and class interests; they offer the same status value for the viewer, the same opportunity for learned display or scholarly analysis. But some of them are undeniably better than others in a way that social categories can't explain. Many artists, too, have offered explanatory recipes for the creation of new works; in fact, since the time of Wordsworth artists have depended more and more upon the theory, the manifesto, and the movement to support their personal innovations. The salvos they launch against the old recipes tend to strike deep, but the new recipes turn out to be short-lived. Each new movement has its power to attack reigning conventions, direct artistic initiative, instill creative morale, launch a parti pris, and conduct the reaction of the audience, but they are still destined to go out of style. The more narrowly explanatory the theory, the less effective in the long run. Artistic programs do not ultimately provide the standards for judging even the works of literature they motivate, not to mention those that were not created with them in mind. Their value is primarily diagnostic and destructive.

The truism about literature's dependence upon inimitable skill would hardly be worth stating if the past century and a half of poetic experiments had left anything else we could plausibly say about what makes a poem worth reading. Until the mid-nineteenth century, the boundaries of poetic innovation were relatively stable and so well worn as to approach the mechanical, but since then poets have pursued a course of relentless explosion, deflation, and subtraction. They have attempted the annihilation of form in the pursuit of content; the evacuation of content in the pursuit of form; the suppression of the oral and the vocal; the automation of language; the spatialization of the page; the refusal of all the traditional demands of poetry including that its interest last longer than a day. And poets have experimented with just about every combination of these. Hence the perennial need for theory. As a result of all this innovation and experiment, all that is left to identify the common properties of poetry is the personal display of skill at putting words on the printed page—to whatever end that can sustain the reader's interest. Poets still bear the burden of providing something you have not seen before, something that is worth experiencing and takes you by surprise. But the fact that surprise has turned out to be the last touchstone we can use for the value of poetry is telling in itself, surprise being an entirely relative and unstable criterion. Surprise can only be accomplished against the background of what is already expected, and that is constantly changing. Surprise is in itself a principle of change and draws our attention back to the ancient insight that poetry is an intrinsically competitive activity. Success in poetry demands leaving one's competitors behind. The experience of poetry is never simply an experience of the text. It is always in response to a performance in context.

The spirit in which recipes are created is entirely different. They represent an attempt to help others less skilled than oneself repeat a performance. The recipes for poetry produced by practitioners like Wordsworth or Pound serve a different goal, the need, as Coleridge put it to Wordsworth, on the part of "every great and original writer, in proportion as he is great and original," to "create the taste by which he is to be relished."[2] To be persuasive, such recipes, being works of propaganda, must be very broad, but to grasp the full useless-ness and irony of poetic recipes, we have to imagine a recipe that actually engages with the details of an extended poetic performance. Here, then, is a recipe for the life's work of the widely recognized American poet Charles Wright as he has been practicing it for six decades. To produce a Wright poem:

1. Greet every new day as the occasion for a poem, and every poem as a new version of the same day. Confine yourself to lyrics, except when stringing them together into a long poem. But be certain that any section of any poem would be at home in any other. Write the same poem over and over again your whole life, but succeed in making it striking, beautiful, and never totally familiar.

2. Never leave a word out of place. Perfect the ear in a single, subtle octave, without ever missing a note. No vulgarity, no relevance, no colloquialism, no idioms, no stress. No italics, changes of tone or register. None of the local inflections of English. Never use a word that would be out of place translating Montale or Rilke. Make every line a pitch-perfect compromise between sound, sense, feel of the mouth, and aura—"One ear to the moon's brass sigh."

3. Set a poem in every place you have ever lived, but make all those places indistinguishable. Notice history in its setting but do not respond to it. Establish local coordinates without local color. Skim only the surface of your life into poetry.

4. Focus exclusively on landscape and the self, moving from the first to the second and back again. Include the landscape of memory, but do not remember actions or events. No politics, no history, no violence, no therapy. No achievements, failures, regrets, or missed opportunities. No love, either Eros or Agape. Meditate upon the permanent features of day and night—sky, wind, water, stars, trees, flowers, birds, and selected beasts. Observe the nuances of light. Never crack a smile or hazard a joke.

5. Admit people—other poets that is—only as memories, traces in the landscape or in the language with which you describe it. Visit one of their landscapes now and again to feel your self in it. But tell no tales, create no drama, and be moved only by the human condition in which you find yourself. Remain observant of the wind, the water, and the sky. Stick to the one poem you are always writing.

6. Honor the line above all, its inner tensions and unexpected resolutions. Never ask a line to begin without the flourish of a capital letter. Achieve beauty without grandiloquence or emphasis. In the vein of Keats, load every rift with ore—"twistwart and starbane."

7. Hover near the brink of sense or just beyond it, "on the far side of the simile." Show that lucidity can do without clarity, that simplicity can keep secrets. Encounter words and ideas as things, things as ideas, and ideas as words. Weigh them against each other and keep them in balance. Live in metaphor, but mostly as a grammatical device, a source of indications for an ungraspable link between things and ideas. Marshal rhetoric and repetition, but only to vary your posture or lend a hint of structure.

8. Philosophize about language and existence, citing occasional authorities. But never be drawn into argument. Let arguments justify themselves by the experience of the lines. Babble wisdom, formulate aphorisms, in a dream you will never leave.

9. Stay in the first person and the present tense—what is happening, now, in your mind, in your world, without ever becoming personal. Share with your reader the benefits of a lifetime of perfect weather, its infinite variations and velleities, from which you never allow yourself to be distracted.

10. Linger in the gentle presence of God, even though he does not exist! Solicit a kind of transcendence guaranteed by all that's missing. But find your ultimate safety in nothing—the nothing that is you confronting the nothing all around you. Yet do not freeze with Stevens's Snowman. The nothing is too rich and abundant to be cold. It is not an unforgiving emptiness. It is warm and full, a night with stars and wind and "the silvery alphabet of the sea." Find it everywhere and in yourself and spend your life filling book after book out of its

inexhaustible hollow center. Offset the hollowness of this via negativa with the acoustical fullness and rightness of your line.

This is the recipe for being Charles Wright. No one could follow it, and following it would be no use. Its value lies entirely in its seeming impossibility, but what is remarkable is how well Wright has proceeded as if by these instructions, poem after poem, for over half a century. This, for example, is "Dog Day Vespers."

Sun like an orange mousse through the trees,
A snowfall of trumpet bells on the oleander;
                              mantis paws
Craning out of the new wistaria; fruit smears in the west . . .
DeStael knifes a sail on the bay;
A mother's summons hangs like a towel on the dusk's hook.

Everything drips and spins
In the pepper trees, the pastel glide of the evening
Slowing to mother-of-pearl and the night sky.
Venus breaks clear in the third heaven.
Quickly the world is capped, and the seal turned.

I drag my chair to the deck's edge and the blue ferns.
I'm writing you now by flashlight,
The same news and the same story I've told you often before.
As the stag-stars begin to shine,
A wing brushes my left hand,
                              but it's not my wing.[3]

The familiar elements of a Wright poem are here: the presence of appearances, the "I" that witnesses the appearances, and the absence that suggests something beyond mere appearances—"not my wing." There is also the "you," the reader, an addressee perhaps among the living, perhaps among the dead. The order in which these elements appear can vary. Wright composes, as he puts it, in "tonal blocks . . . that work off one another,"[4] but the effect is not one of drama or tension, build-up or resolution. The effect is line by line, keeping just the right pitch, with a perfect internal balance of sound. Perceptions emerge in an orchestrated sequence, but that too is mere appearance. It is all quite beautiful, remarkably so, but in a static, placid, or even complacent way—"a gentian snood of twilight in winter."[5] Stendhal's definition of beauty as a promise of happiness seems to fail here. The beauty of the words, the thoughts, and the objects is always a different beauty, each in its own realm. None of them strains toward the other, and the sense of promise does not arise, though, as we shall see, Wright eventually came to experience a sense of disappointed promise.

Here is the "Beauty" sonnet from the sequence "Skins."

> In the brushstroke that holds the angel's wing
> Back from perfection; in
> The synapse of word to word; in the one note
> That would strike the infinite ear
> And save you; and in
> That last leap, the sure and redeeming edge . . .
> In all beauty there lies
> Something inhuman, something you can't know:
> In the pith and marrow of every root
> Of every bloom; in the blood-seam
> Of every rock; in the black lung of every cloud
> The seed, the infinitesimal seed
> That dooms you, that makes you nothing,
> Feeds on its self-containment and grows big.[6]

This is a characteristic example of Wright's soothsaying, though it stands out for the absence of pictorial setting. Wright conjures up a whimsical background of assumptions as if they were proverbial, builds a hive of metaphorical structures, leading toward a proclamation of emptiness and loss that is nevertheless strung upon rich, resonating sequences of sound and image. Beauty is beyond the graspable just like the sense of the words, yet the distance between beauty and the inhuman, the nothing, is delicately bridged by Wright's lyricism. The rhetorical parallels give the poem an insistence and force that contrast with its elusiveness, and the sonnet form, with its double climax, provides a tension and impetus unusual for Wright. The arrival of "nothing" is not deflating. It is an absence, a gap, that keeps the poet at the right contemplative distance—still attentive, still hoping. Authentic presence would be implausible, deflating, and, for Wright, beyond words. Wright's persona is not so much a speaker as a thinker, a muser, whose rhetorical constructions are a vestigial habit and who, with no audience to address, can be guided as much by the sense of sound as by the sound of sense. The Baudelairean crescendo of the ending is uncharacteristic, almost a hint of irony toward the fecundity of emptiness.

Despite his love of Italian poetry, and his fine translations of Eugenio Montale, whose thick verbal texture he ingeniously rarefies, Wright's linguistic register is densely Anglo-Saxon, a panoply of sounds ever on the verge of music, and we are reminded that Hopkins was one of his early discoveries.

> Dog Creek: cat track and bird splay,
> Spindrift and windfall; woodrot;
> Odor of muscadine, the blue creep
> Of kingsnake and copperhead;
> Nightweed; frog spit and floating heart,
> Backwash and snag pool: Dog Creek

> Starts in the leaf reach and shoal run of the blood.[7]

Thinking of Hopkins, we might expect some celebration to follow this revel in the richness of word and thing, but the mention of blood is already unsettling, and the section will end with "false flesh." Wright can flirt with a Heaneyesque confidence in the richness of things, "the music of what's real" where, as he puts it, "The plainsong of being, is happening all the while."[8] "Reconstruct, not deconstruct," he recommends, a warning to unwelcome readers. On the whole, though, it is the emptiness of things that comes through, and the inadequacy of language to make up for it, since "language, always, is just language."[9] Nevertheless, Wright expresses the emptiness of things and the inadequacy of words without dissonance, without what Heaney in the classroom liked to call "acoustical doubt." Indeed, his contemplative poise can seem too placid, too little troubled.

How easily one thing comes and another passes away.
How soon we become the acolytes
Of nothing and nothing's altar
              redeems us and makes us whole.[10]

Wright's poetic faith hinges not upon the power of language but upon the paradox that language keeps speaking through every disappointment, every failure of presence. The landscape of his imagination keeps appearing before him with its endless suggestivity, "the page that heaven and earth make."[11] His is a Berkeleyan intelligence that comes to appearances as mere appearances and uses words in mere particularity. Hence their independent and quite separate beauties. Like Berkeley, Wright looks beyond the appearances and words toward something holding them in place, only where Berkeley finds an improbable God behind the pageant of the senses, Wright finds a nothingness that serves his poetic goals by protecting the screen of landscape from being unsettled by any deeper questions of knowledge. Through the magic of grammar, Wright's "nothing" is transformed from the name for an absence to a positive force. "Nothing forgives," he tells us, replacing the despair of forgiveness with a phantom benediction.[12] We might think that the forgiveness of nothing should depend on its power to defuse the force of accusations, but for Wright the power to flirt with nothing, to feel the inadequacy of what appears as an invitation to what is beyond, is more important than any logic of negation. The lasting power of words spun out of nothing is an enabling consolation—"making a language where nothing stays."[13] This nothing that "stays" is presence and absence at once.

Wright's relation to divinity has a recognizably fideistic character, dwelling upon negation and, to recall Paul's formula, "the substance of things not seen." In a fascinating interview, contrasting himself with Hopkins, a poet "charged with the grandeur of God," Wright describes himself as "charged by the *absence* of God."[14] It is in Emily Dickinson that he finds the true model of his stance, the glimpse, in "There's a certain slant of light," of a God "defined by what he isn't." Wright guesses that this is the "ur-poem" in his unconscious, representing for Dickinson, and for him, "that moment when illumination seems possible. It never actually happens," he adds, "at least not so far, but its possibility is the illumination, I guess, that one is looking for." Nothing could be more Romantic, indeed Keatsian, than this stance of eternal anticipation, although, schooled by Dickinson, Wright is more focused on the appearance of illumination than on the reality behind it. But where Dickinson looks one step higher than the Romantic seeker, Wright takes a step backward. His enabling hope seems to be not that possibility will be fulfilled but that the looming moment of possibility itself will return, one of those "few moments when things seem just the way they're supposed to be." This, he explains, is why he's "so drawn to landscape as opposed to nature. Landscape is a kind of simulacra for the way things can be." It is fascinating to learn that not only is Dickinson the model for the stance of backyard illumination Wright practices but that he thinks of her as his poetic correspondent. "She's the person I'm writing to."

When Wright says that he is a poet of landscapes rather than a poet of nature, he is not only pointing to his sense of nature as a mere screen of appearances; he is also alluding to his sense of nature as a palimpsest, a scene already inflected by the vision of others. When he calls himself a "shallow thinker," it is because he is facing a flat surface.[15] He admires the Italian artist Giorgio Morandi's conceit that you can "increase the presence / Of what is missing" by leaving it out of the picture.[16] And Cézanne is a seminal point of reference. The flatness of Cézanne's canvas, the vivid, half-formed shapes in his landscapes, make a fine analogue for Wright's way of seeing. But Wright's is not a painterly eye that fixes upon the visual detail. He can say that he has "no interest in anything / but the color of leaves,"[17] but it is the color of that thought which interests him, not the leaves. Wright's painterliness is at a higher or meta-level, with a hint of synesthesia. He mixes images, thoughts, and sensations with experimental abandon, the way painters mix colors from their palettes.

> Someone is mourning inconsolably somewhere else.
> Yellow of goldenrod, bronze of the grass.
> By the creek bridge, the aspen leaves are waving good-bye, good-bye.
> Silence of paintbrush and cow pink.[18]

Each of these lines has the integrity of a separate brushstroke. There is a sense of movement in the sequence, but it is not a narrative or even a temporal movement. It is the composition of a scene on a mental canvas.

Like dreams awaiting their dreamers, cloud-figures step forth
Then disappear in the sky, ridgelines are cut,
grass moans
Under the sun's touch and drag:
With a sigh the day explains itself, and reliefs into place . . .[19]

The true model for this contrived landscape of assorted thoughts, images, and sensations is Eliot:

The goat coughs at night in the field overhead;
Rocks, moss, stonecrop, iron, merds.[20]

Wright has transposed Eliot's associative freedom back into a lyric framework and setting, but with the same commitment to the integrity of the unmetered line.

Through the course of Wright's career, he has experimented with different line lengths and paid tribute to various forms. A favorite resource is the journal as a string for historically dated lyrics, well adapted to Wright's "metaphysics of the quotidian."[21] For a time he borrowed Stevens's habit of whimsically irrelevant titles. One of his finest poems, "Homage to Paul Cézanne," shows that he can marshal a rhetoric grand enough to stay longer on the wing. Once in a while, on significant life occasions, he also writes a paraphrasable poem of a more traditional sort, as on the birth of his son, though he gives his son a distinctively poetic recipe for living: "Indenture yourself to the land . . . / Imagine its colors; try / to imitate day by day, / The morning's growth and the dusk."[22] But such intrusions are rare. On the whole, Wright remains in the same posture, writing the same meditation upon the beautiful, empty surfaces of things that only seem to point to something beyond.

It is a kind of believing without belief that we believe in,
This landscape that goes
                              no deeper than the eye, and poises like
A postcard in front of us
As though we'd settled it there, just so,
Halfway between the mind's eye and the mind, just halfway.[23]

As Wright grows older the central theme of nothingness in his poetry grows a little darker, a little less controlled. "Believing without belief" loses some of its consolation, while the link between nothingness, age, and death increasingly looms. As Dan Chiasson puts it, often Wright's "tenacious mellowness seems to fray."[24] The later books show a certain discouragement in the knowledge that his poetic resources, being entirely in the vein of the negative, will turn against Wright in the end. "The strict gospel of silence"[25] gets more difficult to cling to. "It is hard to imagine how unremembered we all become / . . . unremembered and unforgiven."[26] Wright's unforgiven deeds are characteristically unnamed—forgiveness, in his work, seems like a metaphor for memory itself—but while he has always found a Stevensian beauty in the transience of impressions, now

> Death is the mother of nothing.
> > This is a fact of life,
> And exponentially sad.
> All these years—a lifetime, really—thinking it might be otherwise.[27]

It may, of course, be "exponentially sad," but the statement is too bare and explicit to retain the artistic poise that has been Wright's signature. The danger of too much explicitness is one that Wright has long been aware of. "Art tends toward the condition of circularity and completion," he writes. "The artist's job is to keep the circle from joining—to work in the synapse."[28] If this is not true of all art, it is certainly true of his.

The quotations in this chapter make it clear how useless a recipe for replicating Charles Wright would be, how far his talent outstrips any procedural description. The values and standards by which Wright's poems are to be judged must be derived from our experience of the poems themselves in the light of other performances. Only the poems can tell us which of the accomplishments that make poetry valuable they actually achieve. Judgments of value in art are not, of course, a post facto matter. The very pleasure we take in reading a poem is a judgment of its quality made in the wider context of our reading experience. Line by line, we are judging the performance against its intuited purpose, whether that purpose is a generic one, a refusal of all genres, or whether it is, like Wright's, a variant of a familiar form, the Romantic lyric, taken in a peculiar direction. Still, in spite of its unique character, Wright's poetry is more susceptible to recipe than most, helping to make the point that poetic recipes don't work without the special talent to implement them. This is what criticism and theory offer, an artistically useless set of recipes that serve only to pinpoint the relationship between the poet's goals and his or her means of achieving them in order to suggest the character of that achievement. Such recipes, of course, are only reconstructed after the fact; for the poet, the goals are as often contrived to suit the means as the other way around. Still, coming back to Wright, there is a narrowness to his work, a sameness of thinking, stance, and tone, that can only be seen ultimately as a limitation, however admirable his ability to sustain it for so long a career at so high a level. The absence of variety and development even in mood does not suggest the ups and downs of a genuine intellectual or spiritual engagement in the vein of Stevens. Helen Vendler writes that "Wright's verse is the poetry of the transcendent 'I' in revolt against the too easily articulate 'I' of social engagement and social roles,"[29] but I see no inclination in Wright to deal with anything but transcendental matters to start with, nor does he seem to be in revolt against anything in particular. His description of Dickinson's "stationary psyche"—she "sat still, and enclosed, and let it happen, writing always from a stationary point of view"—seems more true of him than it does of her.[30] The mobile dynamism of a poem like "I taste a liquor never brewed" would be unthinkable for Wright. Because his preoccupation with the experience of the transcendent "I" is not authentic enough to make him inquire more boldly behind the postcard of appearances or consider in a more sustained way the implications of there being no transcendence, his spiritual quest can seem more like a pretext than a subject for poetry. Even in his late melancholy, Wright is largely content to keep the world of truth at a teasing distance—"At ease," he says, "because the dark music of what surrounds me / Plays to my misconceptions, and pricks me, and plays on."[31] Is it only the ability to make solipsistic poetry out of these ironically acknowledged misconceptions that gives them their value?

The question might seem to invite an ethical judgment rather than an aesthetic one, but it is inescapably raised by the experience of reading Wright all the way through. He is the author of hundreds of beautifully crafted poems composed of truly exquisite lines. His ear and formal mastery are beyond praise. But taking the work as a whole, the governing theme of the nothing-haunted landscape becomes too predictable to carry the weight of a life's work. And eventually the poet of elusiveness and emptiness becomes too direct and explicit in his confrontation with those things to be suggestive about them, nor is he intense enough in developing their implications to be a persuasive spiritual witness. Wright's game of hide-and-seek with nothing is neither serious enough nor playful enough to keep one wishing for more.

Notes

1. Edward Young, *Conjectures on Original Composition* (Manchester: Manchester University Press, 1918), 11.
2. Samuel Taylor Coleridge, letter to Lady Beaumont, 1807, in *Literary Criticism of William Wordsworth*, ed. Paul M. Zall (Lincoln: University of Nebraska Press, 1966), 83.
3. Charles Wright, "Dog Day Vespers," in *The World of the Ten Thousand Things: Poems 1980–1990* (New York: Farrar, Straus and Giroux, 1991), 32.
4. Charles Wright, *Halflife: Improvisations and Interviews, 1977–87* (Ann Arbor: University of Michigan Press, 1988), 20.
5. "Roma I," *The World*, 96.
6. Charles Wright, "Skins," in *Country Music: Selected Early Poems*, 2nd ed. (Middletown, CT: Wesleyan University Press, 1991), 83.
7. "Dog Creek Mainline," *Country Music*, 36.
8. "Language Journal," *The World*, 217.
9. "Vesper Journal," *The World*, 223.
10. "A Journal of Southern Rivers," *The World*, 226.
11. "Spring Abstract," *The World*, 27.
12. "California Spring," *The World*, 30.
13. "Portrait of the Artist with Hart Crane," *The World*, 33.
14. Thomas Gardner, "Interview with Charles Wright," in *A Door Ajar: Contemporary Writers and Emily Dickinson* (New York: Oxford University Press, 2006), 98.
15. Charles Wright, "Why, It's as Pretty as a Picture," in *Bye-and-Bye: Selected Late Poems* (New York: Farrar, Straus and Giroux, 2011), 41.
16. "Chinese Journal," *The World*, 199.
17. "Journal of the Year of the Ox," *The World*, 186.
18. "Three Poems of Departure," *The World*, 85.
19. "A Journal of One Significant Landscape," *The World*, 196.
20. T. S. Eliot, "Gerontion," in *The Waste Land and Other Poems* (New York: Harcourt, 1934), 19.
21. Wright, *Halflife*, 22.
22. "Firstborn," *Country Music*, 26.

23. "Why, It's as Pretty as a Picture," *Bye-and-Bye*, 41.

24. Dan Chiasson, "So Fluid, So Limpid, So Musical," *New York Review of Books* 61, no. 13 (August 14, 2014): 70–75.

25. "Journal of the Year of the Ox," *The World*, 177.

26. "The Woodpecker Pecks but the Hole Does Not Appear," *Bye-and-Bye*, 197.

27. "Twilight of the Dogs," *Bye-and-Bye*, 334.

28. Wright, *Halflife*, 35

29. Helen Vendler, *Part of Nature, Part of Us: Modern American Poets* (Cambridge, MA: Harvard University Press, 1980), 288.

30. Wright, *Halflife*, 22.

31. "Why, It's as Pretty as a Picture," *Bye-and-Bye*, 41.

CHAPTER 12

The Warm Variety of Risk

Richard Wilbur and Edgar Bowers

KENNETH FIELDS

FORD MADOX FORD believed that "[c]arefully considered, a good—an interesting—style will be found to consist in a constant succession of tiny, unobservable surprises." Richard Wilbur is admired for his formal mastery, his diction, his rhetorical conceptions, but it's important to notice how often he gives us these fine, all-but-unobservable surprises. According to Bruce Michelson, "Wyeth's Milk Cans" is based on a dry-brush sketch. We may say several things about the poem. It's meant to flesh out a sketch. It is set in winter, with the summer road congealing. Wilbur gives us a jolting turn:

> Beyond them, hill and field
> Harden, and summer's easy
> Wheel-ruts lie congealed.

> What if these two bells tolled?
> They'd make the bark-splintered
> Music of pure cold.

What is one to say? The two cans, one light, one dark, become imagined bells and make the music of pure cold? Cold milk is delicious? The passage from summer through fall to winter is as sudden as two bells ringing? I think of it as a reminder that a small turn in a poem has the virtue of leading you into prolonged meditation, like those temple bells in classic haikus.

A short poem from Janet Lewis's *The Indians in the Woods* (1922) uses similar figurative language. The chapbook deals with Ojibways she knew in northern Michigan, and the modernist techniques she uses come from poets from the imagist movement and translations from Japanese haiku and Ojibway songs. The prevailing spirit is the Ojibway shape shifter and culture hero, Manibozho or Nanapush (it's appropriate that he has several names). Lewis sees Manibozho as "the variant principle of life." Enacting simultaneity or synchronicity, the poem contains all four seasons:

LIKE SUMMER HAY

Like summer hay it falls
Over the marshes, over
The cranberry flats,
Places where
the wild deer lay.

Now the deer leave tracks
Down the pine hollow; petals
Laid two by two, brown
Against the snow.

These are not just local effects; they lift a poem up, even express its meaning. Here is Beat poet Lew Welch's little visionary triumph of surprise:

I SAW MYSELF

I saw myself
a ring of bone
in the clear stream
of all of it

and vowed
always to be open to it
that all of it
might flow through
and then heard

"ring of bone" where
ring is what a

bell does

It couldn't be simpler, turn a noun to a verb, but it makes the poem.

This sort of attention to detail is at the heart of Wilbur's poem. I can show more of this, I think, with one of his best-known poems. When he has collected his poems, he starts with the most recent book and works back to his first, a confident move, so every collection ends with the same poem, "The Beautiful Changes," which is also the title of the book.

THE BEAUTIFUL CHANGES

One wading a Fall meadow finds on all sides
The Queen Anne's Lace lying like lilies
On water; it glides
So from the walker, it turns
Dry grass to a lake, as the slightest shade of you
Valleys my mind in fabulous blue Lucernes.

The beautiful changes as a forest is changed
By a chameleon's tuning his skin to it;
As a mantis, arranged
On a green leaf, grows
Into it, makes the leaf leafier, and proves
Any greenness is deeper than anyone knows.

Your hands hold roses always in a way that says
They are not only yours; the beautiful changes
In such kind ways,
Wishing ever to sunder
Things and things' selves for a second finding, to lose
For a moment all that it touches back to wonder.

I have known this poem for more than forty years. I don't think I'm alone in thinking of the title of the poem or book, "Beautiful Changes," as an adjective-noun combination, and that we're meant to read the phrase this way. And every time I read the poem, I feel the shift when the phrase turns into a noun-verb combination (the beautiful changes) that embodies the theme. Similarly, the Queen Anne's Lace "turns / Dry grass to a lake." These changes of direction are what Donald Davie had in mind in his book on syntax, *Articulate Energy*. A similar surprise comes earlier, in line 5, when we realize that the poem is in the second person and is a love poem. The changes "sunder / Things and things' selves for a second finding."

Years ago I was walking along the beach with my young daughter. It was near sundown, the sun low above the water, and she was looking down at her sneakers as she scuffed them in the dry sand, intrigued by the sound the shoes made. I asked, "Erika, what color is the ocean?" Without looking up, she said, "Blue." Brp brp brp. I said, "What color?" and she said, "Green?" When I told her to look at the ocean, she exclaimed, "It's orange and red and black and blue and green!" Her reaction shows the power of the collision of the conventional with the singular perceptual experience. To paraphrase a Wilbur moment, singlenesses floating on the great generality of waters.

The wonder we experience at such moments is perhaps what Pound was thinking of when he quoted Henri Gaudier-Brzeska: "Works of art attract by a resembling unlikeness." Similarly, we can read an elegy or a love poem and note that it is like and unlike other poems in its genre.

Catullus's Carmina 4, "Phaselus Ille," describes a boat (Peter Green translates "cutter") that comes to quiet harbor after a lifetime of braving rough seas. The boat is personified and speaks to the poet, remembering when it was a forest before being made into a boat. It has been the instigation for many poets, including R. P. Blackmur, Yvor Winters, and Edgar Bowers. It is a retirement poem. Wilbur's "Driftwood" is a skillful variant on Catullus's poem.

If we think of the *Odyssey*, "Phaselus Ille" becomes a little epic. Its pattern resembles what R. W. B. Lewis means by the title of his essay on Whitman, paraphrasing Whitman's mother's comment: he was "Always Going Out and Coming In." "Driftwood," whose title offers multiple suggestions, employs a stanza consisting of 5, 3, 4, and 2 feet per line. It's rhymed in pairs of stanzas, which allows for subtle interplays among syntactical units. It begins

imagining the forest that supplied the ships, now driftwood cast on the
shore, and from the start the language is moral.

> In greenwoods once these relics must have known
> A rapt, gradual growing,
> That are cast here like slag of the old
> Engine of grief,
>
> Must have affirmed in annual increase
> Their close selves, knowing
> Their own nature only, and that
> Bringing to leaf.

He imagines that the forest may have been taken in the search for the
mythical Seven Cities of Gold, and the language begins to focus on shaping,
as the ships take shape and move to adventure and loss.

> Say, for the seven cities or a war
> Their solitude was taken,
> They into masts shaven, or milled into
> Oar and plank;
>
> Afterward sailing long and to lost ends,
> By groundless water shaken,
> Well they availed their vessels till they
> Smashed or sank.

And from here on out the real theme emerges, the growth of character, arête,
excellence: the interplay of inborn virtue and experience. The first two lines
marvelously compress character and aesthetics.

> Then on the great generality of waters
> Floated their singleness,
> And in all that deep subsumption they were
> Never dissolved,

But shaped and flowingly fretted by the waves'
Ever surpassing stress,
With the gnarled swerve and tangle of tides
Finely resolved.

The poem concludes with a mythic apotheosis and also the emergence of the speaker, who is likewise transformed. One feels the marine pull of the poem, "the lathe of all the seas," as well as a literary presence, lyric and epic, embodied. It feels like wonder.

Brought in the end where breakers dump and slew
On the glass verge of the land,
Silver they rang to the stones when the sea
Flung them and turned.

Curious crowns and scepters they look to me
Here on the gold sand,
Warped, wry, but having the beauty of
Excellence earned.

In a time of continual dry abdications
And of damp complicities,
They are fit to be taken for signs, these emblems
Royally sane.

Which have ridden to a homeless wreck, and long revolved
In the lathe of all the seas,
But have saved in spite of it all their dense
Ingenerate grain.

"Driftwood," first published in December 1948, appeared in *Ceremony and Other Poems* (1950). I leave it to the reader to ponder the relation of "a time of continual dry abdications / And of damp complicities" to the House Un-American Activities Committee. *Ceremony* is dedicated to F. O. Matthiessen, a famous scholar at Harvard (and author of *American Renaissance: Art and Expression in the Age of Emerson and Whitman*) who many people believe was driven to suicide in April 1950 by the Red Scare, with its increasing hostility toward his Christian socialist politics and his homosexuality. It was a terrible, familiar time.

Texture, text, and *context* are folklorist Alan Dundes's important points of analysis. I've tried indirectly to show how Wilbur's poems yield to a consideration of these categories. I'd like to suggest another—namely, structure.

In his *John Keats: Complete Poems,* Jack Stillinger offers a useful diagram for Keats's odes and for a number of other Romantic poems. A horizontal line divides the "actual world (below)" from "the ideal (above)." Many other pairs may be substituted for these two. An acute angle starts below the line (A) to a point above the line (B) and ends below the line (A′)—the poem returns to a point different from its starting point, with something learned, for example, Frost's "Earth's the right place for love."

This structural scheme allows one to chart variations. Yeats's "Sailing to Byzantium," for example, begins *above* the line "That is no country for old men," and does not return from the ideal world except for a memory, some of the most beautiful lines in Yeats.

The young

> In one another's arms, birds in the trees,
> —Those dying generations—at their song,
> The salmon-falls, the mackerel-crowded seas,
> Fish, flesh, or fowl, commend all summer long
> Whatever is begotten, born, and dies.

The poem concludes with what, for many of us, is a decidedly less attractive option.

> Once out of nature I shall never take
> My bodily form from any natural thing,
> But such a form as Grecian goldsmiths make
> Of hammered gold and gold enamelling
> To keep a drowsy Emperor awake;
> Or set upon a golden bough to sing
> To lords and ladies of Byzantium
> Of what is past, or passing, or to come.

Wilbur's "Love Calls Us to the Things of This World" follows a different path, "this world" contrasting with Yeats's "that is no country." The title, Wilbur tells us, comes from a phrase from Augustine. The title of a related poem, "A World without Objects Is a Sensible Emptiness," comes from another mystic, Thomas Traherne. Both poems celebrate Christian incarnation. The Traherne poem describes the scene in the manger beautifully: "Lampshine blurred in the steam of beasts."

To return to Stillinger's diagram, "Love Calls Us to the Things of This World" begins above the line, in the realm of bodiless sleep. Written in Rome, the setting is apartments with laundry lines strung between buildings. The soul is awakened by the harsh cries of pulleys.

> The eyes open to a cry of pulleys,
> And spirited from sleep, the astounded soul
> Hangs for a moment bodiless and simple
> As false dawn.
>   Outside the open window
> The morning air is all awash with angels.
>
> Some are in bed-sheets, some are in blouses,
> Some are in smocks: but truly there they are.
> Now they are rising together in calm swells
> Of halcyon feeling, filling whatever they wear
> With the deep joy of their impersonal breathing;
>
> Now they are flying in place, conveying
> The terrible speed of their omnipresence, moving
> And staying like white water; and now of a sudden
> They swoon down into so rapt a quiet
> That nobody seems to be there.

Wilbur's initial inspiration was the question of how to write a poem about angels in the contemporary world. And his answer was, bodiless laundry hanging on a line. They move and are in one place and are omnipresent, and when the wind stops they swoon into selfless, impersonal rapture, which leads to the shocking rape of being brought into the ordinary, extraordinary day.

The soul shrinks

From all that it is about to remember,
From the punctual rape of every blessèd day,
And cries,
         "Oh, let there be nothing on earth but laundry,
Nothing but rosy hands in the rising steam
And clear dances done in the sight of heaven."

The soul's descent is understandably reluctant; waking from rapture to the busy intrusive world is seen as a violent intrusion, a punctual rape, and "every blessèd day" carries a double force: every holy day and every goddamned day. The tone of blessedness, albeit bitter, continues to the end.

Yet, as the sun acknowledges
With a warm look the world's hunks and colors,
The soul descends once more in bitter love
To accept the waking body, saying now
In a changed voice as the man yawns and rises,

    "Bring them down from their ruddy gallows;
Let there be clean linen for the backs of thieves;
Let lovers go fresh and sweet to be undone,
And the heaviest nuns walk in a pure floating
Of dark habits,
         keeping their difficult balance."

It's worth remembering Richard Eberhart's remark that not all women would warm to the image of doing the laundry as "rosy hands in . . . rising steam."

The range of feeling in this poem, especially in its concluding lines, is winning. The "world's hunks and colors" is something a painter might say. All this has taken place before the man is fully awake, when he can finally acknowledge and accept, with great charm and wit, the world of murderers, thieves, lovers, and those marvelous nuns who embody the moral difficulty of the poem. It beats an eternity of keeping a drowsy emperor awake.

The power of the poem, it seems to me, comes from Wilbur's skillful variation on a common Romantic way of structuring a poem. R. W. B. Lewis takes the title of his essay on Whitman from a remark of Whitman's mother: he was "Always Going Out and Coming In." (This is essentially the structure of Catullus's "Phaselus Ille.") Wilbur's poem moves from in to out.

Richard Wilbur and Edgar Bowers are in the same generation of poets who served in World War II. They are both masters of traditional forms, and they share some concerns. Both have a wider range of subjects that I am suggesting, especially Bowers in the second half of his career. But I have chosen to focus on some areas they share.

I've discussed Wilbur's use of a theme common in the nineteenth century: the definition (sometimes by opposition) of the self against the other. This is a familiar stance of Emily Dickinson, for whom the other can be God, Eternity, Nature (often the sea), a lover. Sometimes these are metaphors of each other. Is "Wild Nights—Wild Nights!" about God or a lover? My students think the latter, I think the former. In "I started early, took my dog / And visited the sea," the sea is personified as a dangerous seducer, who pursues the speaker:

> And made as He would eat me up—
> As wholly as a Dew
> Opon a Dandelion's Sleeve—
> And then—I started—too—

What quickens her is the realization that she would be wholly obliterated. Yvor Winters says of this poem, "The sea is here the traditional symbol of death; that is, of all the forces and qualities in nature and in human nature that tend toward the dissolution of human character and consciousness." Wilbur's epigraph to "The Terrace," from Baudelaire, gets at this drama: "De la vaporisation et de la centralisation du Moi, Tout est là."

Bowers's "Dark Earth and Summer" begins with a somewhat mysterious, evocative title. The poet is visiting the grave of a loved one:

> Earth is dark where you rest

Though a little winter grass
Glistens in icy furrows.
There, cautious, as I pass,

Squirrels run, leaving stains
Of their nervous, minute feet
Over the tombs, and near them
Birds grey and gravely sweet.

The heavily weighted trimeter begins to run across line and stanza, setting up the extraordinary rhythm of the second half of the poem. The contrast of darkness and light, breath and cold carries the theme of the poem. As the long syntactical units overflow the short lines, we see remarkably powerful turns. The poet desires death, and the vision of brightness and ripe fruit against the backdrop of dissolution takes on the power of a mystical vision:

I have come, warm of breath,
To sustain unbodied cold,
Removed from life and seeking
Darkness where flesh is old,

Flesh old and summer waxing,
Quick eye in the sunny lime,
Sweet apricots in silence
Falling—precious in time,

All radiant as a voice, deep
As their oblivion.

The apricots falling in silence, radiant as a voice deep in their oblivion—the mixture of sensations, precious in time, gives rise to the final term.

Only as I may,
I come, remember, wait,
Ignorant in grief, yet stay,

> What you are will outlast
> The warm variety of risk,
> Caught in the wide, implacable,
> Clear gaze of the basilisk.

The warm variety of risk—this is where we all live, caught in the gaze of the mythical serpent, the little king who rhymes with risk, who can kill with a glance. It is hard to tell if that gaze, modified by three adjectives, brings terror or powerful desire.

Perhaps because of his early Calvinist background, Bowers is drawn to ultimate absolutes—tempted, he used to say—although his criticism of the desire for "[t]he perfect order trusted to the dead" is unequivocally rejected in "The Astronomers of Mont Blanc." Early, he is pulled by the first and final cause toward God, soon phenomenologized in a gorgeous line from "Adam's Song to Heaven": "Beautiful you are, fair deceit!" After God, the obsessive desire, as in the poem just discussed, is for death. He once remarked that the modern desire was to be usurped by an inscrutable muse, and he thought Handel's "Semele" expressed that desire in music.

Bowers takes up this desire in much more casual terms, at least at first, in "Afternoon at the Beach." While teaching at the University of California, Santa Barbara, he lived in Miramar Beach in a small house at the edge of the Pacific. At high tide you could hear and feel the sea dragging at the shingle beneath the living room. "Afternoon at the Beach" quietly states a desire for the classical descent into the underworld:

> I'll go among the dead to see my friend.
> The place I leave is beautiful: the sea
> Repeats the wind's far swell in its long sound,
> And, there beside it, houses solemnly
> Shine with the modest courage of the land,
> While swimmers try the verge of what they see.

Just as casually, he realizes that he cannot go, and yet the imagining has a quietly profound effect on his perceptions:

> I cannot go, although I should pretend

Some final self whose phantom eye could see
Him who because he is not cannot change.
And yet the thought of going makes the sea,
The land, the swimmers, and myself seem strange,
Almost as strange as they will someday be.

The psychological turn is unforgettable. Yes, these things, including myself, will really seem strange when I am not here. He is imagining his beloved coast when he is not there to see it.

The final self in the eighth line leads to the most fascinating of absolutes that haunt Bowers, perhaps a hangover from his discarded Calvinism. This is the final completed self, sum of all you are, have thought or done. Of course, since it is only completed with your death, it is unknowable, which only intensifies its appeal. Bowers is said to have celebrated three birthdays every year: those of Mozart, Pasteur, and Valéry.

Paul Valéry's poem "Le Cimetière Marin" was one of Bowers's favorites (and a favorite of his teacher, Yvor Winters). *Le midi*, noon, is a symbol for the absolute:

Tête complète et parfait diadème,
Je suis en toi le secret changement.

Bowers often spoke of Valéry's brief novel, *Monsieur Teste*, Mr. Head, Witness, or perhaps Testicle, an account of a man of pure consciousness, who is still unknown to himself. At the end, he says: "[P]erhaps I shall behold the entire sum of myself in one terrible flash. . . . Not possible." Valéry thought that this obsession was a "monster idea."

"Autumn Shade," a sequence of ten blank-verse poems, is the masterpiece of Bowers's middle period. He has returned to his homeplace in Stone Mountain, Georgia. He records change in the sound of the logging saw and recalls "[t]hat goddesses have died when their trees died." Nevertheless, he feels a divine presence in the spring he once drank from:

1

The autumn shade is thin. Grey leaves lie faint

Where they will lie, and, where the thick green was,
Light stands up, like a presence, to the sky.
The trees seem merely shadows of its age.
From off the hill, I hear the logging crew,
The furious and indifferent saw, the slow
Response of heavy pine; and I recall
That goddesses have died when their trees died.
Often in summer, drinking from the spring,
I sensed in its cool breath and in its voice
A living form, darker than any shade
And without feature, passionate, yet chill
With lust to fix in ice the buoyant rim—
Ancient of days, the mother of us all.
Now, toward his destined passion there, the strong,
Vivid young man, reluctant, may return
From suffering in his own experience
To lie down in the darkness. In this time,
I stay in doors. I do my work. I sleep.
Each morning, when I wake, I assent to wake.
The shadow of my fist moves on this page,
Though, even now, in the wood, beneath a bank,
Coiled in the leaves and cooling rocks, the snake
Does as it must, and sinks into the cold.

He speaks of himself in the third as well as the first person. He gives the clue
of extreme self-consciousness ("The shadow of my fist moves on this page"),
and he concludes with an image of death.

Bowers's blank verse is supple, with varying syntactical lengths moving
across and against the lines. It allows him to bring a variety of subjects into
play, from the constellations in the night sky to the flowers he "feels" in the
woods to a beautiful, terrible cold that may stand for the completed self that
haunts him:

2

Nights grow colder. The Hunter and the Bear

Follow their tranquil course outside my window.
I feel the gentian waiting in the wood,
Blossoms waxy and blue, and blue-green stems
Of the amaryllis waiting in the garden.
I know, as though I waited what they wait,
The cold that fastens ice about the root,
A heavenly form, the same in all its changes,
Inimitable, terrible, and still,
And beautiful as frost. Fire warms my room.
Its light declares my books and pictures. Gently,
A dead soprano sings Mozart and Bach.
I drink bourbon, then go to bed, and sleep
In the Promethean heat of summer's essence.

Against that ultimate cold he brings Promethean fire: "Fire warms my room."
Other forms of fire are light and books and pictures and music: "A dead
soprano sings Mozart and Bach." And bourbon. And sleep.

3

Awakened by some fear, I watch the sky.
Compelled as though by purposes they know,
The stars, in their blue distance, still affirm
The bond of heaven and earth, the ancient way.
This old assurance haunts small creatures, dazed
In icy mud, though cold may freeze them there
And leave them as they are all summer long.
I cannot sleep. Passion and consequence,
The brutal given, and all I have desired
Evade me, and the lucid majesty
That warmed the dull barbarian to life.
So I lie here, left with self-consciousness,
Enemy whom I love but whom his change
And his forgetfulness again compel,
Impassioned, toward my lost indifference,
Faithful, but to an absence. Who shares my bed?

Who lies beside me, certain of his waking,
Led sleeping, by his own dream, to the day?

In section 4 Bowers invokes a Rilkean angel, desiring to be carried to speech or riot. He's still summoned by the idea of his "[m]ysterious self, / Image of the fabulous alien."

The poem, available online (and in Bowers's *Collected Poems*), is closely argued, and I'll have to compress its progress. In section 5, he asks "Who is it says I *am*?" and considers several options that take him back to his experience in the war and to the present task of writing:

> For there he is,
> In a steel helmet, raging, fearing his death,
> Carrying bread and water to a quiet,
> Placing ten sounds together in one sound:
> Confirming his election, or merely still,
> Sleeping, or in a colloquy with the sun.

Section 9 moves from first to third person as he comes to terms with the other:

> In nameless warmth, sun light in every corner,
> Bending my body over my glowing book,
> I share the room. Is it with a voice or touch
> Or look, as of an absence, learned by love,
> Now, merely mine? Annunciation, specter
> Of the worn out, lost, or broken, telling what future.
> What vivid loss to come, you change the room
> And him who reads here. Restless, he will stir,
> Look round, and see the room renewed and line,
> Color, and shape as, in desire, they are,
> Not shadows but substantial light, explicit,
> Bright as glass, inexhaustible, and true.

Most of us, had we been lucky enough to have written this sequence, would have concluded it here. But the genius of "Autumn Shade" lies in its refusal to come to a sense of an ending—appropriate, given its theme. The feelings are expertly modulated, but the poem still ends with fear:

10

My shadow moves, until, at noon, I stand
Within its seal, as in the finished past.
But in the place where effect and cause are joined,
In the warmth or cold of my remembering,
Of love, of partial freedom, the time to be
Trembles and glitters again in windy light.
For nothing is disposed. The slow soft wind
Tilting the blood-root keeps its gentle edge.
The intimate cry, both sinister and tender,
Once heard, is heard confined in its reserve.
My image of myself, apart, informed
By many deaths, resists me, and I stay
Almost as I have been, intact, aware,
Alive, though proud and cautious, even afraid.

I want to return to the beach for a final poem, "An Elegy: December, 1970." The poem is a meditation on the death of Bowers's sister Eleanor, and it is shrouded in mystery. She married late, and in conversation Bowers made it clear that he did not approve of the husband. He may not have attended the wedding. He felt that he had wounded his sister, with reason. Eleanor was found dead in her bed, and the suspicion was that she had killed herself. It's a sunny southern California Christmas, and what he ponders in Atlanta is as cold as snow. Below the bright surface is the depth of the ocean. The poem is haunted by uncertainty. It conveys, for me, feelings that will neither let you go nor bless you.

Almost four years, and though I merely guess
What happened, I can feel the minutes' rush
Settle like snow upon the breathless bed—
And we who loved you, elsewhere, ignorant.
From my deck, in the sun, I watch boys ride:

Complexities of wind and wet and wave:
Pale shadows, poised a moment on the light's
Archaic and divine indifference.

I know that the theme of this collection is evaluation. This is difficult for me. What I can say is that Wilbur and Bowers are among my favorite poets. Much of evaluation for me is personal. What draws me to Bowers is depth and intensity of feeling, different feelings, that seem to come from below the surface of the poems. I have been reading Bowers for nearly sixty years and have read Wilbur for nearly as long. Bowers seems to be drawn by his concerns. He might have written these two lines by Frederick Goddard Tuckerman on the image of himself before he felt "terror and anguish" of his wife Hannah's death: "I cannot rid the thought nor hold it close, / But dimly dream upon that man alone."

My classmate at Santa Barbara, Jim McMichael, introduced me to Bowers, as he introduced me to many other things. I would not be who I am without McMichael and Bowers. Bowers was my first teacher. The evenings in his living room, with the sound of the surf a few yards below us, gave me a dimly realized sense of what my intellectual life might be. We read Pope, Diderot, Wordsworth (*The Prelude*), Melville, Proust, Stevens, and Hart Crane. When he quoted the conclusion of Crane's "Repose of Rivers"—"I heard wind flaking sapphire, like this summer / And willows could not hold more steady sound"—he said, "I'd sell my soul to have written those lines," adding, "but then I'd buy it back again the next day." He spoke of "Le Cimetière Marin"; he said, "It's worth learning French just to read that poem." When we read "The Comedian as the Letter C," I was struck by "The man in Georgia, waking among pines, / Should be pine-spokesman." I was over my head, but it sure felt nice.

We became friends and corresponded and saw each other over the years. I loved him and his poems. Late in our relationship we had a falling out. The details are unimportant. He moved to San Francisco, and I heard that he had lymphoma. I didn't know how grave he was, but I called him and visited him in his apartment. He was sitting up in bed and seemed his old, bright self. A young Frenchman was sitting with him. Edgar's friend and partner, James

Davis, a distinguished rare book librarian at UCLA, was in Los Angeles for a routine valve replacement surgery and would return soon. In the midst of our chatting, Edgar mentioned a poem of mine that had recently been published in a festschrift for C. Q. Drummond. "That's the real thing." Then he characteristically added, "Of course I didn't like the first line," a remark that would have rattled me as a young man. I said, "Oh hell, Edgar, you know, you have to start them somehow." We laughed, he asked me to come back, and I said I would. I kissed him on the forehead, at which point the young Frenchman interposed, "Non, non, les microbes!" We laughed again, as if to say, "Screw les microbes." I never saw him again.

I had been thinking of him and of the final haiku sequence Masaoka Shiki wrote about the pot of peonies his students brought him on his deathbed. Near the end he wrote (Earl Miner's version):

> The peonies have fallen,
> And what alone is left behind
> Is—Bashō's portrait!

About four days after my visit, I woke up suddenly in the middle of the night and said, "Edgar died." And I wrote down a haiku. The next morning Helen Trimpi called to say that Edgar had died in the night and that James Davis had died unexpectedly at about the same time. Here's the haiku:

> "The Man in Georgia Waking among Pines . . ."

> Peony blossoms scattered,
> On the desk, a photograph,
> Stone Mountain, Edgar Bowers.

> (1924–2000)

MUSICALITY

CHAPTER 13

Songs and Their Lyrics

Any Room at the Feast?

NIGEL SMITH

Perhaps the perceived irrelevance of much of contemporary poetry is a function of poetry's turning its back on song, turning a deaf ear to audience. Dylan doesn't need the Nobel Prize in Literature, it will neither help nor hinder him, but literature is weakened without song.[1]

CRITICISM ON TWENTIETH-CENTURY and contemporary verse has become as complex as the most conceptually wrought examples of poetry itself, not least where the long line has held sway in North American verse. This type of critical discourse, often integrated with literary theory, has become a kind of philosophical work itself, and such a mixture of course is not alien to the longer history of poetry. But what of that other part of the life of poetry, that shadow sibling that is present in the modern world in a very intense way on account of sound recording technology: the song lyric? While song was obviously part and parcel of poetic culture in the nineteenth century, with the development of *Lieder* (art songs) and the setting of a great number of esteemed works of lyric verse, twentieth-century literary development might be said to have put a greater distance between poetry and song lyrics, even as the ever wider and cheaper availability of song recordings made them ever more readily present.[2] It is almost as if the modernist moment reenacted that much earlier divorce between song lyric and poetry when Arnaut Daniel invented the sestina as a mnemonic device for troubadours, but whereby the sophisticated form itself rapidly lent itself to words alone and not music. It is no coincidence that Ezra Pound so venerated Daniel, or that Eliot praising Pound should echo Dante lauding Daniel. The periodical literature of the modernists, such as *Poetry: A Magazine of Verse* (1912–), not only entertained vigorous discussion of the relationship between poetry and music but also sometimes showed a keen interest in indigenous folk songs.[3] This is an overlooked topic much in need of further inquiry, but this interest is not how high modernism is usually remembered. The conferring on Bob Dylan of the Nobel Prize in Literature urges us once again to take popular song lyric, or *some* popular song lyric, seriously as literature, controversial or infuriating as it might be for some.[4] The message was brought home throughout 2016, where in addition to Dylan's honor, many reflected on the deaths of several singer-songwriter heroes, including David Bowie (January) and Leonard Cohen (November), both masters of the form.

If popular song and indeed much art song appeared so distant from nonsong poetry (despite later efforts to prove intimate association[5]), that distance collapses with the advent of rap, that spoken but not sung rhythmic verse, much of it created spontaneously and enunciated against a steady and repeated rhythmic pattern. Rap is rhythmic speech and lends itself to narrative, so that it begins to converge with the longer narrative poetry of the Victorian period. Rap may have begun with the African American community, and it might largely remain there, but there are white and Hispanic rappers, and most young people of all ethnicities worldwide seem to know it. Rap's existence, and its vital place in popular music, makes the conjunction of song lyrics and nonsong verse once again unavoidably proximate. One cannot experience rhythmically strong lines in verse tradition without hearing echoes of rap, and perhaps vice versa. This has been exploited for the better understanding of poetic tradition and rap in the context of the classroom.[6] Rap isn't at all marginal now, of course, as the enormous popularity of the Broadway show *Hamilton* (2015) with libretto by Lin-Manuel Miranda reveals.[7]

Where does that leave us? Well, for one thing, it means that we should take notice of the small body of scholarship that does honor these matters, often in the form of close readings of the work of the past half century's acknowledged masters of songwriting and word setting: Leonard Cohen,

Bob Dylan, Joni Mitchell, Steely Dan, and so on. Behind that sits a virtuous body of commentary on earlier twentieth-century songwriting, not least the wit and romance of the Tin Pan Alley writers.[8] But one feature is common to most of this critical writing: it nearly always avoids confronting a major disciplinary divide. Literary critics are no good at talking about musical structure, and musicologists are singularly bad at talking about words. Despite all of its elegance and impressive, generous attentiveness, and its explicit insistence that music must be considered with words, Adam Bradley's study of the pop lyric is still very largely a piece of literary and cultural as opposed to musical analysis.[9] There was a moment in the late 1960s when Richard Goldstein's study of "serious" popular lyrics seemed to point to a new age of awareness, but the gap in mutual awareness and competence has often seemed as far off as ever.[10] The British folk-rock guitarist Richard Thompson, now long resident in the United States, is revered today first as a guitar hero, the "Eric Clapton of folk-rock," and rightly so, but we should also remember his comment in a recent interview with regard to his first band of the late 1960s and early 1970s, Fairport Convention: "They were known as the 'lyric' band." One then thinks of Thompson's macabre and profoundly melancholic "Walking on a Wire," and the many songs in similar vein that have followed from his pen:

> Too many steps to take
> Too many spells to break
> Too many nights awake
> And no one else
> This grindstone's wearing me
> Your claws are tearing me
> Don't use me endlessly
> It's too long, too long to myself
> Where's the justice and where's the sense?
>
> When all the pain is on my side of the fence
> I'm walking on a wire, I'm walking on a wire
> And I'm falling.[11]

One needs to put this simple but effective lyric, with its deft repetitions and rhymes, into the context of its plangent, heart-rending performance by Thompson and his then wife Linda, with her startlingly powerful voice, set off by Thompson's angular, spiky guitar breaks, quite literally the wire being walked upon.

My argument is that we will only return in criticism to that hopeful earlier moment when we have a critical discourse that facilitates the appreciation of the simultaneous coexistence of words and music. There is in fact some work that does encompass this goal, albeit thus far confined to close analyses of single songwriters, songs, or recordings. A fine example would be Walter Everett's exacting and compelling reading of the complexity that makes up Steely Dan songs: fusing rock and jazz time and harmonics with ironic modernist or postmodernist lyrics.[12] Everett is an accomplished musicologist of classical as well as popular music, and perhaps the greatest and most precise analyst of rock music—certainly one of the most diligent and prolific.[13] To this must now be added from the literary side Timothy Hampton's book-length study and preceding articles on Bob Dylan's crucially transformative songs, written with a sensitivity to musical structure but also to the poetic tradition and poetic structures that Dylan is interested in, indeed extending back to the Middle Ages. It is a sophisticated reading, situating Dylan's particular version of pastiche within an understanding of the *Dialectic of Enlightenment*. Hampton's resurrection of Petrarch rather than Dante as the proclaimed muse of Dylan is highly evident, and not surprising when we learn that Hampton is best known as a professor of Renaissance French.[14] The interest that has hung around Dylan, as high-priest artist, modernist prophet, living legend of the counterculture, and indeed one-man historical event, has always attracted commentary. His dense lyrics may be compared, with liberal engagement, to the entire poetic tradition, as famously intimated by possibly the greatest close reader of his generation, Christopher Ricks.[15] They are certainly very often rich word assemblages, showing how much "music (rhyme and rhythm), contemporary references, high and low registers, political and personal sentiment, and literary allusions could get into a popular and powerful work of words."[16] But Hampton is different because he focuses on a historical moment, and because he can analyze the relationship between lyrics and music:

The inclusion of a G natural in the melody (an accidental in A, but diatonic in D) underscores this impression. This tonal ambiguity, via the striking alternation between A major and G major, perfectly sets up the unstable mobility that is narrated in the lyrics; there is no point of rest. The opening eight lines of each stanza unfold across this wavering musical structure.[17]

The influence of this approach is discernible elsewhere.[18] Hampton also follows the intricate relationship of Dylan with Rimbaud, and that late nineteenth-century French poet of outrage is strongly present by name, by form, and in spirit in the work of the great female poet of rock, Patti Smith, often judged to be the maker of punk rock.[19] Unlike Dylan, Smith began as a poet and transformed into a rocker (by which time she would eventually shake Dylan up with the cohesive power of her performances) after she began to read her poetry live to the accompaniment of an electric guitar. Unacademic, there is a nonetheless and triumphantly pure literariness in her work, from the obviously postsymbolist early poetry through to her acclaimed passionate masterpieces, such as *Horses* (1975) and *Easter* (1978): "the first woman musician to bring poetry to rock and roll, . . . the first poet to bring rock and roll to poetry."[20] It might be no surprise that one of her fellow travelers of her early days in New York City, Tom Verlaine, should take his name from the French symbolist poet, and in knowing parallel with Dylan's own poetic self-naming after the Welsh poet Dylan Thomas. At least in much of Smith's early song work, it would be hard to find instances of the malleable balancing and unbalancing that Dylan explored in the early 1970s, but instead there is a passionate intensity sometimes of poems intoned against music and sometimes of eviscerating cover versions of famous rock songs that become more chaotic as they reach their conclusion: "unconventional, experimental, intensely personal and passionate" (and, it might be added, in the long term, winning huge and affectionate approval for the honesty of this revolt).[21] This must have been unattractively cacophonous for most ears, and it took an outstanding and romantic joint collaboration with Bruce Springsteen, "Because the Night" (1977–1978, Smith adding lyrics to an extant Springsteen title, melody, and arrangement), to give Smith her first major hit, and the breakthrough to a wider audience. Smith's songs remain in search of a proper analytical assessment, although Carrie Jaurès Noland comes close in her consideration of the subversive appearance of the entire package of *Horses*, album art and all: "mixing and thus transgressing a series of hierarchical codes established in order to distinguish popular from high culture."[22]

> In "rock n roll nigger" to transgress the boundary of the word is to transgress material boundaries as well. Excrement becomes "hard gold rythumn," a new "mathematics" makes art (words) "outta soft sold shit."
>   However, even as Smith represents the transgression of ontological orders, she draws attention through the very orthography of the passage to the *distinction* between word and song, text and matter, "art" and "shit."[23]

And perhaps something might be said of the Patti Smith Group playing a three-chord pattern (their favorite A-G-D) tightly and in vigorous, uniform eighth notes behind her voice, both a foundational backdrop and a force of hedonistic abandon, but, alas, by no means a "transgressive experimental musical practice" so much as a rock band firing on all cylinders in a well-worn mode for that time.[24] Here, Noland seems blind to the musical limitations of this kind of punk music, and more still might be made of other song recordings in which Smith's distinctive and unusual pronunciation sits juxtaposed with quite beautiful if orthodox piano playing.

When it comes to lyrics fitting into musical structure, some of the conventional comments about the difference between poetry and lyrics need to be rehearsed. Lyrics often have to be simpler than lines of verse, and to fit into shorter lines. I'm not sure we need to stretch to the chestnut that lyrics can be bad in and of themselves but work very well within songs, but something of that strain should be borne in mind. Certainly we have the general condition of the *consumption* of words within the performance of a song. You cannot have too many words in a song verse, or a line: if you do, you'll break the back of the music. Where there is rapid word consumption, as in Joni Mitchell's "Raised on Robbery," the music either must make space, or, as in this example, be prepared to run as fast in tempo as the words demand. The words and the music must each "lack" something in order to make room for the other; if not, they collide and mutually disrupt each other in a fatal scramble. A "song lyric by Leonard Cohen may coincidentally be published in his *Collected Poems* and yet be rather steadfastly a song lyric. It needs something else. It may be recited as a poem, but for one reason or another, it's missing something. The poem conventionally brings its own music."[25] One can go back to the history of song setting in earlier times and see these principles at work, for instance master lyric setter Henry Lawes being praised for seeming to punctuate poetry more effectively with his setting than was the case with handwritten or printed punctuation marks.[26] Even here, there are those who risk cramming, with exuberant wordplay, and continuity has been seen here between Bruce Springsteen and Paul Muldoon, a most allusively learned poet who has ventured into rock lyrics.[27]

It is with these things in mind that one can turn to a songwriter as poised and lyrically precise as Paul Simon. It is not surprising that his lyrics are so accomplished, so measured, so worthy of being collected as a book of poems, when we remember that he was an English major and carries a particular fondness for Yeats. One of his greatest songs, from his middle period, is "Graceland" (1986), in which the journey that is so often implied in the transit through performance of a song is literally present in the lyric's content, a journey to the roots of popular music in the Mississippi Valley, and to Elvis Presley's home, which turns out to be the point of reconciliation between the persona of the song's singer and his son, for they are on a voyage of discovery, led ever closer by the insistent southern stomp that is the rhythm of the song. Rhythm is everything in this middle phase of Simon's creativity. He has said that a song might start simply by tapping out a rhythm on a car's dashboard while driving.

On the vexed question of whether words or music come first, in Simon's case it is the music in its rhythmic foundation from which all else grows.[28] The musical distinction is to use the African instrumentation and arrangement that works throughout the *Graceland* album (most famously on "Diamonds on the Souls of Her Shoes," in which Simon sings in collaboration with the South African vocal group Ladysmith Black Mambazo), so that the African roots of Mississippi Valley and Delta music are literally present: it is African into American music addressing a southern landscape associated as much with African American experience as with early rock 'n' roll.[29] The shuffling, two-beat rhythm is a key characteristic, along with the arpeggio slide guitar in a high register sliding onto its note above the rapidly strummed rhythm guitar, and perhaps above all else the strongly present fretless electric bass sliding up to the tonic and then pushing the song along in octaves—very much distinctive elements of African electric music in the 1980s. However, the minor guitar chords are not characteristic of African music but were introduced as an imitation of American country music by guitarist Ray Phiri.[30]

Like all great Simon lyrics, in "Graceland" there is a strongly coherent story, set off with some rather mysterious references left to the reader to puzzle. Graceland is heaven: that's where Simon and his nine-year-old son are heading, north from Louisiana on Route 61 to Memphis to find the former Presley residence. The song is quite literal, then, as an event, but the landscape is embellished with the starkly figurative language for which the early Simon was famous (as in the personification and synesthesia of "Hello darkness my old friend" in "The Sound of Silence"). Here we have "The Mississippi Delta / Was shining like a National guitar," and that brings home the link: African music but a resonator guitar, preferred instrument of many a black bluesman.[31] There is a sharp contrast between the relatively languid and reflective verses and the pulsating, jumping, dancing choruses: "I'm going to Graceland / Graceland / In Memphis, Tennessee / I'm going to Graceland."

The next twist is the introduction of the nebulous woman, no doubt the mother of the son, the estranged first wife, brought on by association with the son, reappearing Laura-like in the poet's vision when she is absent. She is the Cold Heaven of the poem, and the recollection combines a touching personal detail: "The way she brushed her hair from her forehead" with the prophecy that will be repeated through the lyric. It is almost a cliché but in the song context is an acceptable way of registering the emotional exposure that comes with loss, that something from you goes missing, that everyone around you sees it, and, whether you like it or not, everyone can empathize with it:

> "Losing love
> Is like a window in your heart
> Everybody sees you're blown apart
> Everybody feels the wind blow."

Milton's dead second wife did not even speak in "Methought I saw my late-espoused saint." In the third verse, the prophecy becomes the speaker's own words, no longer a quotation. Before this, he is released to contemplate a second female, this time a more distant figure, who exemplifies his sense of disconnection, the girl from New York City on the trampoline, emblematizing the Zen moment of being extracted from all of that to which one is connected:

> There is a girl in New York City
> Who calls herself the human trampoline
> And sometimes when I'm falling, flying
> Or tumbling in turmoil I say
> Whoa, so this is what she means
> She means we're bouncing into Graceland

As discrete, disconnected souls, but all joined together by the recognition of our common pain: "Everybody sees you're blown apart."

There's little end rhyme, but plenty of near rhyme and alliteration, and this seems to be required by the loose but persistent rhythm of the music: "cradle . . . Civil War," "Poor boy and pilgrims," "losing love," "falling, flying . . . tumbling in turmoil," "every ending," "highway . . . War." Just a tendency to end-rhyme in the third- and second-to-last lines of both verse and chorus stanzas: "believe/received," "heart/apart," both of course thematically significant. To return to the altar of the song, the heaven that is Graceland, the point where we must come clean, fess up, or we cannot sing:

> And I may be obliged to defend
> Every love, every ending
> Or maybe there's no obligations now
> Maybe I've a reason to believe
> We all will be received
> In Graceland

Lines 1–2 imagine an inquest at the Last Judgment: then one must answer for the correctness or failure of every act. Line 3 supposes instead that "now" that kind of judgment seems utterly false. Now, in our self-forgiving era, there are no obligations to be met. Lines 4–6 therefore conclude that the singer has a reason, in light of line 3, to understand that we will all be forgiven. The sense of redemption as release from previous unhappiness and guilt might be frustrated by a syntax that threatens not to connect, but if it doesn't of course the music will.[32] There's no perfect regularity in the delivery of the lyric in the recording but some pleasing moments of variation, suggesting the memory of the speaker coming to life. "There is a girl in New York City / Who calls herself the human trampoline" is almost delivered as speech, and two spoken "Whoas" of amazement suspend in the third verse and the outro (or concluding section) chorus.[33] Perhaps memory, too, isn't necessary because all experience is common as we enter Graceland, where the closeness of father and son in the second chorus is replaced by "ghosts and empty sockets . . . ghosts and empties."

These elements make up what we might say is a singer-songwriter's style.[34] The idea is to register and then develop a popular and recognizable lyrical and musical signature. The whimsical, ethereal harmonies of the 1960s Simon and Garfunkel, plus Simon's rhythmically inventive solo work, open to a variety of US and global ethnic music of the 1970s and 1980s: funk from New Orleans, reggae from the Caribbean, and so on. That injunction for style is perhaps remembered in the highest "artistic" way in Bob Dylan. Quite apart from the debt to modernist poetics, and its French symbolist prequel, there is in Dylan a production of words that ventures against what we feel should be the proper distribution of syllables or metrical feet into the available musical space, as in "Highway 61 Revisited":

Oh God said to Abraham, "Kill me a son"
Abe says, "Man, you must be puttin' me on"
God say, "No." Abe say, "What?"
God say, "You can do what you want Abe, but
The next time you see me comin' you better run"
Well Abe says, "Where do you want this killin' done?"
God says, "Out on Highway 61"[35]

In particular here it is the enjambed lines 4–5, and especially the linear powertrain syntax of line 5, that suggests the overfull exuberance of excited speech, the speaker's accommodated version of the vengeful God. As is often the case with Dylan, the sung voice is close to, not far from, a speaking one, with whole lines or more, or nearly whole ones, delivered in one pitch. This is not quite the adjusted "speaking blues" of "Subterranean Homesick Blues," but it is certainly related. As the stanzas are performed, so Dylan's strange apocalyptic landscape becomes apparent. And as in many Dylan songs, there is no chorus and no relief in a middle eight or bridge: the narrative exposition is relentless, underlined by the annoying whistle blown by Al Kooper in the original recording. In these various ways, Dylan's mysterious song manifests its distinctive style, and in this moment of 1965, Dylan confirms his move away from his early identity as a folk-protest singer.

Dylan's light, agile, rock 'n' roll style is there for all to hear, with no compromises. It is rough, authentic rock 'n' roll, with a big debt to the blues, and in stylistic and production terms quite the opposite of the polished early Simon and Garfunkel, and Simon's heavily produced later solo work. The sense of excess also features centrally in the extended lyric of "Like a Rolling Stone," described by Dylan as a "long piece of vomit," "a rhythm thing on paper, all about my steady hatred directed at some point that was honest."[36] Here the music was, so we are told, quickly put together to make a platform for a lyric whose anger breaks the regularity of song verse form. As well as catching its verbal exuberance, Christopher Ricks sees, too, that the lyric is distinctive for its unusual moods and mood changes:

> The right characterization of the animus within the song, in my judgment, is not gloating but exulting. . . . [It is] the source of the song's delight (energy is delight, as Blake sensed), and since delight often overflows its bounds, then if the Princess is indeed like a rolling stone, some of this sense of delight just might roll her way. She can't simply be anathema to him, for the song rolls like an anthem.[37]

It is the extraordinary complexity of mood, indicating psychological depth, that makes these songs stand out.

If ever there was a songwriter who was able to fuse the interest of lyrics with that of the music, it would have to be Joni Mitchell, whose distinctive melodies and voices, and openness to unusual harmonies and instrument tunings, enabled her to escape the constraints of the late 1960s–1970s conventional singer-songwriter mode into an innovative fusion of folk-rock-jazz with impressionistic lyrics that never quite let go of their roots in protest music and personal romantic ballads. One *New York Times* review described her songs as "glistening with her elegant way with language, her pointed splashes of irony and her perfect shaping of images. Never does Mitchell voice a thought or feeling commonly. She's a songwriter and singer of genius who can't help but make us feel we are not alone."[38]

Many of the songs feature a rapid pace of word consumption that is striking, but most notable of all is the sheer color of the musical tone painting, facilitating a lyric that comprises both narrative record and introspective reflection. Take "Free Man in Paris" as an example.[39] The lyric looks like a modernist poem on the page and is purportedly in the voice of an American record executive in Paris, temporarily free of his responsibilities. It is usually supposed to be David Geffen. The rich, elaborate setting converts the speaker's voice, his voiced consciousness, into what we might call an angelic, paradisal ode of delight, imparted and in terms of texture and timbre dramatically enhanced with Mitchell's multilayered vocal harmonies (and helped by male angel collaborators David Crosby and Graham Nash), these then cleverly dispersed in the stereo mix: they sound like a choir all around you. The rhythmic conversion from the intro's compound quintuple meter of 15/8 (which then becomes an instrumental refrain played by the entire band) into the regular 4/4 of the verse and chorus is effortlessly held up by a performance from some of the greatest jazz and fusion players of the day: Tom Scott (woodwinds), José Feliciano and Larry Carlton (electric guitars), Wilton Felder (bass), and John Guerin (drums). The exuberance of walking down the banks of the Seine or through the Marais is internalized as a delightful experience in the listener. If this is not musical poetry, I do not know what is. The complete song makes poetry of conversational musing and dignifies what would otherwise be trite rhyming. Ordinary speech repetition becomes interesting and "arranged," like a fine libretto:

> "The way I see it," he said,
> "You just can't win it.
> Ev'rybody's in it for their own gain;
> you can't please 'em all.
> There's always somebody calling you down.
> I do my best
> and I do a good business.
> There's a lot of people asking for my time.
> They're trying to get ahead.
> They're trying to be a good friend of mine.

I was a free man in Paris,
I felt unfettered and alive.
There was nobody calling me up for favors
and no one's future to decide.
You know I'd go back there tomorrow
but for the work I've taken on,
stoking the star maker machin'ry
behind the popular song."[40]

There's an extra element to this excellence of word and music combination that comes when we reckon with a song that is a parody of another song. The case I offer is David Bowie's "Life on Mars?," fine enough itself as a great song, with an intricate and intelligent lyric that has also been the inspiration for acclaimed poetry, as for instance in the case of Tracy K. Smith.[41] Bowie's eclecticism at this early point in his career displays an uncommon mastery of many forms, while the themes of isolation, mental instability, and transformation speak to an excellence that was about to be readily acclaimed. The embodiment of change in the chorus of "Changes"—"Ch-ch-ch-ch-an-ges"— seems to imitate the way that at first we are reluctant to acknowledge, understand, and accept change. We are pulled forward by its inevitability, just as the syllables pull the word from the conceptual present into a future: the mimesis of change is in the pronunciation.

"Life on Mars?" (1971) is actually a parody of the popular song (in jazz mode) "My Way," made famous by Frank Sinatra (recorded in late 1968 and released the following year), with a lyric written by Paul Anka and set to the music of the French song "Comme d'habitude," co-composed, cowritten, and performed in 1967 by Claude François and Jacques Revaux. Anka's words certainly rhyme, but that's about it as they offer an overview of a life very unspecified and leave themselves open to mockery: the lyrics are anodyne, unimaginative clichés. That might have been fine for its imagined market, and singers from Sinatra and Elvis Presley to Sid Vicious have had the chance to let their voices shine or not as they sing over the musical characteristic of the verse—the descending pattern of the chords, each phrase nonetheless starting higher than the last.

Enter Bowie with a descending scale that parodies François and Revaux's music, but that also finds renewal with its unusual landing places or points of resolution, and the wholly surprising chord changes that greet the pre-chorus. This view has been upheld in an interview with the virtuoso keyboardist Rick Wakeman, who played piano on the session and worked much with Bowie at this time. With this comes a lyric of distinct verbal strangeness and *Alice in Wonderland* surrealism. It is anything but trite. The impetus on "My Way" is toward the bottom of scale, to the landing that comes to the accomplished man of integrity who sings the song. Bowie's response descends and then ascends dramatically and triumphantly. It is a rejection of resignation, though we look at a girl whose world is very real and very restricted:

It's a God-awful small affair
To the girl with the mousy hair
But her mummy is yelling no
And her daddy has told her to go
But her friend is nowhere to be seen
Now she walks through her sunken dream
To the seat with the clearest view
And she's hooked to the silver screen.

There are rhymes in couplets and in other schemes, near-rhymes and pointed enjambments, on which the sense turns, and the movie that's at the heart of the song, which seems something from the world of silent film, is echoed by the somewhat doomy and dramatic mood of the music, especially during the description of the sailors' brawl: "Oh man! look at those cavemen go / It's the freakiest show."[42] In this passage, there is modulation to something a little happier at "Take a look at the lawman / Beating up the wrong guy," but then the menace returns as the chorus ends with the acknowledgment of alienation and the quest to escape: "Is there life on Mars?" While Paul Anka's lyric ends with self-satisfied platitudes, Bowie slips into the most glorious symbolism, fusing the ghost of Hollywood with extraordinary imagery of the British public, both striking workers and "mice," all alienated from their sources of entertainment ("Lennon") or their icons of authority ("Rule Britannia"). Of course, David Bowie was British, but he spent much of his later adulthood in the United States. Like much of his art, "Life on Mars?" is forged in a triangulation of French, American (Tin Pan Alley), and English perspectives, each dependent on the other.

There is now good evidence of gathering energy for a new cross-media, cross-disciplinary approach, alongside Timothy Hampton, from intensely detailed perception of precise, rhythmic diversity in African American verse, literary but so rhythmic in focus that it has become musical, or, starting from the approach of musicology, and considering as an example the rap of Kendrick Lamar, so attentive to metrical ambiguity that it makes the case for the innovative musical-poetic simultaneity of protest art.[43]

The reservoir of popular song is vast, and not every lyric will by any means be considered worthy of consideration in a volume of essays on the virtues of contemporary verse. But to remove popular song from the picture would be a huge loss, and a failure to acknowledge the extent to which most contemporary poetry is invested in the interaction of "highbrow" and "lowbrow" culture. What I have tried to do is to suggest that the popular song lyric cannot be analyzed just as a lyric, and that to monumentalize it or dismiss it without understanding its relationship with music is to miss something quintessential about it. To avoid that element is to risk misunderstanding its nature entirely, as some examples I discuss reveal. I've tried here to show some ways forward. We now need a developed critical language that pays attention to the interaction of popular song lyric and music to do justice to its essential nature; "else a great prince in prison lies."

Notes

1. A. E. Stallings, "Bob Dylan: Song as Poetry," *Times Literary Supplement*, October 14, 2016, https://www.the-tls.co.uk/articles/bob-dylan-song-poetry, accessed September 2, 2021.

2. See Daniel Karlin, "The Figure of the Singer," *Essays in Criticism* 50, no. 2 (April 2000): 99–124; see also Daniel Karlin, *The Figure of the Singer* (Oxford: Oxford University Press, 2013), esp. chap. 9; and Daniel Karlin, *Street Songs: Writers and Urban Songs and Cries, 1800–1925* (Oxford : Oxford University Press, 2018).

3. See, for example, essays by Harriet Monroe, *Poetry* 3, no. 2 (November 1913) and 3, no. 3 (December 1913); and Vachel Lindsey, *Poetry* 4, no. 4 (July 1914). Thanks to Sylvie Thode for help with accessing and understanding this material.

4. Among negative comments, the *Guardian* reported charges of mere nostalgia and a lame avoidance of demanding literary merit. Comparisons with Homer were made by the report from the Swedish Academy. Hannah Ellis-Petersen

and Alison Flood, "Bob Dylan Wins Nobel Prize in Literature," *Guardian*, October 13, 2016.

5. Ronald Schleifer, *Modernism and Popular Music* (Cambridge: Cambridge University Press, 2011), chap. 4.

6. Adam Bradley, *Book of Rhymes: The Poetics of Hip Hop* (New York: Basic Civitas, 2009).

7. Now generating its own body of analytical commentary: see, for instance, Jeffrey Severs's penetrating "'Is It Like a Beat without a Melody?': Rap and Revolution in *Hamilton*," *Studies in Musical Theatre* 12, no. 2 (June 2018): 141–52.

8. Robert von Hallberg, *Lyric Powers* (Chicago: University of Chicago Press, 2008), chap. 5.

9. Adam Bradley, *The Poetry of Pop* (New Haven, CT: Yale University Press, 2017).

10. Richard Goldstein, ed., *The Poetry of Rock* (New York: Bantam Books, 1969); see also Pete Astor, "The Poetry of Rock: Song Lyrics Are Not Poems but the Words Still Matter; Another Look at Richard Goldstein's Collection of Rock Lyrics," *Popular Music* 29, no. 1 (January 2010): 143–48.

11. Richard Thompson, "Walking on a Wire," on Richard and Linda Thompson, *Shoot Out the Lights* (Rykodisc, 1982).

12. Walter Everett, "A Royal Scam: The Abstruse and Ironic Bop-Rock Harmony of Steely Dan," *Music Theory Spectrum* 26, no. 2 (Fall 2004): 201–36.

13. See for instance, Walter Everett, *The Beatles as Musicians: "Revolver" through the "Anthology"* (New York: Oxford University Press, 1999); Walter Everett, *The Beatles as Musicians: The Quarry Men through "Rubber Soul"* (New York: Oxford University Press, 2001); and Walter Everett, *The Foundations of Rock: From "Blue Suede Shoes" to "Suite: Judy Blue Eyes"* (New York: Oxford University Press, 2009).

14. Timothy Hampton, *Bob Dylan's Poetics: How the Songs Work* (New York: Zone Books, 2019); Timothy Hampton, "Tangled Generation: Dylan, Kerouac, Petrarch, and the Poetics of Escape," *Critical Inquiry* 39, no. 4 (Summer 2013): 703–31; and Max Horkheimer and Theodor W. Adorno, *Dialectic of Enlightenment*, trans. Edmund Jephcott, ed. Gunzelin Schmid Noerr (Stanford, CA: Stanford University Press, 2004), 103, quoted in Hampton, "Tangled Generation," 726–27.

15. Christopher Ricks, *Dylan's Visions of Sin* (London: Viking, 2003). I wonder what William Empson might have said about Dylan.

16. Stallings, "Bob Dylan: Song as Poetry."

17. Hampton, "Tangled Generation," 718; and Hampton, *Bob Dylan's Poetics*, 133–34.

18. Andrew Cutrofello, "'The Wind Began to Howl': Dylan's Antinomianism," *Journal of Speculative Philosophy* 34, no. 3 (2020): 232–47.

19. Timothy Hampton, "Absolutely Modern: Dylan, Rimbaud, and Visionary Song," *Representations* 132, no. 1 (Fall 2015): 1–29.

20. Greg Smith, "'And All the Sinners, Saints': Patti Smith, Pioneer Musician and Poet," *Midwest Quarterly* 41, no. 2 (2000), 175.

21. Ibid., 185.

22. Carrie Jaurès Noland, "Rimbaud and Patti Smith: Style as Social Deviance," *Critical Inquiry* 21, no. 3 (Spring 1995): 591.

23. Ibid., 596.

24. Ibid., 601.

25. Paul Muldoon, "In Conversation," Academy of American Poets, June 10, 2011, https://www.poets.org/poetsorg/text/paul-muldoon-conversation.

26. See Nigel Smith, "Lyric and the English Revolution," in *The Lyric Poem: Formations and Transformations*, ed. Marion Thain (Cambridge: Cambridge University Press, 2013), 71–91.

27. M. H. Miller writes: "'Jezebel Was a Jersey Belle' is something like 'Kitty's Back'—Mr. Springsteen's anthem of a Jersey chick who falls for a 'city dude'—mixed with the Beach Boys' 'California Girls.' Mr. Muldoon lists female companions from across the country—Delilah from Delaware, Ilana from Illinois ('she wasn't at all double-dealing / though she dealt heroin')—before going into the refrain: 'Even the dogs in the street could tell / Jezebel was a Jersey belle.'" M. H. Miller, "Poet Crossing: Regarding 'Word on the Street,' Rock Lyrics by Paul Muldoon," *Observer*, February 12, 2013. A version of the song may be found as track 4 on Chris Harford, *Shimmering Waste* (2018), with Ray Kubian, Noriko Manabe, and Nigel Smith, recorded during the June 2011 sessions for Wayside Shrines' *The Word on the Street* (2013).

28. This appears to be missed by James Bennighof's earlier analysis of "Graceland": "Fluidity in Paul Simon's 'Graceland': On Text and Music in a Popular Song," *College Music Symposium* 33–34 (1993–1994): 232: "Simon's technique of using specific instrumental and performer choices to support central ideas of the song is, in fact, typical of his personal compositional style." The musical analysis in this article is important in the establishment of the presence of "fluidity" in the song; in my view, the lyric analysis is less satisfactory.

29. Issues of integrating African musicians into American recording practices, or not, have been a subject of controversy surrounding the reception and reputation of the *Graceland* album.

30. "*Graceland* by Paul Simon," Songfacts, https://www.songfacts.com/facts/paul-simon/graceland.

31. Paul Simon, *Lyrics 1964–2008* (New York: Simon and Schuster, 2008), 181–82.

32. Thanks to Robert von Hallberg, the source of this comment.

33. "Outro: A concluding section, esp. of a piece of music or a broadcast programme," *Oxford English Dictionary*. An outro was recorded in Vivian Stanshall's 1967 piece "The Intro and the Outro" by the Bonzo Dog Doo-Dah Band.

34. See Bradley, *The Poetry of Pop*, chap. 8.

35. Bob Dylan, *Lyrics: 1962–2012* (New York: Simon and Schuster, 2013), 178.

36. Clinton Heylin, *Revolution in the Air: The Songs of Bob Dylan, 1957–1973* (Chicago: Chicago Review Press, 2009), 240.

37. Ricks, *Dylan's Visions of Sin*, 181, 186.

38. Loraine Alterman, "Songs for the New Woman," *New York Times*, February 11, 1973.

39. Joni Mitchell, "Free Man in Paris," on *Court and Spark* (Asylum Records, 1974).

40. Joni Mitchell, *Hits* (New York: Alfred Publishing, 1997), 80–90.

41. Tracy K. Smith, *Life on Mars: Poems* (Minneapolis: Graywolf Press, 2011). I am indebted in the following remarks on Bowie, Smith, Frank Sinatra, and Paul Anka to an unpublished presentation by Jonathan Wells and discussions with him afterward. See also Jonathan Wells, ed., *Third Rail: The Poetry of Rock and Roll* (New York: MTV Books, 2007).

42. This quotation is from a 1960 novelty song, "Alley Oop," written by Dallas Frazier in 1957 and performed by the Hollywood Argyles, a group of studio musicians. Thanks to Robert von Hallberg for this information.

43. Michael Skansgaard, "How Not to Introduce Blues Prosody: Langston Hughes and the Rhythms of the African American Vernacular Tradition," *Poetics Today* 40, no. 4 (December 2019): 645–81; and Noriko Manabe, "We Gon' Be Alright? The Ambiguities of Kendrick Lamar's Protest Anthem," *MTO: A Journal of the Society for Music Theory* 25, no. 1 (May 2019), https://mtosmt.org/issues/mto.19.25.1/mto.19.25.1.manabe.pdf.

CHAPTER 14

Jay Wright

A Few Words of Appreciation

DANIELLE S. ALLEN

JAY WRIGHT HAS published fifteen books of poetry. Sixteen if you count his very first, *Death as History*, a small pamphlet published in 1967. He has won the highest literary honors: Yale University's Bollingen Prize, a MacArthur Fellowship, the Lannan Literary Award. He has published plays. He was born in 1935. He has lived in New Mexico, Scotland, and Vermont, as well as having spent time in Mexico and Africa. I do not know the whole of his itinerary and I don't think my job in this chapter is to tell you about his biography. I have been invited to be a *reader* just as, in each one of his poems, Wright calls each of us to read, and thereby to transfigure ourselves.

What does Jay Wright invite each of us to do when we enter one of his poems?

Much has been made of the fact that he is an African American poet who draws on the resources of African cosmologies—the tradition of the Dogon, for instance. He invokes figures like Robert Hayden and Ralph Ellison in telling his own education. But it is a mistake to think that the frame that should govern our thinking about Jay Wright's poetry might be labeled with terms like "representation," "authenticity," or "solidarity." Wright's poetry instead is oriented by the stars of argument, aspiration, and social and aesthetic experimentation.

Literary history was dealt a cruel blow in the nineteenth century when German theorists fused into a unity the ideas of culture, nation, language, and *Volk*, as if the peoples of the world live in isolated and separable units or islands. We have reproduced this view of humanity in our universities with Departments of English and French and German and East Asian Languages and Cultures and so on. But people don't live this way. They never have. They didn't do so in the nineteenth century and don't do so now. How then to write a poetry for how people live, for the omnivorous character of our lives in language and culture? This is the question Jay Wright has been seeking to answer for the whole of his writerly life.

First, there is music. The human body knows rhythm; the spirit knows rhythm. The ear knows sonic texture—rhyme, assonance, sibilance. The eye and the mind's eye work together to turn image into words. That, just that, the music of rhythm and sonic texture, the union of vision and word, is the stuff of language, the material humans use everywhere to explore their experience and render it memorable. Jay Wright is a brilliant, underappreciated prosodist, whether writing in iambic pentameter, dactylic hexameter, the jazz rhythms of Sonny Rollins, subtle lyric structures, or free verse. A critic has described Wright's poems as characterized by "incantatory intensity." So they are, and the incantation is all, I would say, in the rhythm. Wright aspires to write music.

"Entering New Mexico" begins:

Here on the porch,
with the lights going out
all over the neighborhood,
we can see the moon rise
from hour to hour,
as red as the flat,
round top of the stove.
Voices seem to harmonize
with the quiet belling of spoons and dishes.[1]

The thundering anapests that we know from comic verse or from Byron ("The Assyrian came down like a wolf on the fold") here find a new valence—simple and quietly pleased ("Here on the porch / with the lights going out"). Five lines down, we get a subtle in-between rhythm in "from hour to hour"; the line almost slips from anapests into iambs but not quite, and it doesn't really flip to dactyls either. The most rhythmic object in the poem—the moon in its circling of the earth—thus eludes the poetic net. Yet it serves as the gravitational center for the anapestic lines lapping around it, before and after, like waves. Wright has rhythmically captured the moon in his poet's net after all, since gravity is what the moon gives us, its celestial rhythms grounding all of our earthly rhythms.

Even much later, Wright still finds resolution in the anapest. In "The Double Invention of Kọmọ," he begins with an invocation, which, for an English-speaking reader, must be all and only rhythm and sonic texture:

This is the language of desire.

> banã yírí kọrọ
> banã ba yírí kọrọ
> dyigini yírí kọrọ
> yẹlẹni yírí kọrọ

Through this you will be fulfilled.

> I place myself under the sign of the divine spirit
> under the sign of the great divine spirit
> under the tree of sacred signs
> under the tree of ascension of souls (*T*, 316)

The last four lines downshift from five beats to four, to three, and then a final anapestic trimeter—desire for rhythmic equilibrium fulfilled.

Wright's corpus is in fact vast, though it is hard to access. The collected poems take us only to 2000, and the four books that postdate its publication are kept unevenly in print. A short essay must necessarily shortchange, because there is as much in the way of concrete image and coherent lines of thought as of rhythm. Yet rhythmic pleasures of the kind noted above, and of far more complex forms, abound. You cannot pick up a page of Wright without being reconnected to the moon, in the sense of being pulled into experience patterned against cosmic patterns. Wright knows this about his poetry and knew it from an early point. He writes in the early poem, "Benjamin Banneker Sends His 'Almanac' to Thomas Jefferson,"

> At night,
> the stars submit themselves
> to the remembered way you turn them;

the moon gloats under your attention.
I, who know so little of stars,
whose only acquaintance with the moon
is to read a myth, or to listen
to the surge
of songs the women know,
sit in your marvelous reading
of all movements,
of all relations.

Yet Wright also doubts both the perfection and the comprehensiveness of the celestial rhythms:

Surely, there must be a flaw.
These perfect calculations fall apart.
There are silences
that no perfect number can retrieve,
omissions no perfect line could catch.
. . .
So you go over the pages again,
Looking for the one thing
that will not reveal itself,
judging what you have received
what you have shaped,
believing it cannot be strange
to the man you address.

Wright then jarringly shifts from the celestial to the political. He stubs his toe on race in this poem, figuring the relationship of Banneker, an eighteenth-century African American naturalist (a small category), to Jefferson. The distant moons are less strange to us than we are to one another, thus of Banneker from Jefferson's point of view:

But you are strange to him
  —your skin, your tongue,
the movement of your body,
even your mysterious ways with stars. (T, 108–9)

For Wright, the racialized modern world must be read as something of a wormhole in the cosmos, where rhythm has failed. This is a remarkable thing. Wright's integration of Dogon mythologies and rhythms into poetry in which "the Florentine" and "his Roman guide, / arguing out the first sense of justice" also live comfortably repairs damage to space-time. I take the time not merely to appreciate individual poems but also to interpret the work done across the corpus as a whole because this ambition—and its vision of human beings' relations to the cosmos, the divine, and one another—moves me profoundly. Why does it do so? To use the categories of social analysis, one could say that Wright offers a vision of neither assimilation nor multiculturalism. He acts instead as a creator, making the mental cosmos anew, as if a rhythmic explosion in the here and now could make the universe run differently. This effort moves me because it expresses such a strong desire that the world be right and such a full-throated, impassioned effort to bring that rightness into being via the instrument that links humanity to all creation—rhythm.

The collected poems close with rhythmic fireworks—three codas, one (numbered "IV") in almost singsong rhyming iambs, a second (numbered "V") in a form of alphabetized spondaic compression with nearly no unaccented syllables, and a third (numbered "VI") in Wright's familiar personal rhythms, which resolve, once again, in a concluding anapest.

Coda IV
Hummingbird of hummingbird
wing of air no one has heard.
Now the wing contains a flaw,
red lines on a box of straw,
threaded veil, bone root or shale,
bred of a corrupted tail.
All bereft, you are death's tree.
Nothing here remembers me.
How I marvel that your bill
has incensed my tongue and will.

Coda V
Blessèd be bright brood birches
bred blithely beyond bridges
clustered clutched crustily close

cunningly composed cover
demure dire docents doubtless
December's decent double
endogenous eloquence
enchiridion essence
ferns' ferrous ferocious friends
fit fetish freighted forged found.

Coda VI
Starlight is my measure,
that one clairvoyant texture
set upon the plane
            of the tau.
Dark light is my nature,
the spirit's own erasure,
creative domain
            of the tao;
creative domain—
            ask me now. (*T*, 619)

What does Wright do with the stunning, gorgeous musicality that he deploys with ease like water's flow? He gives back to us our world and his, as if with a new moon. That is what his rhythmic work does. But he also gives us our world through arguments—deploying Dogon ritual but also Parmenides, Democritus, Xenophanes, all the pre-Socratics, not to mention the ancient poets and medieval philosophers and theologians like Nicholas di Cusa, and modern poets, too. His contemporaries do not so orient themselves. James Merrill, not at all. John Ashbery sounds as if he is seriously putting together thoughts and propositions, but then a kind of dissolution sets in. Robert Pinsky is someone who does construct arguments, but that is not, in all likelihood, what his audience likes best; many are turned off by his knowingness. Poets have more easily oriented themselves on symbols, images, moments of exceptional experience. In Wright's phrasing, alone one sees how comfortable he is with the idioms of argumentation. It is as if he had not heard that poetry should not concern itself with ideas as essays do.

For instance, he gives us arguments about being and nothingness. How can any of us come to be unless there was nothing out of which we came? Yet if there was nothing, then how can we be? He probes the great metaphysical problems of all peoples and places, attaching to them metaphors of stirring power.

> Such is the scandal of nature
> an awakening to nothingness,
> a metrical insistence upon
> small shapes.[2]

The rhythmic project is reprised in argument. The point I am trying to make is that Wright follows language toward understanding of being as he has lived it. Any and every helpful tradition is pulled into his net to make a language spoken nowhere on this globe; it has no stable geography. "My gacelita knows I have no home" (GS, 80). But that homelessness gives Wright's language access to everything, everywhere, with rhythm as a great unifying point of reference. And this, Wright proposes, is how we should all build our identities in the future. In an early interview, he said that his poetry "[o]ffers itself in the service of a new and capable personality at home in the transformative and transformed world." His is not the language of homelessness after all, but of being at home in the world.

A new and capable personality, that is what Jay Wright calls each of us to be as people and as readers, and he demonstrates the linguistic tools to facilitate just that.

> Argue me another mode,
> the quality of an imprisoned bird,
> trepando el aire,
> free of its pain,
> and singing that no one will die.
> These measures you know,
> the techne of an infinite desire,
> the negation of a self,
> the constituent argument of one and one,
> the undecidable certainty embodied in grace. (GS, 74)

So he calls us, as readers, writers, thinkers. And he shows us the way with poems that "speak of the difficult birth of a mind that measures its own transfiguration" (*GS*, 75).

Notes

1. Jay Wright, *Transfigurations: Collected Poems* (Baton Rouge: Louisiana State University Press, 2000), 110, hereafter abbreviated as *T*.
2. Jay Wright, *The Guide Signs: Book One and Book Two* (Baton Rouge: Louisiana State University Press, 2007), 69, hereafter abbreviated as *GS*.

CHAPTER 15

Nathaniel Mackey and the Music

ROBERT VON HALLBERG

WHEN POUND WAS starting the Cantos, and floundering, he asked himself: "Has it a place in music?" Maybe his capacious project was insufficiently lyrical . . . or not poetry. An ambitious poet's ugly worry. Nathaniel Mackey is a free-verse poet with a sound so distinctive that it counts in the development of US poetry. Much of his verse is iambic, though this is to say little more than that it is a version of speech; against that ground, he disposes stress unexpectedly at the outset of lines, and inside the lines stressed syllables gather in spondaic patterns. The edges of lines, beginnings and ends, take special force even though semantically and syntactically a memorable solitary line is not his objective. He prints his verse in patterns that appear stanzaic; the mostly unscheduled dropping of a final word or two at the right end of a line contributes to an analogue of stanzaic form. Those dropped words gain rhetorical emphasis and mark something like the end of a free-verse strophe. He's a strophic poet who seeks movement and gatherings. He characterizes his music as a fraying of the iambic conventions of English verse; one often hears iambic tetrameter. Resistance is audible—raspiness, he calls it in Song 50.

> Came to it sooner
> than we could see but soon enough
> saw we were there. Some who'd
> come before us called it Bray . . .
>
> Sound's own principality it was, a

```
        pocket of air flexed mouthlike,
    meaning's mime and regret, a squib of
        something said, so intent it
    seemed. At our backs a blown
                            conch,
    bamboo flute, tropic remnant (SA 66)[1]
```

Bray, the sound of an ass, the stubborn peculiarity of one who squanders resources. Or it may be a tropical richness, as in "of the tropics" (where African and European sensibilities mix), but also "a byproduct of tropes," turns through which phrases and clauses are put, to register a distinctive voice.

The sounds of a voice establish human presence, though not necessarily social identity. Mackey's fictional prose goes as far as can be imagined in paraphrasing instrumental music. That music is altered even through *talk of* performance. The sounding of words, even in interpretive talk, expresses hope. For what? Change, mobility; it might be otherwise. Whatever one's initial sense of a song-text as utterance and one's sense, too, of previous versions, a new singer takes all that somewhere else, moves the song. N. asks, "Did song imply a forfeiture of speech or was it speech's fulfillment?" (*DBR* 160). The falsetto voice is an extreme instance of angular interpretation. "By this I mean," N. writes, "the deliberately forced, deliberately 'false' voice we get from someone like Al Green [who] creatively hallucinates a 'new world,' indicts the more insidious falseness of the world as we know it" (*BH* 62). "Like the moan or the shout, I'm suggesting, the falsetto explores a redemptive, unworded realm" (*BH* 63). The paraphrasable sense of a song is not a reasonable measure of art. "What made us laugh was the incongruity— the unreality and the inappropriateness of singing, the gap between song and circumstance. That gap, that incongruity, obeyed a principle of non-equivalence, an upfront absence of adequation . . ." (*DBR* 49). Performance can free a song from the constraints of recognized sentiments. "I think of such things as scat, where the apparent mangling of articulate speech testifies to an 'unspeakable' history such singers are both vanquishers and victims of" (*BH* 83). Unspeakable because abominable, or because one cannot affirm the implications of some idioms? Both, assuredly.

> Sang with a catch in our throats,
>   cough caught in our throats . . .
>   Sang to
>   have been done with singing,
>   song
> not enough (*SA* 33)

An expression of desire not of possession, song is. The conventional structure is that possession lies in the future, desire fulfilled. Carpe diem. Mackey imagines instead a beauty carried forward by loss. Song may express what was known and then lost, and now a memory (*SA* 92). Standard romance: "now my consolation is in the stardust of a song." The difference from Hoagy Carmichael is that, for Mackey, loss survives as mutilation rather than revery; deliberate damage evident still in the sound of the music he admires. The poems cannot move swiftly to their objectives; they circle back in worry, reconsideration.

> Abbey Lincoln sang a Sufi lament.
>   Truth blurred if not blue, blue, bereft,
> face never seen they say . . . Lookless,
>   faceless, voice heard in hell, life love
>   alluded
>   to lifted, love's
>   laryngitic
> address (*SA* 119)

This is the intellectual support for Mackey's stylistic idiosyncrasies, his wounded music.

The general issue raised by Mackey's work is the proper function of sonic structures. He makes an especially strong case for the determining role of sonic resemblances in the construction of phrases, lines, and poems. Critics commonly hold that sound properly echoes or ornaments sense, that sense not sound ought to determine what is said by poets, insofar as that is distinguishable from a manner of saying. This is not to say that Pope's is the only view preserved in the English tradition. Shakespeare tracks sounds so closely that resemblances obviously generate phrases, and phrases, lines. At some density, however, the sonic structures of poetry have traditionally been understood to reduce intellectuality. Tropical richness, a siren song. Geoffrey Hartman put the matter well in regard to Hopkins:

> Hopkins tends to use rather simple ideas without theological complication, as if his purpose were confined to the medieval *manifestatio*—an illustration, not argumentation, of sacred doctrine. But his poems do not seem to progress by thought to which word and image are subordinate, rather by word and image distilling thought. . . . Consciousness of the word is so strong in "The Windhover" that the poem's continuity seems to derive from an on-the-wing multiplication of the sound of one word in the next, like a series of a accelerating explosions.[2]

The challenge posed by echoic poems is acute with regard to religious and philosophical poetry. Hopkins proceeds in accord with the contours of sound, but an intellectual discipline, theology, trims his topics in accord with the disciplines of grammar and logic. Basil Bunting said that "strong song tows." Hopkins seems to derive better guidance from sonic resemblances than from the protocols of disciplined intellectual discourse. Poetry critics speak of pleasure taken in sonority. Georges Bataille described the problem: "Pleasure, whether art, permissible debauchery, or play, is definitively reduced, in the intellectual representations *in circulation*, to a concession; in other words it is reduced to a diversion whose role is subsidiary."[3] Sonic lushness is a sign of insubordination.

This is why, in Song 50, Mackey may speak of meaning's regret of sonority. Sounds lure one away from transportable sense. One asks repeatedly what sonority means, where it leads, and on what ground it commends one syllable over another. That questioning is constant as one reads Mackey's poems. As Song 50 proceeds, Mackey elaborates a sense in which sonority produces something like a textile.

> Antiphonal thread
> attended by thread. Keening string
> by thrum, inwardness, netherness . . .
>
> Violin

strings tied their hair high, limbo
the headrags they wore . . . The admission
   of cloth that it was cover, what
was imminent out of reach,   given

                              what

went for real, unreal,

                  split,

   silhouetted
redress (*SA* 67)

Reparation for a loss: sonority covers what is inadequately stated otherwise, however imminent the unstated may seem. The full body has been partly lost. The work of a poem is recovery. Redress is compensation for a loss, and also to dress again (rehabilitate), to cover over, as a headrag does. And the poems, like dancers, bend to pass between a bar above and the dirt below. They are neither prose sense nor entirely musical. To be *in* the music is the poet's aspiration:

        It was only
there we wanted to be, the everywhere
   we'd always wanted, ours,
              albeit
   only an instant, forever, never to be
                 heard
from again (*SA* 35)

One's access to the music: intermittent, at best. Songs pass through air, and are gone. In *Bedouin Hornbook*, Mackey quotes Victor Zuckerkandl about the dynamism of music: "Listening to music, we are not first *in* one tone, then in the next, and so forth. We are always *between* the tones, *on the way* from tone to tone; our hearing does not remain with the tone, it reaches through it and beyond it" (*BH* 22). Restlessness is constant; uncertainty, resolved only temporarily when an unforeseen stress lands. "I'm struck by how the echoes are already there in advance of themselves, that maybe it's all only next year's nostalgia heard ahead of time" (*BH* 49). Moments of satisfaction seem discovered more than made. They inhere in language, there before the poems.

I was once in a reading group that each week interpreted one of Pound's Cantos. The evening we disbanded, after a year, each reader reflected on the experience. Most of us referred to the labor of looking up references, and several spoke of Pound's repugnant politics. Mackey said that he did not look up any of Pound's references, that his interest was Pound's ear. I had looked up too many references to count and for that reason didn't understand how serious his remark was. He saw in *The Cantos*, first, a poet's liberty in tracking the sounds of words, and second, the capacity of very specific proper nouns (of the sort I had glossed) to serve general semantic objectives. His own poems too are metaphysical and general where they seem on the surface to be specific. I should add that Mackey's remark was made in 1972, a moment of strenuous realism in US poetry. Think of Robert Lowell's *Notebook* (1969), Robert Bly's *The Teeth Mother Naked at Last* (1970), Adrienne Rich's *The Will to Change* (1971). The allegorical mode Mackey later developed is a reaction to the proud political engagement of a preceding generation. It is surprising that in the current literary context greater explicitness is not required of him.

Allegory proposes near-equivalences, not identity. One term may stand for another without misrepresentation. One reads with some skeptical awareness of discrepancies, as one lives: a degree of blur among concepts, propositions, people, and things is a constitutive feature of social existence. A just representation of mental activity retains some fluidity of reference. This may be why Mackey writes in a manner that seems clearest when most allegorical. In "On Antiphon Island" he writes of a phase of oppression that may be understood as the Middle Passage endured by African slaves. An "antiphon" is a versicle sung by one of two choirs—a partisan form. It also signifies a sentence that precedes song, a kind of epigraph in advance of a psalm or canticle. Here are lines 23–33.

> Where we
> were was the hold of a ship we were
> caught
> in. Soaked wood kept us afloat . . . It
> wasn't limbo we were in albeit we
> limbo'd our way there. Where we
> were was what we meant by "mu."
> Where

    we were was real, reminiscent
    arrest we resisted, bodies briefly
                                                    had,
        held on
    to (*SA* 64)

The main reference is to slaves incarcerated for transport in a soggy hold. A Christian imagination might characterize that transitory phase of oppression as especially vague, "limbo"-like, neither entirely here nor there. "Limbo" as noun derives from Latin for edge or border: the abode of the just on the border of Hell, occupied by those excluded from the new covenant, unbaptized infants and those who lived before Christ. These lines liken the ship's hold to a state of arrest. This section concludes by likening resistance to arrest to a holding on to one's body. An opening section (lines 1–17) refers to the assumption of a bowed bearing, like that of limbo dancers, a display of subordination accepted. The movement among these analogies entails some blur. The act of resisting arrest is familiar now in reports of civil cases when police justify the use of extreme violence to subdue a prisoner. Our contemporary civil order is separated by more than a century from the Middle Passage: how speak of the Middle Passage as "reminiscent" of a later period, unless the temporal intervals and legal changes of the nineteenth and twentieth centuries are inconsequential? (As they are in a global sense.) Yet the topic of resistance, particularly to authority, is there in the word "limbo." A limber person is pliant, bends easily. As a verb "limbo" refers to a Jamaican dance in which one bends backward to pass under a bar. Resistance to arrest or compliance with authority? How behave in the hold? Has the hold really opened? "How low can you go?" was a bass-y refrain to Chubby Checker's 1962 hit "Limbo Rock."

    A trickle of water lit by the sun
        I saw with an injured eye, captive   40
    music ran our legs and we danced . . .
                                    Knees
    bent, asses all but on the floor, love's
        bittersweet largesse . . . I wanted
    trickle turned into flow, flood,   45

two made one by music, bodied
                    edge
gone up into air, aura, atmosphere
              the garment we wore. We were on
a ship's deck dancing, drawn in a   50
                    dream
above hold . . . The world was ever after,
                         elsewhere.
Where we were they said likkle for little, lick
    ran with trickle, weird what we took it   55
for . . . The world was ever after, elsewhere,
                         no
    way where we were
was there (SA 65)

Blood (line 35) has become water (39), and with that change an aesthetic perspective has displaced a realistic one. Blood injuries entail ideas of justice and punishment. But a trickle of water hit by sunlight is a different matter altogether. The Middle Passage as a site of adversity, the experience of being supine. The dream-response of the prisoners is an indirect uprising. The supine one hears a drop of water and imagines a music, then a dance on the deck. Ever after life is on the deck with the sun overhead, not in the hold. A glimpse can change things. The music begins there (41), "and we danced." He chastises himself for wanting, or expecting, grandeur, "two made one by music" (45). But what is little if music transforms blood into "water lit by the sun"? *Likkle*, not little. Captivity was not the last word, once the music began. African American song begins in that moment when blood becomes water. This is an extraordinarily independent-minded way to write about the sufferings of slaves. Out of misery the music is born, everyone knows. Should the stress fall on *out of* or on *misery*? Slaves dance on the deck, in imagination, because life is ruled by aesthetic values, not by trickles of blood alone. Many others, including Robert Hayden, have written of atrocity, injustice, retribution in regard to the Middle Passage. Mackey gainsays none of the suffering, but he has something else to say: that music makes a world, and that, too, has turned out to be true.

In a political context, realism indicates a willingness to adjust one's objectives to achievable ends; in a literary one, it refers to the representation of social activity in some apparently actual time and place. With that appearance of actuality goes, too, a sense of decorum: certain concerns and activities are understood as realistic; others as implausible. The generation of American poets who came to prominence in the two decades following World War II were accustomed to leaving realism to fiction writers, though African American poets, then as ever, regarded the American social order as a subject for poetry. Lowell, Rich, Merwin, and Bly, however, came to political and social engagement on their own schedules; they determined, mid-career, that US politics demanded attention. Rich wrote sentimentally in "The Blue Ghazals" of taking instruction from Amiri Baraka. Mackey has not been engaged by political or literary realism. He has not allowed the expectations of his contemporaries to shape his work. Strange diction, odd syntax, and a sweet tooth for abstractness take much of the heat away from political subjects in his poems.

> Asked had he been hit he
> answered yes. Ouab'da he
>   called it as if it was a
>   place,   made-up name he
>   made mean "beat with clubs,
>   kicked,"
>   what as-if there was long
>   since fallen away. It was
>   a place brought boots
> to the ribs, batons to the
>   back . . .
> Ouab'da he called it, said it
> was a place, knew, if not already,
>   he'd be hit . . .
>   Split lift,
>   sat ravished, over-
>   taken, overwhelmed . . .
>   Ouab'da
>   he named it, said it was a
>   place,

> never go back
> there again (*WSS* 44)

These lines, sandwiched between Songs 24 and 25, address state violence, the grand spectacles of which, for Mackey's generation, were photographed in the South. The police effort to suppress the civil rights movement is a special subject: an overwhelming ethical consensus now renders political questions concerning such social change beside the point. In the background is "Manteca," written by Dizzy Gillespie, Chano Pozo, and Gil Fuller in 1947; later, Dizzy chanted a refrain, "I'll Never Go Back to Georgia." And it gave a poignant political sense to the big hit that Gladys Knight and the Pips had with "Midnight Train to Georgia" in 1973. Why "Ouab'da," a nonce-term? To contain terror and outrage, and then to leave them behind, as if they were places, like Georgia, or Mississippi. By the late 1960s, it was apparent that northern cities were not short on Ouab'da. The explicit racism of the South, "a simpler place and time," was clear and distinct; there is that to say for it. The next installment of Mackey's series focuses on a march on Washington, on what to do about Ouab'da. Civil war, or Ouar generally, is undesirable, but the contradictions between the enlightenment ideals of the constitution and the activities of the US state keep in view visions of civil war, or Ouar.

> Saw Ouagadou, sought Ouadada. No
> point protesting warned a mouth
>   made of catfish teeth . . .
>   Chanted
> *Where is your love*, chanted *Run,*
>   *come, rally*, chanted *What, blood,*
> *put it in place, pull it*
>   *apart,*
>   chanted Chant down Babylon . . .
> On its rise we the dismembered
> winced. Inasmuch as what we want
>   was unreal there it stood, "four
> times fallen asleep" not even
>   close,
> came to where they'd always been.

>   Bombed
> origins, splendorless, war their
> one resolve. Reich without end its
>   aim, omnibus hitlist . . .
>   Hurtless.
>   Unctuous.
> Oiled . . . (*WSS* 45)

Before the poet: an inert nation wielding an imperial war machine, the air aswarm with contesting imperatives. Milton and Blake had imagined a sleeping giant—and felt the appeal of exotic nomenclature. Mackey uses anagrams: that becomes ahtt and so on. His work switches into code terms, constantly reminding one of his distance from mainstream civility. He makes an idiom, partly out of substitutions, partly out of a stress on strangely abstract and recondite modifiers: asymptotic is an easy one; andoumboulouous is more fun. Concrete verbs are used as abstract nouns, and the familiar systemic words—pronouns and prepositions—often become, of all things, abstract nouns. He twists common usage into peculiarity by fixing on abstract qualities, on terms for characterizing forms—of walking, feeling surfaces. Adjectives are pushed into unfamiliar syntactic formulations in order to concoct names for rare, indistinct phenomena. This is a poetry of angular definition. One might recall similar liberties taken in academic prose, but the more instructive model is that of vocal music that improvises departures from ordinary language and thought. "I think of such things as scat," N. says, "where the apparent mangling of articulate speech testifies to an 'unspeakable' history such singers are both vanquishers and victims of" (*BH* 90). Al Green's falsetto, remember, "explores a redemptive, unworded realm . . . where the implied critique or the momentary eclipse of the word curiously rescues, restores and renews it: new word, new world" (*BH* 63).

In the face of a monumental war state,

>   Better
> to be somewhere else we thought,
>   called
> elsewhere Mozambique, Might've-Been . . .

                                    B'Legless.
        Last resort . . . (WSS 46)

Those odd terms evoke an elsewhere of thought and hope (an Africa of the imagination); Spenser, Milton, Blake, Pound, not Dryden, not Wordsworth, not Eliot—not Pinsky. Mackey is attracted to a mythic more than a civic mode of representation. He is right to focus on relatively uncontroversial political subject matter, because he is not interested in the refinement of controversy, nor in political instruments generally: "I do think it is important to acknowledge . . . the differences between poetry and politics" (PH 274). Rather than curate microaggressions, he generates peculiar terms and inclusive concepts at some distance from political particulars. He writes as if to think differently were to summon another nation, place, people, language. The master topos of the Songs of the Andoumboulou is migration; the road, intellectual.

Mackey's words are like cloths over a beloved subject; one labors to follow a single thread through several sections, for two reasons. One is that the work tracks a mind that moves insistently back and forth—crablike, he says. But behind the movement are lines of thought, zigzag; some allegorical reading is necessary to hold that track, some patience, too. His characteristic syntactic structures are those oriented more on substantives than on verbs. Those structures that allow one to say something before one is certain what to say. One might prune the first two words of this poem, for instance, and thereby eliminate one of many instances of the least active English verb. One might continue editing many of the "what" and "where" formulations that generate return to the verb "to be." The economy one might achieve would eliminate some vagueness, but with that would go a sense of the mind in its most recognizable motions, those that show persistence rather than cleverness, say. The poems bear an uneasy relation to the here and now. Mackey is uncompromising in holding the poems to the indefiniteness of life in the mind, though readers intermittently find some grounding in time and space, as in the beautiful Song 48, which begins:

        It was a freeway overpass we
    were on, an overpass east of
        La Brea. There we stood watching

cars pass under us, desert
    flutes gargling wind at
                our
    backs, an overpass we stood
                  on
    looking west . . . (*SA* 57)

This poem, or its first section, moves gently from this concrete frame to a gorgeous Dantesque vision of the double flow of traffic as a stream of souls. He is referring to the Santa Monica Freeway, which carries traffic from downtown Los Angeles to the ocean and back again (the one discussed in *L.A. Confidential*). This scene, on the Crenshaw overpass, is uncharacteristically specific; he more frequently speaks of abstract qualities having person-like abilities, as if qualities and feelings were themselves as active and alive as we are. Scenes are uncommon because the poems are set in thought and imagination rather than recollection. It is easy enough to prefer the idealistic, less experiential mode, but one must recognize that the scenic mode does present thought in relation to lived experience. In Song 48, Mackey brings his pilgrimage into hazardous proximity to some of the greatest literary pilgrims, Heraclitus and Eliot, but especially Dante.

      What there
  was wasn't music but music was
    there. Where it came from
  was nowhere, we heard it
    nonetheless, not hearing
             it
  before put us there . . . So we
             thought
  but wrongly thought, wrong to have
    thought we could. There we stood
  atop the world looking out at
    the world. L.A. it now was we
            were in . . .

Inside each car someone bore the

world away, each a fleeting guest
　　whose going we lamented, kin we
could've sworn we saw . . . It was
　　a bridge over the river of
　　　　　　　　souls
　　we were on. Lower than we thought
　　we stood we stood looking, eyes
　　all but shut by glare . . . It was
a river never stepped into less
　　than twice. A river of light, it
　　　　　　　was
a river of lies we were told, the
　　biggest we'd outrun river's end . . . (*SA* 57)

The souls of the underworld move through LA, some in the fast lane, others in the slow, but all souls. The scenic mode makes the point nicely that what presents itself to the eyes of contemporary US poets is wholly adequate to the needs of poetry; the glare of southern California light, reminiscent of the paradisal brilliance Dante invokes. Mackey's account of the pilgrims' relation to the music is deeply traditional. The pilgrims' mistaken notion that they were obliged to return to LA because they had previously failed to hear the music suggests that their movements are directed by a guide determined to educate them. Mackey refers to a music out of "nowhere," out of the heavens, that readers of English poetry know well. This sense of the music of the universe is behind the many references to recent jazz and world music, as the pilgrims proceed from poem to poem, place to place. They are listening for a deep music. "World" and "souls" are among Mackey's most recurrent terms. His orientation is grandly global, not national, not ethnic, and spiritual. When he speaks of the biggest lie, in the diction of a child, he refers to the notion that one can escape judgment. His words are strange—Raz, Zar, Ouadada—but the ideas are nothing if not familiar in Western thought.

This first section of Song 48 is followed by two others and then by three ancillary poems. These subsequent texts elaborate the consequences of the vision in a stuttering idiom familiar to Mackey's readers. The first words of the second section are "Head of echoic welter." Then, a recollection of Ouab'da: "Head I was / hit upside." The traffic of souls in contrary directions, out and back, like an echo. They are different from neither one another nor from the visionary company. All apparently headed nowhere. Beyond that is Mackey's conviction that one pursues knowledge, understanding, and art in a welter, and with head injuries. Five linked texts follow this lucid opening, because movement through confusions is the only path before us.

In the presence of ruin, music preserves a memory of fulfillment. Faith is an element of sonority. One takes music in, without skepticism, as one does a beloved, too. The pathos is that the beloved herself then vanishes; music is left behind—like "Stardust," or a memory of Laura.

> To abide by hearing was
>   what love was . . . To
> love was to hear without
> looking. Sound was the
>   beloved's
> mummy cloth . . . (SA 93)

Mackey thinks of troubadour love songs, of Petrarch, and later Wyatt. The materiality of existence—bricks, diseases, neighbors—is not the ground of the pilgrimage. What is soul? the poet asks. Mecca is of the spirit.

> It wasn't an epic we sang had
> there been a song we sang, heroic
>   waste
>   around us though there was. The
> beloved's long-distance voice
> was what it was. Muse meant lost
>   in thought it reminded us, erstwhile
>   epiphany, snuffed . . . It was all
>   a wrong
>   turn or we took a wrong turn. All the
> roads ran off to the side and we as
> well, we of the interminable skid . . . We
>   were they of the imagined exit (SA 115)

Blocked desire—an inaccessible beloved—the poet's objective. The resolution might be to bring the lover and the beloved together to mate. These "two," their desire, leads the poems: union is the meaning of Mecca. A kiss would do the work of the art. The beloved inspires because she is lost, and dwells in thought. I stress the traditionality of Mackey's work because it is unapparent but deep. The expository character of the Songs recalls the *Purgatorio*; their repetitiveness, Petrarch's *Rime*. It matters too that the model of fulfillment is heterosexuality—but seen abstractly: a kiss. However improvised the series, the plot entails a static vision of the end, like a tapestry behind every Song.

Where do the pilgrims seek to arrive? At Sophia, a state of wisdom, or in literary terms at the body of the beloved.

> Climbed a ladder he said she climbed
>   ahead of him, looked up her
> dress. Saw planets, furtive hair,
>   the insides of her thighs . . .
>   Sometimes
>   called it a tree, sometimes called
>   it a ladder. (*WSS* 32)

This is a mythic account of the destination, "a glimpse he said she gave / him into what lay beyond the grave." He speaks of this, in Song 22, as a "Rude epiphany," vague, from which the speaker was removed—only an observer of the two lovers. He returns to it in Song 24, wanting more from it. He had formerly said the pilgrims got off the train to pick loquats. Here they detrain in order to urinate. And as the women squat, they metamorphose into birds. This is a figure of implausible change on the order of "Now I've seen everything . . . a chicken with lips." And with the transfiguration came an altered sense of community, of "we."

> What we they exacted spread as
> myth insisted, so that we for
>   whom the word was long dead
>   said so
> be it, that on such-and-such a
>   day So-and-So woke up to
>   a new

life,   rid of wish, moot
would-it-were-so, moot
                          remorse,
out no less a part of it
     than in, in out,
such the one place they
                    might meet,
mute School-of-What-Hurts
                              her
     husk of a voice
revive
     them in (*WSS* 41)

The point of view of the series is that of an indefinite "we." We travel as in a pilgrimage (or hajj). This handsome lyric examines the formation of community in adversity. The voices of some are constrained, which retards the community's progress. But they manage to come together as a hoarse chorus, joined but a little unlike.

                    Stra Hajj was behind us now.
          It seemed it was a train we
               were on, church we were
                                   in,
          stuck voices all but
          tugged us down . . .
          Plucked strings made the
          floorboards buckle, tenuous
                              hold on
          what we had more tenuous.
                              Hoarse
               Chorus the congress of souls
               we exacted,   soul serenade,
                                        whatsaid
          surmount . . .
                    So that the he
          we heard sing stayed

> with us, haunted
> us, allowed us to move
>   like music,
>   but in
> boxcars, hobos it
>   seemed   (*WSS* 95)

The voice of one singer has the power of the music to render a weakened group to gather and move, even if they must do so in shabby circumstances. "We" move by various conveyances: trains, buses, boats, and feet; that hardly matters. The beauty of this short passage owes much to the play of irregular, unpredictable stress patterns. Strong stresses tend here to huddle together, especially at the outset of lines (stra Hajj, stuck voices, plucked strings), or just to move to the fronts of words. The rhythm has an uncertain tendency toward trochees and spondees. One thinks of Creeley as a predecessor, but Mackey's force is greater. The movement is hesitating, but tough too—and sufficiently persistent to come to an end.

Poets labor at forms and destinations—actually one thing.

> I don't know how humanity stands it
>   with a painted paradise at the end of it
>   without a painted paradise at the end of it (Canto 74)

Pound came to see that closure was not in his hands.

> Let the wind speak
> that is paradise.
> Let the Gods forgive what I
> have made
> Let those I love try to forgive
> what I have made. (Canto 120)

Where does Mackey mean to arrive?

>   arkical
>   city soon to be founded we thought,

glimpse gotten of God under loquat
leaves . . .
    That it wasn't there or that it was
but unreachable,   hard to say
    which was worse,   the Soon-Come
Congress no sooner come than gone, train
    we thought we'd asked how long about,
minds
    ever only half there. (*WSS* 100)

This odd term, arkical, nonce as an adjective, otherwise heavy with usage. Ark is a ready figure for survival, preservation, delivery—above all, for God's covenant, a promise. The Bill of Rights, an American ark; its city, a nation-to-come, whose satisfaction is devoutly to be feared. The sound alone of that funny first word establishes a cool perspective on the grand suggestions of a city of the hill. Say it: "arkical." Say: "glimpse gotten of God." Visionary, yes; ecstatic, no. The speaker is amused, quizzical. Thinking as he goes, not rushing conclusions, patient in process. The style is fanciful without vanity.

A stranger walks into a bar, drops coins in a jukebox, and the atmosphere changes. These poems are based on mobility: arrival at an unfamiliar place may make all the difference. Want a different life? Move, with the discontent of migrants. "We" are constantly moving, checking out new places. At the site of arrival may be a fresh atmosphere, emotionally so, heard in a tune in the air. The pilgrims repeatedly move to yet another place, as if environment, however determinative, were not changing enough to warrant a prolonged stay. The repetitive form of the narrative encourages doubt about quick change. And what about temporal changes? "Moment's Gnosis" begins in a recollection of John Coltrane's 1957 classic, "Moment's Notice." Mackey reflects on the fallacies concerning that which is apparently "of the moment," as if time were determinative. Were it so, we might elude the past by surviving from one moment to the next. The issue is liberty, and the constraints of space and time.

How
    to make moment more than
    moment, they kept asking,

                                    how
      to make moment not elapse . . .
      "Moment shall abide" was
        everyone's gambit, moment's
                                more
      than momentary life. "Moment's
        gnosis," everyone clamored,
      "moment's gnosis," though
                          mo-
        ment's gnosis meant each
        moment has its way . . . Thus
      they'd have had it both ways,
        philosophic beginners, . . . (BF 23)

This analysis of cant proceeds through sonic resemblances: notice→gnosis, a question of knowledge but also a mystery. Philosophic→phosphor, the brief light of the morning star; Venus in disguise as Lucifer. A moment is no sooner recognized than it has passed. To live for the moment, as we approvingly say, is to orient oneself on nothing at all.

                        Not to
        know moment or no sooner
      know than not, moment's know-
          ing nothing if not vanquishment,
                                  relin-
        quishment they called it instead . . .

That linkage of contraries by means of "quish" (vanquish, relinquish) gets Mackey to the notion that an aspiration to contemporaneity is a *surrender* to circumstance. It is an insufficiently examined concept of liberty that affirms, instead of a principle, the easily claimed authority of contemporaneity. The recursive procedure has the poet not just expressing his thoughts about the romance of the moment but worrying a way past notions of which he is sharply critical. The form itself suggests that he has these notions in his head, that he writes of them to get free of them. Read the poem aloud and quickly, all its syllables through, to hear his immersion in the movement of moments. For all the coolness of his tone, recursiveness has him writing his own misgivings even when he seems to dissect others' follies. The pilgrims' objective is to arrive at an account of spirit, not just to keep moving, place to place, moment to moment. Mackey sees poetry as a site of invention and extreme liberty. He writes as if he were clear to all, as if his diction and syntax had currency, though he means to come out at the far end of what is most current.

The series stalls, in Song 106, at the lead-up to the 2016 presidential election—not at its outcome—at a moment, that is, when the poem is most realistic in its reference. "Tales / of / outrage regaled us now, / trumped-up fire we camped / around" (*BF* 128). The ugly hubbub of campaign rhetoric is muffling the utopic aspiration of the Songs. Everyone is speaking of urgently needed changes. "Trumped-up" means invented to serve an ulterior motive—inauthentic. All seemed fakery, the rage of right and left. Even "The kingdom of the loquat" that the pilgrims sought, moving from site to site, listening for something new on the box, seems not the poem's destination. Nothing real lies around the next bend in the road. Dante wound around the Mount of Purgatory, but he did make it to Paradise eventually. Mackey is now doubtful. "It was all bend, we / went / around and around, not / getting around it" (*BF* 129). The crisis is one of confidence in thought. Something said to be real has brought even the pilgrims to anger and impatience. This is a surprising critique, because the poem had not seemed based on what is said to be actual. Mackey's utopian ambition appears insufficiently vigorous to withstand a strong shift of political discourse, the prominence of candidate Trump's rightist diatribes. Readers learn from Mackey's first pages to prize peculiar locutions and articulation; his diction, syntax, and prosody require this of readers. Why should rightist bluster bring the poem to a crisis? Because forces that had formerly seemed distant—that of white supremacy, for instance—suddenly seemed immediate. Mackey's cultivation of differences of expression are designed less to represent a wide array of thought than to establish distance from the immediacy of political advocacy, or the "poverty of politics," as he calls it in the preface to *Blue Fasa* (*BF* xv).

Mackey's recent volume, *Blue Fasa*, brings Songs of the Andoumboulou to what momentarily seems a conclusion. He speaks of the pilgrims' need for a reminder of their quest to remake themselves. In the poem's terms, they are pursuing a "second" existence—an ideal that survives the decline of the discourse of the first "world," as described in Song 106. Here is the first section of the last poem, Song 110:

We took to the road, Wagadu
revisited, more times fallen asleep
  than we could count. "Were
                        all
  as we would want," we re-   5
minded ourselves, the we that
  we were on our way toward . . .
All else behind, Wagadu no
                    way,
  Baltimore it was we were in.
    Baltimore it was, then Cincin-   10
  nati, stone buildings meant to
mean forever, squat stone stacked
  against time . . . So it was away
                        was
  all there was of it, it the inside   15
we were after, not there where
  we were or not there when we
were, said to've been there but
                    gone . . .
  Second bodies carried us far-   20
ther. We were truly blue Fasa
  now. *Live at the Apollo* was
                      on
  the box and we sang along,
                      each   25
    the Apollonian someone we
  sang about, lost Apollonian some-
    one, second body we lagged be-
hind . . . We the Andoumboulou,
                      we   30
    the blue Fasa, we the hurt com-
  mencement whose hurt kept rip-
    pling, we the ones who thought of
                        them
  still (*BF* 148)   35

The spiritual destination of Wagadu was not where the pilgrims had arrived. Wagadu is a historical place-name of the city-state of the Soninke people. Leo Frobenius, the anthropologist celebrated by Pound, recorded the epic of the Sudan, *Gassire's Lute*, in 1909. Gassire is a son of the aged king Nganamba and wishes to succeed his father and set the state in order. But the prophecy is that Wagadu shall fall due to vanity, and Gassire will leave the sword behind to take up a lute—from struggle to song. Wagadu, it is said, "is not of stone."

> not of wood,
> nor of earth.
> Wagadu is the strength
> Which lives in the hearts of men.[4]

They were in pursuit of someplace antithetical to the materialism of Baltimore and Cincinnati. The distinction registered here is between stone and the "inside." The object of desire, the beloved, is an Apollonian figure. We the pilgrims are incomplete beings, a kind of error of breeding, like the Andoumboulou.[5] "Hooh! / Fasa!" is the greeting repeated in the poem and cited by Pound in Canto 74. Mackey calls his last book *Blue Fasa* to indicate some distance from the ancient conditions of the Soninke. Wagadu fell four times, and the poem prophesies that Wagadu "will live with much power / in the minds of men / that she can never again be lost."[6] Gassire makes the transition from warrior to bard, satisfied by song. There, the idea of the aesthetic is founded. The pilgrimage seems to end in this Song. The pilgrims want not to strive for somewhere else.

> There
> wasn't anything we were after
> any-
> more. (*BF* 149)

The music of these lines is composed of the insistent echoing of the small words that connect terms through grammatical references and indications of temporal and modal shifts: we, were, was, when, would. These systemic signs are an abstract, austere basis for musicality. They are different from the referential, realistic terms that provide an imitative sort of music: "squat stone stacked" (line 12). The latter phrase is effective in a familiar fashion, and this, too, of course is part of Mackey's art. But the former expects readers to respond to the sounds of much leaner terms.

A critic wants to advocate by citing a poet's strongest poems, but this procedure serves some poets better than others.[7] Before he published *Eroding Witness* (1985), his first book, Mackey had resolved to bring all his poems within a single long project, as Pound, Charles Olson, and Robert Duncan had done. But he also wrote epistolary fiction in conversation with the greatest African American artists—the musicians. This he still does in thematic forms repeated in the poems. His writings hang together. Coleridge speaks of the value of a poet's work as spread through many pages, "a continuous *undercurrent* of feeling."[8] That is a feeling for language.[9] Recursive, he calls his poems, and returns repeatedly to their subjects, even their lines and phrases, to test variants. Should one sentence be indicative? Is it improved by being rendered conditional? Or is a subjunctive warranted to acknowledge the uncertainty it actually entails? This method of revision, repeatedly evident, is driven by self-skepticism. The pilgrims are in fact on the road still; the series proceeds. One assents as reader to a conviction that first thoughts—contra Ginsberg—are rarely best thoughts. Behind this method is an admission that the poems are imperfect, flawed, even wounded by loss; partial, not all there.[10] They come in sections, and at the bottom of many pages are poem-notes on the poems that precede them, or occasionally other versions of the same lines. In the larger forms, too, one moves along an edge, back and forth in small steps, between non-sense and allegory, as one assembles a lexicon with which to resist the prefabrications of sense that reproduce a mental status quo. One reads with obvious uncertainty, as one does in Blake's *Jerusalem*, say, fretful that one here or there misconstrues an ambiguity. The price of misconstrual would be a merely familiar sense—an old story.

Who, then, tracks his path? Mackey prefers not to look back. On every page is evident the liberty to speak idiosyncratically where ideologues are heard: Ouab'da rather than criminal police brutality; Ouagadou rather than Washington. Ouadada rather than art capital. He is a loner in a literary culture eager for the warmth of identity communities. Collaborating jazz musicians are his model; no one accuses them of conformity or docility. Pound's question—"Has it a place in music?"—was grand enough, but think how that sounds to him. African American musicians of Mackey's parents' generation—never mind any others—expanded the music loved throughout and well beyond the English-speaking world. For African American poets, that fact is at the center of the history of art. Mackey has kept it in view in everything he writes. He is closer, among African American poets, to the stalwart Robert Hayden than to Brooks, Hughes, or Baraka. "I don't think about the given categories of audience," he said.

> I think about doing what makes sense to me, what is meaningful to me, with the conviction that there are other peoples that it will make sense to, be meaningful to, and with the hope that what I'm doing will find its way to them and they'll find their way to it. That's the sense of audience I work with. To me it's more the work finding or defining, proposing an audience, than the work being shaped out of some idea of an audience.[11]

Notions of representation dog African American writers; their audiences gather in an all-too-familiar ideological context. Speaking-for and speaking-to are usually liabilities, nearly always so in African American letters. Mackey's achievement is an imaginative regime, with its own idioms and music—a model of self-reliance. "Be not conformed to this world," Paul told the Romans (Romans 12:1). One wants the news to be had from poems to be deeply different from what passes for news elsewhere.

Notes

1. I have used the following abbreviations to cite books by Nathaniel Mackey:

> BH = *Bedouin Hornbook* (Charlottesville, VA: Callaloo, 1986);
> DBR = *Djbot Baghostus's Run* (Los Angeles: Sun & Moon Press, 1993);
> WSS = *What Said Serif* (San Francisco: City Lights, 1998);
> SA = *Splay Anthem* (New York: New Directions, 2006);
> NH = *Nod House* (New York: New Directions, 2011); and
> BF = *Blue Fasa* (New York: New Directions, 2015).

2. Geoffrey H. Hartman, "The Dialectic of Sense-Perception," in *Hopkins: A Collection of Critical Essays*, ed. Geoffrey H. Hartman (Englewood Cliffs, NJ: Prentice-Hall, 1966), 117.

3. Georges Bataille, *Visions of Excess: Selected Writings, 1927–1939*, ed. Allan Stoekl (Minneapolis: University of Minnesota Press, 1985), 117.

4. Alta Jablow, trans., *Gassire's Lute: A West African Epic* (Long Grove, IL: Waveland, 1971), 40.

5. Nathaniel Mackey, *Paracritical Hinge: Essays, Talks, Notes, Interviews* (Madison: University of Wisconsin Press, 2005), 316.

6. Jablow, *Gassire's Lute*, 40–41.

7. Here is my list of the strongest of Mackey's poems. These are the poems with which to begin: In *Song of Udhra*, "Alphabet of Ahtt." In *What Said Serif*, Song 22, Song 24. In *Splay Anthem*, Song 48, "On Antiphon Island," "Sound and Cerement." In *Nod House*, Song 70, "Anouman Sandrofia." In *Blue Fasa*, "Moment's Gnosis," "Sound and Supplement," Song 106, Song 110.

8. Samuel Taylor Coleridge, *Biographia Literaria*, ed. James Engell and Walter Jackson Bate (Princeton, NJ: Princeton University Press, 1983), 1:23.

9. See, too, Albert Gelpi's recent overview of the theme of language among postwar US poets: *American Poetry after Modernism: The Power of the Word* (Cambridge: Cambridge University Press, 2015).

10. Peter O'Leary has a far-reaching analysis of illness in Mackey's work and in Duncan's. See *Gnostic Contagion: Robert Duncan and the Poetry of Illness* (Middletown, CT: Wesleyan University Press, 2002), esp. chap. 4. I am grateful to him for saving me from some errors in the pages above, and for advancing my understanding of Mackey's work in other instances. See, too, the essays collected by Jeanne Heuving in *Nathaniel Mackey, Destination Out: Essays on His Work* (Iowa City: University of Iowa Press, 2021).

11. Mackey, *Paracritical Hinge*, 254–55.

CONTRIBUTORS

LINDA GREGERSON is the Caroline Walker Bynum Distinguished University Professor of English at the University of Michigan. Her most recent book of poems is *Fire in the Conservatory*. She is the author of several studies of early modern poetry, and her essays have been collected in *Negative Capability*.

STEPHEN YENSER is a Distinguished Research Professor of English at the University of California, Los Angeles. His most recent book of poems is *Stone Fruit*. He is the author of critical studies of Robert Lowell and James Merrill, and his critical essays have been gathered in *Boundless Field: American Poetry at Large*. He and Langdon Hammer have edited *A Whole World: Letters from James Merrill*.

LANGDON HAMMER is the Niel Gray Jr. Professor of English at Yale. He is the author of *Hart Crane and Allen Tate: Janus-Faced Modernism* and *James Merrill: Life and Art*, and poetry editor of the *American Scholar*. He is now writing a biography of Elizabeth Bishop.

STEPHANIE BURT is a professor of English at Harvard. Her most recent book of poetry is *Advice from the Lights*. She and Mark Payne collaborated on translations in *After Callimachus*. She is the author of *Don't Read Poetry: A Book about How to Read Poems* and *Close Calls with Nonsense*.

ROBERT FAGGEN is the Barton Evans and H. Andrea Neves Professor of Literature at Claremont McKenna College. He is the author of *Robert Frost and the Challenge of Darwin* and the *Cambridge Introduction to Robert Frost*. He is writing a biography of Ken Kesey.

JOHN WILKINSON is a professor of English at the University of Chicago. His most recent book of poems is *My Reef My Manifest Array*. He is the author of *The Lyric Touch: Essays on the Poetry of Excess* and *Lyric in Its Times: Temporalities in Verse, Breath and Stone*.

KATERINA STERGIOPOULOU is an assistant professor of classics and Hellenic studies at Princeton. She is the author of the forthcoming *Modernist Hellenism: Pound, Eliot, H.D. and the Translation of Greece*.

SCARLETT HIGGINS is an associate professor of English at the University of New Mexico. She is at work on a critical study of collage.

CHARLES BERNSTEIN is the Donald T. Regan Professor of English and Comparative Literature emeritus at the University of Pennsylvania. His most recent book of poems is *Topsy/Turvy*. He is the author of *The Pitch of Poetry* and *Attack of the Difficult Poems*.

MARJORIE PERLOFF is the Sadie Dernham Patek Professor of the Humanities emerita at Stanford and the Florence R. Scott Professor of English emerita at the University of Southern California. She is the author of two forthcoming books: *Infrathin: An Experiment in Micropoetics* and an edition and translation of *Wittgenstein's Private War Diaries, 1914–1916*.

JOHN FARRELL is the Waldo W. Neikirk Professor of Literature at Claremont McKenna College. He is the author of *Varieties of Authorial Intention* and *Paranoia and Modernity*. He is writing a critical study of literary utopias.

KENNETH FIELDS is a professor of English and creative writing emeritus at Stanford. His most recent book of poems is *Classic Rough News*.

NIGEL SMITH is the William and Annie S. Paton Foundation Professor of

Ancient and Modern Literature at Princeton. He is the author of *Is Milton Better than Shakespeare?* and *Andrew Marvell: The Chameleon*. He is currently writing a study of the relation of words to music.

DANIELLE S. ALLEN is the James Bryant Conant University Professor of Government at Harvard. She is the author of *Education and Equality* and *Cuz: The Life and Times of Michael A.*

ROBERT VON HALLBERG is a professor of literature at Claremont McKenna College. He is the author of *The Maltese Falcon to Body of Lies* and the forthcoming *Monogamy, Its Poems and Songs*.

INDEX